ECONOMIC WISDOM

Economic References from
Scriptural, Philosophical and
Classical Sources

Edited by

RAYMOND MAKEWELL

The Ramayana, translated by Hari Prasad Shastri
Published by Shanti Sadan ©
29 Chepstow Villas London W11 3DR

The Man Who Wanted to Meet God
Published by Bell Tower
for The Society for the Study of Normal Psychology ©
Colet House, 151 Talgarth Road, London W14 9DA

Conversations with Shantanand Saraswati
Unpublished, The School of Economic Science ©
90 Queen's Gate, London SW7 5AB

The Letters of Marsilio Ficino
Published by Shepheard-Walwyn for the School of Economic Science ©
90 Queen's Gate, London SW7 5AB

The Editor wishes to express his thanks to the above for their
permission to use these works.

ISBN 0 646 41070 9

First Edition 2001

Published by Raymond Makewell,
64 Boundary Rd, Roseville NSW 2069 Australia   61-2 9417 4120

Produced by New Frontier Creative Services Pty Ltd
6 Merle St, Epping 2121 NSW Australia   61-2 9876 1050

Contents

Introduction i
Glossary of Economic Concepts v

The Texts
Atharva Veda 1
Holy Bible - Old Testament 5
Holy Bible - New Testament 29
Other Biblical Writings 34
Brihadaranyaka Upanisad 35
Brihaspati Smriti 39
Cicero 41
Confucius 47
Marsilio Ficino 49
Hammurabi's Code of Laws 53
Hesiod 59
Lao Tsze 63
Laws of Manu 65
Mahabharata 75
Mencius 109
Narada Smriti 120
Philo 121
Plato 127
Ramayana 143
Shantanand Saraswati 149
The Shû King 155
Šrimad Bhagavata 161
Sukra-Niti 167
Yajnavalkya Smriti 187
Zarathushtra 191

Lexicon of Non English Terms 193
Notes on Texts 197
A Scriptural History of Time 204
Abbreviations 209
Bibliography 210
Index to References 211

"In the olden days, rulers used to take advice from the sages in matters of state. With the wealth of their inner experience and purified intellect, they often came out with bold solutions to political problems. Their advice was untainted by selfish considerations and was given without fear or favour, and was generally one that benefited both the ruler and the ruled. The severance of this contact between Rajas and Maharishis has eroded the quality of administration and brought about discontent. Ethics and politics are not two separate entities. In fact, policies based on their integration are the most far sighted policies and yield the best results. We always advise the citizens to live righteously and the more righteously they live, the easier is the job of the administrator."

Shri Gurudeva - Shankaracharya of Jyotirmath
to Dr Rajendra Prasad - President of India
4th December 1952

Introduction

The desire for happiness is the ultimate cause of all human activity. This desire is in the nature of things, common to all men, at all times, and in all places. Nature, the material of the universe, is modified by men to create wealth so that this desire might be satisfied, in the form of support of the body, for cultural purposes, as well as in religious duties. There is an ancient Sanskrit prayer which begins:-

> May all creatures be happy,
> May all be without disease,
> May all be prosperous,
> And none suffer misery of any kind.

But for his happiness man also requires the opportunity to express his talents. And this expression of his talents (work) produces wealth. The natural corollary is that it is each man's duty to support himself and his family.

And since in nature, no two things are precisely the same, men, in co-operation with others in society are able to express this diversity in the occupations they engage in, resulting in a glorious variety of produce.

Nature, therefore, has created the need and the means of satisfying it. This fundamental truth has two corollaries. Firstly, the means of satisfying the need for happiness must accord with nature, and in accordance with nature, such means will be by nature virtuous. Failure to follow the dictates of nature will lead to unrighteous beahviour. "All wealth" say Plato, "arises from Virtue, both public and private[1]". The second corollary is this: if all men work, expressing their natural talents and taking only what they need, there must be sufficient wealth for all, and happiness will result. But if any do not work (either from their own choice, or because they are denied the opportunity), or take more than they need, then prosperity and happiness cannot be assured for any. The consequence is fear and misery. In this situation, men will attempt to hold wealth and control access to it for their own protection, thus denying others.

Thus begins the study of 'Economics', the science of the laws governing the relationships between men in society, especially where it relates to the creation and distribution of wealth. If the laws governing Economics are understood by the rulers or their advisors, men in society can live a happy and virtuous life. On the other hand, as Keynes observed, fifty years ago, "The outstanding faults of the economic society in which we live are its failure to provide for full employment and

---

[1] Plato's Apology, 30b

its arbitrary and inequitable distribution of wealth and incomes". This is true both in domestic and international terms, and few would be prepared to say that progress has been made in dealing with these issues over the last half century. Has society lost touch with the laws of Economics? Were these laws known previously? How was society previously guided? If the principles are the same for all mankind, can we look to other civilisations for guidance in Economic affairs?

This collection of material is the outcome of a search for that economic wisdom which is available from previous civilisations. The search has been grounded on the premise that Economics has three primary factors: the land, human endeavour, and the environmental dynamics prevailing where these two meet. In this threefold relationship, land includes the entire material universe; human endeavour includes every effort expended by man in this material universe; and environmental dynamics include the condition of the physical world and the state of society prevailing at the place and in the time this effort is expended. These three primary factors cover a lot of ground, and the search for material covering them has therefore been broad; but then, as Keynes observed, the scope of economic study must be broad:

"The study of economics does not seem to require any specialised gifts of an unusually high order. Is it not, intellectually regarded, a very easy subject compared with the higher branches of philosophy or pure science? An easy subject, at which very few excel. The paradox finds its explanation, perhaps, in that the master-economist must possess a rare combination of gifts. He must be a mathematician, historian, statesman, philosopher - in some degree. He must understand symbols and speak in words. He must contemplate the particular in terms of the general, and touch abstract and concrete in the same flight of thought. He must study the present in the light of the past for the purposes of the future. No part of man's nature or his institutions must lie entirely outside his regard. He must be purposeful and disinterested in a simultaneous mood; as aloof and incorruptible as an artist, yet sometimes as near the earth as a politician."

The principles of Economics are common to all mankind. These common principles are reflected across the entire range of civilisations and cultures from which this material is drawn, and they will be expressed differently according to the different emotional, intellectual and physical ground in which they rise. Some of these expressions may not readily find acceptance in contemporary western civilisation. But they cannot be dismissed on this basis. Where the texts speak of the duty of a king, is this not the duty of all forms of government? And if we find in every tradition the principle that 'wealth arises from virtue', should there not be some suspicion that the same may be true in our own civilisation?

The most beneficial approach to studying these texts seems to be to accept the authority of these sages, to assume that these are statements of Natural Law, and to allow the intellect to strip away what is related to time and place, and then, to re-assess them in the context of the Christian Civilisation at the outset of the third millennium - to see what application they may have today.

Why should so much material on Economics be found in Scriptural and Philosophical writings? Because they both have the same end, that all may live in happiness. But if a man must scramble continually for the satisfaction of the basic needs to ensure his physical survival, he will not have time or energy to address the needs of mind, heart and spirit. And for those who are freed from the necessity of struggle for existence, Ficino wrote:-

> '... Of everything that is ours, wisdom alone is good in itself. Only ignorance is bad in itself. Since therefore we all wish to be happy, and happiness cannot be obtained without the right use of our gifts, and since knowledge reveals their proper use, we should leave aside all else and strive with the full support of philosophy and religion to become as wise as possible.'[2].

Scope of this Collection

This anthology represents the oldest extant source material from most traditions. The Egyptian and Buddhist traditions have been excluded - the first on the basis that, despite the fact that so much is known about the organisation of Egyptian Society, most of the available material is secondary, and no source material is available until the Eighteenth Dynasty[3]. The Bhuddist tradition has been excluded because no early material was found which relates to economics and later material draws heavily on older traditions that have been included in this collection.

Some material produced after the beginning of the Christian era has been included for specific reasons. Within the Islamic tradition a body of law has arisen the 'Shariah', 'the path to be followed'.[4] It is derived from Koranic injunctions, statements by the prophet which are not part of the Koran, and statements made by the principle disciples of Muhammad. Within the Shariah there is a substantial section on Economic matters which may prove a fruitful area of study. Two other sources have been included from outside the primary time frame: Santananda Saraswati, on the basis that he was the twentieth century's greatest exponent of the Vedantic tradition; and Marsilio Ficino who was the chief catalyst for the renaissance of the Platonic tradition in the west.

There is still much to discover. Despite the variety of materials represented herein, this anthology only represents a starting-point for an examination of the science of wealth.

Organisation of this Book

The material has been arranged in alphabetical order by author, or by the name of the text,

---

[2] Letters of Marsillio Ficino, Volume 1 letter 2
[3] Curiously, amongst the earliest written laws are injunctions against those in authority to prevent abuse of the people such as excessive tax collection, and other sorts of bureaucratic corruption.
[4] An Arabic word, literally translated as 'the path to a watering place'.

whichever is the most commonly referred to. The texts have been laid out as closely as possible to the original and the original source of numbering has been retained, as has been the spelling, which has led to some variations of spelling appearing within the collection[5]. Extracts have sometimes been abridged, where intervening text does not add to the current subject.

Beside the extracts, have been included notes which may add to the understanding of the text. Sometimes commentaries from other writers, and cross references to other texts that either support or expand on the subject matter have been included. Occasionally, reference to other translations has been included, where variations are useful. Two forms of cross reference are provided, 'see' xyz (meaning that this reference has been included within this collection), and 'refer' xyz (which means that it is not included in this collection). Where translations have been included, they are shown with '='. Foreign terms not so marked are contained in an appendix.

The material is preceded by an alphabetic list of Economic terms and summaries of what is said within this text, and references back to the principal texts that mention these matters.

Two appendices are provided as background to the material in this collection. The first provides notes on the texts themselves and the traditions from which they arise. The second provides an overview of the concepts of time used in all these scriptural traditions, which puts some of the documents into context, and fills out some of the references made by these documents.

---

[5]   Especially in transliteration of foreign names, so that the Sanskrit word for 'King' appears as both 'Kshatriya' and 'Ksatriya'

Glossary of Economic Concepts

The terms included here are both economic, and those which, in the context of the extracts have some bearing on the understanding of economic terms. Dictionary definitions have been provided in many cases, because a full dictionary definition usually provides wider ranges of interpretation than is commonly in use. The descriptions have been written only referring to the material contained herein unless otherwise mentioned, and as such should not be regarded as a complete commentary on the subject, especially where the concepts cross into other disciplines (such as the word 'Justice') where other references are sure to be available from the same sources.

Accountancy - *Technically meaning 'reckoning' or 'valuation', from Latin roots with similar meanings.* The earliest suggestion of records associated with economic activity are injunctions that title to land should be recorded, and any transfer of title should similarly be recorded. The case is similar with loans and contracts. In the absence of written records the scriptures recommend the use of witnesses. The objective is clearly to assist in the resolution of dispute whether benign or malicious.

The Mahabharata extols the king to be fully aware of his income and expenditure on a daily basis as part of his normal house-keeping duties, and the Sukra Niti suggests that one of the kings officers should be responsible to communicate these details to the king (2, 214) and a scribe should record them (2, 672). The Sukra Niti also provides a structure of government accounts (2, 641).

Ages (of man) - A view of history wide spread in religious and philosophical works (and in all the works in this collection), that the origins of man, and society were in a simple but virtuous state in which all man's needs were provided for, and in which he lived in supreme happiness and abundance.

At some time the balance is upset by personal desires, and the level of virtue and happiness diminishes successively from one age to the next until, at the end of the fourth and final age, virtue is almost unknown and misery and poverty are pre-dominant.

These ages are usually referred to as the golden, silver, bronze and iron ages respectively. In the bible, the Garden of Eden story is a description of the golden age. In the Vedantic tradition, these ages are referred to as 'Yugas'. A full description of these is provided in the section entitled 'A Scriptural History of Time'.

Anarchy - *literally, 'want of government'. From the Greek, ἀναρχία, 'a being' ἄναρχος, 'without a head or chief'.* Within the context of these extracts it usually relates to a fearful state of society where there is no protection for the people. Described in the MhB (Santi 67) as 'a state which soon becomes weak and afflicted by robbers. Where the inhabitants devour one another, and righteousness cannot exist'.

Aristocracy - *In the context of Plato, and literally from the Greek the word simply means 'government by the best' (from the Greek ἀριστοκραία - from ἄριο (for ἄριστος, 'best'); and κρατεῖυ- 'to be strong', 'rule' or 'govern'. Some dictionaries note that ἄριστος* *is from the same root as the English word arm - the Vedic ruling class (kshatriyas) were said to come from the arm of the creator. Later the word Aristocracy became applied to a class in society who were said to embody these qualities and who exercised political power (usually by inheritance). The Platonic context is to be found in the Republic and partially in the extracts herein (Book 8, 543a).*

Assets - *Originally from the Latin 'ad satis' carrying the meaning 'to have sufficient'. The root 'sat' being from Sanskrit meaning variously 'being' or ' bliss'. Coming into current usage in the legal context of enough being available in a deceased estate to satisfy debts payable by the estate. In current usage, meaning the entire property of a person or organisation, particularly that part of it which can be sold or exchanged.* The concept of 'assets' as we currently refer to them does not arise within these texts. It is usually referred to as wealth (or treasure). However, taken from the concept that assets enable desires to be realised, the following can be deduced:-

1. The primary asset of a king (government) is land (MhB, Bishma 9).

2. The king may hold assets which require protection (army, fortifications, armament, supplies and reserves), and nourishment (public works in the form of wells and tanks, planting trees, roads, draining swamps etc). These are the collateral assets of the king. The Sukra Niti says that sufficient wealth should be held to maintain the army for 20 years without further revenues (4, 2, 25).

3. Assets can also arise from relationships with others (in the forms of debts due and treaties), which may be considered contingent assets.

Banking - *The English term is derived from renaissance Italian usage of 'Banca', being a bench or table used by money exchangers or lenders.*

Although there is no mention within these texts of an entity which performs the function of a modern bank, many aspects of banking are mentioned in these texts, including lending (with and without security) foreign exchange, money (and debt as money) and letters of credit all of which are dealt with below.

Boundaries - *The word is derived from 'bound' meaning a limit.* The concept of 'boundaries' does not appear to have existed in the Golden Age. Plato suggests that in the ideal state 'all property is genuinely shared' (Laws 739). Boundaries then only arise with a concept of property, whether being the produce of the land, or the land itself (some claim to it must arise when wealth is divided, the land being the source of all wealth).

A number of the texts then make specific references to boundaries, the importance of establishing clear and durable identification, and the offence of tampering with these (Plato, Laws 843; Bible, Deut 19, 14; L of M 8, 245). The Laws of Manu recommends public amenities such as tanks and places of worship should be used as distinguishing marks for boundaries which satisfies clarity, durability and has a great public utility. It also implies that land was shared within the village.

Plato and the old testament prohibit interference with boundary marks.

Mencius goes on to indicate the consequences of the failure to recognise and maintain boundaries, being that taxation dues will not be clear if these are not clear - taxation being calculated on the land and not the product of it (Book 3, A, 3). He further adds that corrupt and despotic rulers always neglect boundaries, and benevolent government begins with land demarcation.

Cicero supports this argument with the observation that 'nothing is more destructive of peace than re-distribution of estates' (Offices 2, 21).

Capital - *From the French 'capital' meaning*

worth, wealth, but originally Latin 'capitalis' the head of a column (from 'caput' a head). *Capital is taken here as defined by the classical economists, being 'accumulated wealth employed reproductively'.*

There are remarkably few references to capital (or forms of capital) in the scriptures and philosophical text.

The advantages of capital works are acknowledged. The MhB speaks of the virtues of planting trees and digging tanks and wells (Anusasana 48), and the Sukra Niti states that extra tax should be payable on irrigated lands (Sukra 2, 665 & 4, 2, 227). The Laws of Manu only mentions the preferred places for building these.

Public amenities such as fortifications, markets, meeting halls and temples are mentioned in most of the scriptures as well as professions such as engineering required to build thcse (Ramayana 1, 5). Cicero notes that all these things (that we would regard as capital works) are the product of men's (usually collective) endeavours (Offices 2, 4).

The Legendary founders of both the Chinese & Egyptian civilisations have attributed to them massive capital works programs required to make the land habitable, productive, healthy and indeed capable of being taxed (Shu King part 3 book 1).

Merchants, says the Sukra Niti, trade with their capital not with the interest (4, 2, 46).

Charity - *Originally from the Latin 'caritas' meaning 'dearness', 'high regard' or 'love'. Some dictionaries show it as originally from the Sanskrit 'kam' meaning 'to wish' or 'to love'. Most commonly meaning 'benevolence', especially to the poor.* MhB notes that acquisition of wealth is easier than charity (Vana 257). See both poverty and gift below.

Citizen - *Technically, the inhabitant of a city, but in common usage, a member of a state,* country or nation (especially if the same is not a kingdom).

Ficino (directly) and Plato (indirectly) write that it is the duty of a citizen to regard the state as a single being formed of parts which are the citizens, and for the parts to serve the whole and not the whole to serve the parts (Ficino, Letters 1, 78).

Collateral - *Literally 'situated or running side by side' from the Latin root with the same meaning, but in Economics, security which a lender can claim in the event of default on repayment of a loan.*

Mention of security for loans is found in most of the traditions herein. The final security being the borrower himself (and is family) who may go into service (or slavery).

Common Land - *Land, enclosed or otherwise held commonly by a community for pleasurable or commercial purposes. In England, usually referred to as 'commons'.*

The Laws of Manu states that Common Land shall be provided around towns (8, 237), and Yaj adds that common land shall exist between villages (2, 166).

Common Land was also provided for under the Mosaic Law (Lev 25, 34) around towns, perhaps especially for livestock. Hammurabi (Babylon 1780 BC) also alludes to Common Land (58) around towns. There is no mention of Common Land in the Chinese texts, the nearest form being a system where eight families would farm nine plots of land, the produce of the ninth being for government revenue (Supplementary notes on Mencius).

Consumption - *The activity of using up, from the Latin meaning 'to take together' in earlier times it carried the meaning 'to make away with', or 'destroy'.*

The concept is not present in classical texts, except in the context that effort is continually required, and in the virtue of continual endeavour (to satisfy demands).

Debt - *An old English word meaning 'an amount due'.* Whilst all of the texts here acknowledge the role of lending, and condone (within limits) usury, they highlight that 'credit takes away people's wealth by compound rate of interest' (Sukra 4, 5, 633), and propose measures to protect the debtor against the extremes that may arise. Among these are:-

1. The Sukra Niti limits the total interest payable to no more than twice the principle (4, 5, 631).

2. The Bible prohibits usury mutually among the Jews (but not between Jews and others), and provides that at the Jubilee year, all property and persons should return to the original owner (Exodus 22, 25 & Leviticus 25, 8).

3. Hammurabi's Code requires persons that sacrificed their liberty to repay a debt to be released after no more than three years (117).

4. Limits on the rate of interest are also provided for (L of M 8, 141).

5. Tax on interest is also prescribed in the Sukra Niti (4, 2, 255).

As with other arrangements, the general advice is that this transaction should be either documented or witnessed, and extensive details are provided on the settlement of disputes that may arise.

There is a reference in the Yagnavalkya Smriti (2, 90) which could be taken to imply that debt was circulated or traded and hence even in early times was used as a form of money.

Demand - *From the Latin word with a similar meaning. The term was first applied in economics by Adam Smith and used subsequently as 'the call for a commodity by consumers with the power to purchase the same'.*

The concept does not arise within these references. See however 'Desire' below.

Democracy - *Originally from the Greek word with the same meaning, and generally defined as 'government by the people'.*

With the exception of Plato none of these texts give any acknowledgement to Democracy. Plato (Republic 556) argues that Democracy arises out of Oligarchy when the thirst for freedom arises from the oppressive behaviour of the oligarches. It is 'full of freedom and frankness, and a man may say and do what he likes'. What he likes can be harmonious with the rest of society or not (such as going to war when the rest of the nation is at war, or not). As a consequence, the society becomes an amalgam of various values and customs and is eventually unruleable.

Desire -*From a Latin root with the same meaning - 'to have a strong wish for', 'to long for' or 'to crave for'.* This term is not usually used in the context of economics, where 'demand' is used to capture the sense of desire with the means for gratification immediately (see demand above).

Desire is the cause of all activity (L of M 2, 1-5). Desire is divided by the Sanskrit texts into four heads, desire for emancipation (which is outside of the considerations of economic activity), desire for attaining virtue, wealth and pleasure (MhB, Santi 123). These may be intermixed and the dominance of one of these factors over another will determine the nature of goods and services produced, and the nature of society (The true satisfaction arises out of pursuit of Virtue). Plato (Republic, Book 8) shows clearly how the desires vary as these elements change in different conditions of society.

The root of all desire is the pursuit of happiness (MhB, Santi 190).

Distribution of Wealth - In times before the current age, wealth was said to belong to Brahmanas (priests and sages) because only they were capable of enjoying it, although in practice they do not take possession of wealth (L of M 1, 100). Other texts state that wealth belongs to the Kshatriya - kings and soldiers - (MhB, Santi 136) presumably because only they can retain and protect it.

Wealth falls first into the hands of the Vaisya (merchants and farmers) who are the only class that can produce it. Indeed some of these are extremely powerful by virtue of their wealth, and the Mahabharata recommends that kings should cultivate these wealthy individuals. The Sudras (servants) are not permitted to accumulate wealth.

Plato demonstrates how the distribution of wealth changes as society changes, and the effects of this change in distribution (Republic, Book 8).

Plato and the Bible both provide for measures to ensure that the distribution of wealth does not become too distorted, so that citizens still share the same concerns and cannot oppress each other. Similarly, Plato (Republic 462b), the Bible (eg Leviticus 25, 8) and Hammurabi's code (117) all provide measures to protect the poor from oppression by the rich, particularly from the oppression of debt.

The Mahabharata also deals with distribution of wealth between the king and the people (Santi 87 & 88). Taxation is the means of achieving this. Excessive taxation and impoverishment of the people discourages production and limits the wealth available to the king.

Plato also notes that the proper function of trade is to make more even the distribution of wealth (Laws 918).

Division of Labour - *The classical use of this term in economics is that work is divided so that individuals specialise in one or a few functions of the productive process, on the basis that this provides greater skill and efficiency for production.*

The Sanskrit texts identify the first form of specialisation as the natural division of society into the four castes, based upon the mix of qualities in their natures (the Brahmans having the quality of serenity and intelligence, Kshatriyas a mixture of this and the qualities of activity and power, Vaisyas this quality of activity and clinging (or desire for acquisition) and the Sudras an absence of both power and intelligence (Brihad 1, 4, 11).

Plato (Republic 2, 370) perceives this propensity for specialisation as enabling men to fulfill their individual natures, and a natural outcome of men in society. He goes on to illustrate how particular functions in society require specific qualities in the man for them to perform the function well (A doctor, he says, must have some personal experience of disease to appreciate the condition and treat appropriately his patient). Mencius (Book 3, A, 4) describes how it is, in fact, essential for society and that society cannot operate as a unit unless specialisation (Division of Labour) takes place, and that failure to have specialisation would be incessant toil for everybody.

Duty - *a word apparently of Anglo-French origin which in its earliest usage caries the sense of 'due debt'. In contemporary usage, it has come to mean that which is due in the form of a payment or service by of way obligation, moral legal or otherwise.*

The extracts here dictate that every class and every function in society has duties associated with it and that duties arise immediately on any intercourse with others in society (see L of M 1, 88-91 for duties of classes, and Ficino 2, 53 for the duties associated with jobs and professions).

Duty (as taxation) - (see also taxation below). The term is also applied to a form of taxation, or impost usually applied to goods when passing through borders, roads and by ferries. Collection of these duties appears in the oldest of the texts herein, which specifically nominates that the rate should not be so high that it impacts the capital of the merchant (see eg

Sukra Niti 2, 351). Further specific definitions and dictates on the imposition of duty are also provided (Sukra 4, 2, 212). Duty here appears to be levied only on trade. Duty should only be levied once, and not through cunning on the part of the collector. Duty should not be collected from both the buyer and the seller, and the collector should only collect duty from the seller when it is evident that the seller has gained from the transaction. Sukra suggests a rate of 1/32, and states that a rate of twice this should not affect the price, implying that modest taxes of this nature need not affect trade.

Earth - (see also - Land) *A word of old English origin for which the meaning has not changed, related to an old usage of 'ear' meaning 'to plow'*. All the scriptures refer to the Earth as a goddess (see index), and even the Bible (Leviticus 18, 25) ascribes to the earth powers, as an independent being, to evict the unrighteous. The earth is mother of all creatures (eg Genesis 1, 24-25), the father being the creative force in the universe (MhB, Santi 190). The earth is eternal, and if cared for becomes an 'ever yielding cow' which for all objectives of human life may be 'milked' (MhB, Bishma 9).

The abundance of the earth is directly related to the virtuousness of men occupying it. In the golden age, the earth was abundant, and no effort was required to reap this abundance (Hesiod 106 to 201 & MhB, Adi 68). In subsequent ages, where virtue has progressively decreased, the effort required to harvest the produce of the earth has increased commensurately.

Ecology - *A word not found in older dictionaries*.

In the context of economics, the earth is the source of all wealth (Atharva Veda 12, 6 & 35), and care of the earth is required to ensure that it is developed properly (MhB, Bishma 4 & 9). Among the aspects of care that should be taken

are the creation of 'tanks' and planting of trees, not just for the benefits to farmers, but also for the benefits of other creatures, and to please the gods (MhB, Anusasana 48). Trees that produce fruit etc should not be cut down (MhB, Santi 89).

It is important then that man should not take more than he needs from the earth (Gospel According to Thomas 81, 28), and by the same token taking more than the land can support is also discouraged (MhB, Vana 256).

Economics - *The source of the word is the Greek οἰκονομία. This is traditionally translated as 'management of a household'. Both Webster's Dictionary and the Oxford Etymological Dictionary of the English Language show the Greek word as being composed of 'οἶκος', a 'house' and 'νομίς', meaning 'usage, law, rule'. νομίς is a form of 'νέμειν', meaning 'to deal out', 'to distribute' and 'to manage'. The literal meaning includes both the construction of a house and the proper setting up and running of a household. The Greek word occurs in the New Testament where it is consistently translated as 'dispensation'. The word 'economy' is widely used in theological works, but its popular modern use fails to convey the idea of Divine bounty, and provision for the ordering of every detail of the processes of the created Universe.*

The French founders of the modern study of Economics were known as the physiocrats from the Greek Φύσις (nature) and ρατεῖν (to rule).

The Sanskrit language has a word (गृहकर्म्मनिर्वाहसमन्धी) for household management, but for 'economics' the nearest word is नीतिविद्याकुशल, which translates as 'the knowledge, laws or science (विद्या) of government (Niti नीति), leading to health, prosperity, and happiness (कुशलत्त).

Whilst the subject matter of economics does arise with these texts, the subject is not dealt with as a specific issue, and especially within the bounds of the contemporary definition. The Sanskrit texts speak of the Laws of Government and the Laws involved in the creation of wealth as two entirely different and unrelated sciences. Specifically where taxation is mentioned, it is emphasised that this is taking wealth from someone else (which clearly distinguishes from the skills involved in the creation of wealth). The science of government then, in this respect ensures that the sources of wealth grow, are protected and are not harmed or discouraged by taxation.

Economic Cycles - Mentioned obliquely in the Mahabharata in the context that destruction causes growth (Santi 97). Shantanand Saraswati observes that world wide recession follows when production costs at some place are too cheap, and local recession when local production costs are too high (Conversations 1982).

Employment - *From the same Latin word (implicare) as the word 'implicate'. The original meaning was 'to fold into, or to involve'.*

All scriptural traditions encourage activity and enterprise and abhor idleness (Hesiod 293 & Zarathushtra). The concept of unemployment is foreign to these texts, and poverty (often associated with it) is perceived as a state of sinfulness (MhB, Santi 8). The Mahabharata states that it is the duty of any higher caste person to offer work to the lower caste when approached (MhB, Santi 60), so that unemployment should not arise. On this basis any economic system in which full employment is not the normal state does not conform to the requirements of the scriptures.

Exchange - *a compound word from old French (eschanger) being 'es' - out or away from, and*

'change' - change.
See trade, and specialisation.

Expenditure - *from the Latin 'expendere' made up of ex - 'out' or 'away from', and pendere -' to weigh'.*

At the level of government, for accounting purposes the Sukra Niti suggests that expenditure be divided into two heads: that which will come back, and that which destroys the right forever (2, 674). Further subheadings are also provided, the principle being expenditure on sacrifices and worldly disbursements. The Sanskrit literature identifies two primary areas of expenditure, sacrifice (MhB, Santi 20) and for the army (MhB, Santi 136) - safety of the citizens is the first priority of government (Cicero, Offices 1, 25).

Expenditure should be provided to support the arts and sciences (Sukra 1, 741), charity and entertainment of the people as well as support for the sick and the elderly (especially those former employees of the king and their dependents), salaries and support for the servants or the king, as well as rewards for service and valour. Useless expenditure should be stopped (MhB, Santi 133).

Farming - *from the Latin 'firma', a fixed payment. A farm is traditionally ground let for cultivation, but also carries meanings of 'food', 'hospitality', 'tribute' and 'a lasting oath'. In Old English the word was 'ferme' which meant - 'rent' or 'lease'. The word 'farm' did not come to mean practising agriculture until the early part of the eighteenth century.*

In all of these quotations farming is the major part of the economy. A wise king should always gratify farmers (and merchants) for they increase the strength of the kingdom (MhB, Santi 87). They should not be taxed in such a way as to emasculate them (ibid).

The methods of organisation of farming are not

detailed, but the indications are that these are principally small holdings, where either tax was paid, or rent was paid for access to the land. From the outset, a substantial amount of infrastructure appears to be provided. The Sanskrit literature refers to variations in taxation based on whether water was provided naturally, from tanks, from rivers or from canals. The early Chinese history speaks of the work done by the king to drain swamps and clear forests so that it was useable for agriculture (Shu King). Hammurabi's Code also mentions a system of dams and irrigation canals (Ham 53).

Regional specialisation is also apparent in the Shu King and the variety of agricultural produce mentioned in earliest China is extraordinary.

Fine - *Originally from the Latin 'finis' meaning 'end'. Both Latin and old French senses carry the meaning 'ending a dispute', 'settlement', 'payment by way of compensation'.*

Fines are shown in the Sukra Niti as normal, non territorial income for the king. There is further commentary in the Laws of Manu that states punishment should suit the person and that in the case of the warrior class it should be removal of property and in the case of farmers and merchants forfeiture of possessions (L of M 7, 14).

Foreign Exchange - is only mentioned by Plato (Laws 741) who suggests that domestic currency should be of no value but the state should hold supplies of currency that could be used by traders and others having dealings outside the state, to be exchanged for domestic currency on return to the country.

Gambling - *Derived from the word 'Game' and from an Anglo Saxon word of the same meaning. Sometimes referred to as gaming). Playing games of chance for money.*

Mentioned in the Mahabharata as drinking houses and public women, as something that should be discouraged (Santi 88).

Gift - *A voluntary transfer of property in a thing without the expectation of a receipt. From the same Anglo Saxon root as 'give'.*

All scriptures encourage the practice of gift and attribute to the practice benefits to the giver both in this life and in others. The L of M (1, 86) states that 'gift' (liberality) is the principal duty of this age. Receipt of gifts is a lawful mode of acquisition of property (L of M Chapter 10).

Gifts should be made to 'worthy' recipients. In fact gifts made to unworthy recipients are of limited value (MhB, Santi 191), but something should always be given when it is asked (L of M 4, 227).

The Mahabharata states that nothing can be enjoyed unless gift is made of some part of it (MhB, Vana 199).

Specific Forms of gift are associated with particular results; gifts of food produce happiness for the giver, gift of a light produces good eye sight etc (L of M 4, 229).

Gifts of land, made by the king, are specifically encouraged, the implication being that this is productive land (MhB, Anussana 62) and gifts of land are encouraged for the gods, parks and dwelling houses for peasants (Sukra 1, 423).

Gift is dealt with more extensively by Brihaspati and Narada, both of whom include as valid gifts wages, and the price of merchandise, which represents both a different attitude towards day to day transactions (including acknowledgement that what is received is from the bounty of the creation), and, perhaps a recognition that for both wages and exchange of merchandise there is no mechanism for ensuring that equal value is rendered to both parties.

Goods - *From the word 'good' in the sense of 'suitable' or 'apt to fit the need'. Akin to a range of words both in English and in other Germanic languages, such as 'gather', and perhaps originally from the Sanskrit वध्*

(ghadh) meaning 'to grasp', or to 'fit'. In economics, 'merchandise' or 'wares'.

The Mahabharata (Santi 139) speaks of goods as being of two classes: a man's own virtues (knowledge, courage etc) and his acquisitions (houses, land, wife, wealth & friends).

Ficino, Letters (2, 53) speaking of the second category says that these nourish the state and the people.

Govern - *Arriving in English from the Latin 'gubernare',· 'to steer, pilot, or govern'. Originally from the Greek κυβερνᾶν, meaning 'to steer', 'to direct' and 'to control the actions and conduct of men, either by established laws or by arbitrary will', but especially in the context of this collection, 'to exercise of the power of the state'.*

Government - *[see govern]*

There are extensive ancient sources on government. Beyond those quotes herein, the entire Santi Parva within the Mahabharata is devoted to this subject, and a complete volume was written in Sanskrit (The Artha Sashtra), Confucius makes extensive references, Plato, Aristotle and Cicero also wrote on the subject. From the quotations herein, the following can be summarised:-

Government was not required in the Golden Age, but has been required ever since. Without government people's behaviour lapses and lawlessness arises (MhB, Santi 68). The principle duty of government is to protect the people (MhB, Santi 58) and supplementary duties are to ensure that the people perform their proper duties (ibid) and that land is made available to the people (MhB, Santi 65). The Laws of Manu and other sources state that finally it is punishment which governs (L of M 7, 13) because fear of punishment provides the restraint among the people. The art of government is hence referred to as 'Dundaniti' or the Science of Chastisement. It is inevitable

that in the practise of government some will be hurt (MhB, Santi 130 & 133), but this should be minimised.

The primary form of Government mentioned in these texts is a Kingdom. Plato identifies a number of other forms of government (Republic, Book 8), an Aristocracy, or government by the best (ie the wisest); a Timocracy, roughly the equivalent of a Kingdom; Oligarchy, government by the rich; Democracy, government by the people, and Tyranny, a government which oppresses the people (all dealt with as separate topics). Mencius and Confucius both are devoted to education of the rulers so that their rule is benign for the people.

Government is said to have seven arms (anga), the cabinet, capital, land, treasury, army and allies (L of M 9, 294).

Revenue is required for government. And attention should be given to this revenue on a daily basis (L of M 7, 56).

Great attention is given to selection and appointment of ministers (Rama 1, 7). Men of wisdom & knowledge should be appointed (MhB, Santi 69), who have proven backgrounds (L of M 7, 54). No minister should hold the same portfolio for an excessive amount of time because the temptation for corruption may be too great (L of M 7, 123).

Hire - *An old English word meaning 'temporary use of something (by contract) in exchange for payment (payment usually governed in some way by time)'. The same word is used in different contexts for the 'act of hiring' (from the point of view of either party, or the action itself), and 'the payment made in exchange'.*

The concept is not found in these texts except in the context of renting land.

See Rent below.

Income - *Revenue derived from ones work,*

business, lands or investments.

Amongst the Vedic texts specific sources of income were allocated to each order of society; being, for a Brahmana gift, for a Kshatriya taxes and tribute, for a Vyasa farming and trade, and for a Sudra service (Srimad 7, 11). The income of government here is indistinguishable from the income of the governing class. The Srimad also comments on the virtue or otherwise of these different classes of income (ibid).

There is a much used analogy in all these scriptures 'that the King should take his from the people in the same way as a leech takes blood, so as not to cause harm to the host'. Notwithstanding this the Mahabharata observes that no wealth is earned without doing some harm to others (Santi 8).

Interest - *Originally from the Latin and meaning 'participation in advantage', 'profit and responsibility', 'share', 'portion' or 'part'. Specifically and more commonly today 'a premium paid for the use of money', usually reckoned as a percentage payable over a period of time.*

See notes on Usury below.

Investment - *Originally from the Latin 'inuestire', literally 'to clother in'.*

New enterprises should not be taxed until they have return to the investor twice the amount in profit (Sukra 4, 2, 242).

Justice - *Introduced into English from the Latin 'iustitia' which translates with the same meaning as the contemporary word, but originally from the Sanskrit* य *(yu) which translates as' to join'.*

Although not the subject of these extracts, some comments can be drawn from them.

Firstly, behaviour which is 'just' is applicable to time and place, and the same behaviour may be quite unjust in another situation. Hence human law cannot be expected to yield perfect justice in every situation (Cicero, Offices 1,10). The Vedic tradition however expects the king to inflict just punishment on all offenders (L of M 7, 16) and requires that this be according to time and place. If the king does this virtue, wealth and enjoyment will abound (Sukra 1, 133).

Economic justice is dealt with in the Vedic tradition by establishing the duties of the different orders of society, and the rightful forms in which income can be drawn (Srimad 7, 11). These also state that there is a proper share of the wealth produced that is due to the producer and a share that is due to the king (L of M 7, 128), and given that the King's only duty is protection the king's share must arise for this protection (and hence also the taking of it must not cause harm. Other measures are introduced in a variety of texts to ensure that wealth does not become concentrated in the hands of a few people (such as the Jubilee Year - Bible, Leviticus 25, 8-17), the protection of the weak against the excesses of usury, and the protection against perpetual slavery arising from debt (Ham 117). Nothing in these texts discusses a just level of wages, however, the requirement of the employer to support and protect his servant and his dependants (even when sick, and after he is deceased) is a common theme (eg Sukra 2, 819). Fair and honest trade is a particular theme, in most texts, the Srimad describing it as a mixture of truth and falsehood (7, 11).

King - *Originally from the old English 'cynn' meaning 'kin' and explained as either 'scion of the tribe' or 'noble kin'. In modern usage it is equivalent to 'Prince' which is from the Latin roots 'primus' first + 'capere' to take. The Sanskrit equivalent (Kshatriya) is the embodiment of the divine powers required to rule.*

Manu describes the king's principal duty as being to protect this whole world (7, 2), by ensuring that all creatures fulfill their duties (7, 15). This is achieved through the fear of punishment, which when inflicted justly leads to universal happiness. His great qualities are prowess, strength, intelligence and valour (Sukra 1, 349).

The first requirement then is an army, to protect the kingdom and to enforce punishment. The army must be supported, and thus the king must take revenue (7, 80), gained in such a manner that both the king and the subjects receive their due reward (7, 128). Under no circumstances must the taxes levied be such that they hurt the source of the revenue (MhB, Santi 72). The other principal duties are to reclaim land for cultivation, and for sacrifice (MhB, Santi 65). The peace, prosperity and sufficiency of the kingdom are dependant on the king's conduct (MhB, Santi 141). Although from one point of view, the entire wealth of the kingdom belongs to the king (MhB, Santi 136), in reality he has no private property (MhB, Santi 321).

Plato describes how virtue diminishes gradually, and how other forms of government arise in the dissatisfaction that this creates (Republic 543 onwards).

The Ramayana contains some lucid descriptions of a kingdom ruled by a virtuous king (Book 1, Chapters 5, 6, 7). By comparison, the prologue to Hammurabi's Code contains a reflection of these principles.

Ficino wraps this up as 'the duty of a prince is to watch over all; mercy in justice, humility in greatness and greatness in humility' (2, 53).

Labour - *Originally from the Latin 'labor' which has the same meaning (bodily or mental toil), but which may be allied to 'labare' which translates as 'to totter' or 'to sink', from the idea of struggling with a heavy weight. Some lexicons trace the word through the Greek to the Sanskrit लभ् (labh) meaning 'to get', or 'to seize'.*

No labour was required in the Golden Age (MhB, Varna 148). Only a few references are made to labour directly. In Vedantic times this was (more or less) restricted to the class of Sudras (L of M 10, 115-131). Not having the ability to accumulate money, taxes from these people could be paid in the form of labour (L of M 7, 138).

Mencius quoting from 'The Book of Odes', observes that labour is constant (3, A, 3), and merely changes according to seasons etc. See also work below.

Land - *An Anglo-Saxon word for which the meaning does not appear to have changed.*

The importance of Land is paramount in these texts and recognition of this goes back to the most ancient sources. The Atharva Veda lists at length the products and pleasures derived from land (12, 1, 1-63). Manu notes that the benefit of any enterprise goes first to the 'owner' of the land, unless some specific agreement has been reached (L of M 9, 48-56). As such, maintenance of boundaries is extremely important (Bible, Deut 19, 14). Desirous of the fruit of land men fight one another for possession of it (MhB, Bishma 9). Private ownership of land however is not in the nature of things, and arises from ancient seizure, conquest or by some law or compact (Cicero, Offices 1, 7).

It is therefore the duty of the king to ensure that land is available to his subjects (MhB, Anusasana 62). This includes, where applicable, clearing forests, draining swamps, constructing roads and irrigation channels, and, extending the boundaries of the kingdom.

Other texts have provisions to ensure that families do not lose access their ancestral heritage (eg Bible, Leviticus 25, 23-34), and inheritance provisions are of significance in establishing this (Bible, Numbers 27, 6 & Plato, Laws 923). Similar constraints are advised against too much land falling into too few hands (Bible, Isaiah 5, 8).

Re-distribution of land is one of the most difficult feats of government (Plato, Laws 736). The Mahabharata distinguishes between land and wealth, the latter being the product of land (Aswamedha 89).

Land Tenure - *The method by which access to land is granted to the users of land.*

Any system of land tenure requires government and law, so that men can enjoy the land that they hold for production and leisure (Cicero, Offices 2, 21). A variety of forms of land tenure are mentioned, or alluded to, within these texts:-

The Mosaic System held that the land always belonged to God and that the occupant was merely a sojourner. Within Israel, land was divided between the tribes, and allocated to families. The land could not be sold, but was always passed on within the family (usually to a male heir). There is no mention of whether possession also included any duty to pay taxation, or other contribution to the community. Common land is provided around towns.

The Assyrian system (Hammurabi's Code) originally required all land holders to pay a 'quit rent', but by the time this code was framed many landholders had been granted exemption from this liability. Fields still subject to this rent could not be sold nor assigned (Ham 37). The rent was based on the productivity of surrounding sites (in case the land holder was lazy). Fields not subject to quit rents could be sold and assigned. Common land is also provided (Ham 58).

The implication in Manu is that ownership of the land always remains vested in the king (8, 265). Boundaries are only mentioned between villages (8, 254), but private access seems also to be provided for (9, 48). Common land is also provided around villages and towns (8, 237).

The Mahabharata mentions a form of land tenure something akin to the feudal system (Santi 87).

Mencius mentions a variety of systems, including one in which the people had to work in a public field to have access to land for their own use (Book 2 A), and another (the 'ching' system) where eight families worked nine plots of land. The product of the ninth was for the king (Book 3, A, 3).

Law - *'A rule of action, which is prescribed by some Superior, and which the inferior is bound to obey' - Blackstone.*

The majority of extracts contained herein are observations of Natural Law and are reflected in accepted legal tradition (such as expressed in the Laws of Manu, which even today is the basis of Indian Law).

There are a few statements on Law as it pertains to human affairs.

Plato makes two specific observations on Law, that the primary objective is to achieve unity and harmony within the state, and that no law can be expected to provide perfect justice due to differences in human situations (of time and place).

Shantanand Saraswati stresses that law needs to be in accordance with the natural laws, but that these need to be expressed in a manner that is suitable for this age. He says that expressions of natural law from previous ages (such as in the Laws of Manu) will not be effective for contemporary society.

Law of Rent - *The natural law which governs the primary distribution of production between land holders and employers, and sets the level of wages within a community (Refer to Ricardo or Henry George for complete descriptions).*

No examination of the Law of Rent has been found prior to the C18th. Not withstanding this, many of the quotations in this collection contain statements which conform to its principles.

The Laws of Manu states that the possessor of

the land is the recipient of its produce (9, 48-56). Common land shall be provided around towns (8, 237), and Yajnavalkya adds that common land shall exist between villages (2, 166). Taxes must not be harmful or discourage production (7, 129) [which can only occur if taxation is not taken on the least productive land]. They are taken from net production (7, 127), and vary according to the productivity of the site (7, 130) [Sukra describes different rates of tax depending on the reliability of water (4, 2, 227)]. The MhB goes on to add the duty of a king is to make more land available - and to people it (Santi 65 & Anussasana 62). Sukra is more specific. Speaking about land revenues, he specifically instructs that taxation should be related to the productivity of the site (4, 2, 220), and includes all sites, houses and retail sites to be treated identically (4, 2, 256-7).

Confucius and Lao Tsze are silent on this subject, but the Confucian student Mencius, lists a hierarchy of preferences of taxation, placing taxation of ground as the highest (Book 2 A).

The Bible contains two famous quotations which rail against the concept of enclosing unused Land - 'The land shall not be sold... for the land is mine' (Bible, Leviticus 25, 23), and 'The earth is the LORD's' (Bible, Psalm 24, 1). Common land was also provided for under the Mosaic Law (Bible, Leviticus 25, 34).

Contemporary with the Mosaic Law, Hammurabi's Code provides similar restrictions against the sale of Land and the payment of rent to the king (36-41), but it seems that at the time the code was written, already grants had been made that removed this obligation to specific land holders.

Law of Wages - The inverse of the Law of Rent (see above).

Lending - *To grant temporary possession of (a thing) on condition of return of the same (or the equivalent). The Hebrew word which is translated as the same also means 'to twine', ie (by implication) 'to unite', 'to borrow' (as a form of obligation).*

Lending was permitted from the earliest times (in the form of money, as well as goods and land) and interest was permitted (L of M 1, 90). Limits were established on the interest that was chargeable to protect the weak (see usury below).

Liabilities - *From the word 'liable' and originally from the Latin word 'ligare' meaning 'to bind'. In modern usage 'debts' or 'obligations' due at law (See debt above). Usually used as an accounting term.* The Sukra Niti shows a structure for keeping accounts which includes income where the proprietary rights belong to another, and provides for debts both due and owed. No other reference is included for 'liability'.

Manufacture - *From two Latin roots, 'facere' meaning 'to make' and 'manu' pertaining to hands, and hence literally 'to make by hand', but more commonly simply 'to produce'. The term covers any modification of resources for satisfying human desires.*

There are few references to this subject, however various discussions on specialisation imply this is a separate activity. The Laws of Manu (7, 138) mentions 'Mechanics and Artisans' as a separate group of people, which implies that manufacturing was organised from the earliest times. Taxation on production should be only after ascertaining all receipts and expenditure so that tax does not harm the producer (MhB, Santi 87). Shantanand Saraswati mentions that production is righteous if both the individual and the society gain from it (Conversations 74).

Market - *A meeting together of people for the purchase and sale of goods. From the Latin 'mercatum' meaning 'to traffic' or 'to trade'.* The only mention of markets within these texts are: Mencius who says the greatest advantage arises 'if goods are exempted when premises are taxed, and premises are exempted when land is taxed' (Book 2, A), and, Sukra (4, 2, 213) who says that one of the collection points of 'Sulka' is the market place. Both suggest that markets have a very long history, and taxation within market places has long been an issue. In the more conceptual sense of a market, Mencius notes (Book 3, A) that inequality of things is part of their nature, hence prices will always vary. Cicero notes that it is a long standing Roman Law that the seller should always disclose the faults in things to be sold (Offices 3, 16).

Merchant - *A 'trader', from the Latin 'mercari' meaning 'to barter', and perhaps associated with the Latin word 'merere', meaning 'to gain', 'to buy' or 'to purchase'.*

Merchants are seen in two contexts, as one who brings goods from afar; and in the context of a retailer. Both engage in trade, which is a mixture of good and evil (Srimad 7, 11). When prosperity is high, merchants abound (MhB, Adi 109). The duty of the merchant is to nourish the state and himself with good things from abroad (Ficino, Letters 2, 53). Merchants should be taxed after consideration of the length of the journey, the difficulty, costs of food etc, and the profits on the sale (MhB, Santi 87), and never in such a way as to destroy the trade. The Bible gives a picture of the extent of trade and the range of the merchant (circa 600 BC) in Ezekiel, 27.

The Retailer's function is to 'collect useful commodities...keep them in good order, place them before his customers when they need them, and charge a reasonable living (Shantanand Saraswati 1974). They should pay 'land tax' (Sukra 4, 2, 257).

Money *From the Latin 'mone ta', which is the surname of the goddess Juno in whose Temple money was coined. The literal sense of 'mone*

ta' is 'the warning one' from 'monere', 'to warn', 'to admonish', or 'to cause to remember'.

There are few references to money in these extracts. Of these, some appear in translation to be equating 'wealth' and 'money'. In the Bible (Genesis 47, 14) for example reads 'And Joseph gathered up all the money in the land', when the Hebrew word used is literally 'silver'. Plato sees two types of money: an internal currency which has no value outside the state, to be used for (especially retail) trade within the state, and for international trade, traders should be given access to the state's reserves of the 'gold' and 'silver' coinage of other Greek States. If traders returned with a surplus, this was to be surrendered to the state in return for domestic currency (Laws 741).

Plato makes two observations about the function of money; firstly that it was invented for the 'care of soul and body' (Laws 743), and secondly that it has an effective role in retail trade (Laws 918), which says Plato, is for the re-distribution of wealth.

The domestic currency for Plato, was not wealth, nor was it a store of value (he stresses in other parts of the Laws, measures to be taken to prevent the mal-distribution of wealth that such accumulation would lead to), but an instrument which facilitates trade (and hence specialisation, hence the education required for care of the soul and body).

Hammurabi provides a law (51) that produce can be used to settle debt (at rates published by the government) when the debtor does not have money. The translators note that where the supply of money is limited, abuse of a debtor is possible if he is obliged to find money the satisfy the debt.

Shantanand Saraswati observes that money is power. Perhaps a reflection on the claims that it holders have on wealth rather than being wealth itself.

The Sukra Niti (2, 720) notes the importance of not debasing the currency. Cicero argues that the issue of money is a proper function of the state (Laws 3, 5).

There is a reference in Yagnavalkya (2, 90) regarding debts remaining in use until they are paid, which implies that they could be traded, and hence were a form of money.

Monopoly - *From the Greek μονοπώλιον - 'sole seller'.* A veiled reference to this occurs in Isaiah who states 'woe unto them that join house to house, that lay field to field.'. Yagnavalkya (2, 250) specifically prohibits merchants collaborating to fix prices. Given the other constraints mentioned to maintain a just distribution of wealth, it is clear that it would be discouraged. Not withstanding this, the Mahabharata should honour subjects that are rich and encourage them to advance the interests of the people (Santi 88).

Nation - *In contemporary usage, a people with common history organised into a separate political organisation and occupying a definite territory. From the Latin 'nationem' the accusative form of 'natio', 'a race'.*

By implication a nation is a group of people who see their own interest and that of the community as the same (Ficino, Letters 1, 78). In practice this can be embodied in the identification of the people with their leader (Confucius, Analects 12, 9).

Within these extracts, the concepts arise of a 'kingdom', a 'state' and a 'city'. The nearest reflection of a 'nation' is the People of Israel.

Nature - *From the Latin 'natus' meaning 'born' or 'produced'. From an economic point of view, 'things as they exist before any intervention from mankind'.*

The Mahabharata says, that nature cannot be the property of any person (Varna 154).

Oligarchy - The term is used by Plato to describe a state which is ruled by the wealthy and acquisitive (few). The major defect of this state is the division created between the rich and the poor (Plato, Republic 550c). The state represents a change from the situation where virtue is the predominant interest of the governors to a state where wealth is the predominant interest (MhB, Santi 123).

Ownership - see property.

Pension - *Originally from the Latin 'pensio' and in turn from the roots 'pendere' and 'pendum' meaning 'to weigh' or 'to pay'. In English, 'a payment' or 'a tribute' but in modern use 'an allowance or payment made in recognition of past service'.*

This duty of care for employees is highlighted in the Sukra Niti (2, 819), where provisions are provided to support the sick, elderly and children and widows of former employees. The basis of these provisions is a responsibility taken on by the employer, and a general understanding that wages will not be sufficient to make provisions for future needs, and further, that employees (Sudras) are not capable of making such provisions.

Poverty - *From the same root as 'pauper' the most common usage is 'the state of having little or no wealth'.*

The earth is abundant and if treated properly able to supply all desires (MhB, Bishma 190), so poverty does not arise through a shortage of resources. On the contrary, poverty did not exist in the 'age of virtue' -the Golden Age (Hesiod, Works & Days) Poverty, argues Plato 'is a matter of increased greed rather than diminished wealth' (Plato, Laws 736). Poverty 'is a state of sinfulness' (MhB, Santi 8), reflecting both cause (virtue is the source of all wealth - Plato, Apology 30b), and the effect (wealth is required for both virtue and pleasure - MhB, Santi 167). The poor, said Christ will always be with us (Bible, Matthew 26, 11).

Price - *The amount paid for something (usually*

with money). *From the Latin 'pretorium' with the same meaning.*

A range of observations are made. Firstly that by nature things are different, and hence prices will vary (even of the same commodity). Price fixing therefore leads to corruption (Mencius 3, A).

The Sukra Niti (2, 718) observes that prices vary according to the ease of obtaining and the attributes of the item, which is the ability of the item to satisfy the desire (or need). It goes on to say that on the one hand there is no price for a worthless thing and on the other, that prices of very fine things are determined entirely by fancy. Taxation (and presumably other costs) with certain ranges do not influence the price (4, 2, 217).

Santanand Saraswati (Conversations 1974) mentions the difficulties caused by inflation.

Production - *From the Latin 'pro - ducere' meaning 'to bring' or 'to lead forward'. In contemporary economic terms it can mean either 'the act of producing', or 'that which is produced'.*

Production is righteous if the individual and the society gain from it. (Shantanand Saraswati).

Profit - *From the Latin 'profectus' meaning 'advance', 'progress' or 'profit'. In contemporary use, 'the advantage or benefit gained (by a person or community be it subtle or pecuniary gain), from any transaction or activity'. Specifically in Economics 'the surplus product of industry after deducting wages, cost of materials, rent, and charges'.*

No activity would be undertaken unless there is profit to be gained from it (MhB, Santi 167). The general approach taken in the Vedantic literature is that there is a rightful part of the profit which is due to the business man (ie farmer or merchant) and a rightful proportion that is due to the king. With regard to taxation, the texts stress that sufficient profit must remain so as to encourage the business to continue with the venture.

Property - *From Latin 'proprius', meaning 'one's own' - in turn from. 'Priuus', 'single' or 'peculiar'. In English meaning 'the exclusive right of possessing, enjoying, and disposing of a thing'.*

Property neither exists in the original scheme of things (Ficino, Letters 1, 73), nor exists by any right of nature (Cicero, The Offices 1, 7). All concepts of property are in fact an illusion (Shantanand Saraswati - The Man who wanted to meet God). The Mahabharata further illustrates this principle by analysing the disposition of all a king's wealth (Santi 321). The Bible states that all land, and all it's fruits belong to the Lord (Psalms 24, 1), and specifically identifies the land as the Lord's property in Leviticus (25, 23). The Mahabharata states that no concept of property can exist over nature unless some work has been done on it (Vana 154) and, elsewhere, that the right falls to the person who has done the work (a deer, for example, belongs to the person who first shot it). The Laws of Manu (1, 100) ascribes all property as belonging to the most godly and first created caste of men, the Brahmana or priestly caste. Plato describes the end of the Golden Age as that time when, on dispute arising, they distribute the land and houses among individual owners (Republic 547), where previously no concept of property existed.

Not existing in nature, property requires an artificial instrument to support it, being 'Law' (Cicero, The Offices 1, 7), and a power to support and uphold that law (a king, or civil authority). This law is reflected in various traditions and times in different ways. Nor is possession ownership (L of M 8, 200). A variety of forms of title are observed, especially that arising from payment of rent for possession.

The Laws of Manu (10, 115) provides a number ways by which property may be legitimately acquired, Viz inheritance, finding or friendly donation, purchase, conquest, lending at interest, performance of work and acceptance of donations - from virtuous men. The Bible and Hammurabi's Code both provide laws to prevent a person losing all his property and freedom, by insisting that if it is lost to satisfy debts, it must be returned after a period of time.

Property in Land - see also property above.

All wealth arises from land, and the owner of the land has first claim on the wealth produced (L of M 9, 48). Cicero observes that property in land arises either by conquest, by ancient and immemorial seizure or by legal contrivance such as by lot. In some of the cultures described herein rent was required from the property owner by the king for possession of the land.

There are a number of descriptions of common land also within these texts (See Common Land above). Forms of property in land vary (see Land tenure above).

Prosperity - *From a Latin word 'prosperare' meaning 'to cause a thing to succeed', in contemporary usage it is used to mean 'good fortune', or 'success' or 'the state of individuals possessing more than they require for basic existence at their station in society'.*

There is a magnificent description of the prosperity of the silver age in the extracts from the Ramayana (1, 5). The Vedic goddess of prosperity is Lakshmi, also associated with success, happiness, beauty, grace and charm. The Mahabharata suggests that all women embody this quality, and honouring women implicitly honours the goddess (MhB, Anusasana 46).

In other places it is stated that prosperity requires co-operation and specialisation (Cicero, Offices 2, 4). The Mahabharata adds that divine co-operation is also required (Udyoga 79). The Bible (Job 8, 3-6) extends this, requiring virtue (see also - wealth).

The Mahabharata also acknowledges that the earth is the essence of prosperity (Anusasana 62).

Public Works - Public works can be considered in three classes. Of these, the first is: Those undertaken to expedite the functions of government, including courts, audience halls and fortifications (a chapter in the Sukra Niti is devoted to fortifications). The second class are those provided for the well being of the community, such as meeting halls, temples and parks, which are largely considered as gifts to the people, or in some cases are financed by a special levy on the people (eg Solomon's temple).

The final category are those which directly benefit production. Little mention is made of these. The Laws of Manu encourages the construction of tanks and cisterns (8, 248). The Mahabharata extols also the virtue of such acts (Annusasana 48). Mencius cites the virtue of Yu, the founder of the Chinese civilisation, who spent years draining swamps and dredging rivers so that the land was habitable and productive, which is one of the duties of government (MhB, Santi 65).

Rent - *'A source or item of revenue, a tribute or tax, levied or paid to a person, the return or payment made by a tenant to a landlord for use of land or houses. Originally from the Latin 'rendere' meaning 'to tear' or 'to separate.*

Rent on land is mentioned in all these traditions, either as paid to a Landlord or as source of government revenue. Manu provides that the king should extract revenue from farmers and that this should be a reflection of the productivity of the site (7, 130).

The Sukra Niti (4, 2, 222) is more explicit, saying that the king should receive rent from peasants (again based on the productivity of the site).

Hammurabi (43) notes that rent should be paid whether the land is worked or not, and the productivity of the neighbours' land should be used as the measure for calculating the rent in this event.

Retail Trade - *'Retail' coming from old French translated literally as 'a piece cut off', and ultimately meaning 'trading in small quantities', usually associated with sales to householders.*

Plato (Laws 918) describes retail trade as part of the process of re-distribution of wealth. Ficino (2, 53) describes the duty of retailers as 'honestly distributing the provisions from the merchants (see trade below) to each member of the state'. Shantanand Saraswati is more explicit (1974), describing the job as 'to collect useful commodities from the main markets or producers, keep them in good order, place them before his customers when they need them and charge a reasonable living for his services'. The requirement for honesty in dealing is paramount. The Srimad (7, 11) describes trade as a mixture of truth and falsehood. The duty of the seller to make the buyer aware of the state of goods he is to purchase seems to be very old, and is mentioned as such by Cicero (Offices 3, 16). Yagnavalkya (2, 244) describes a number of measures for the regulation of trade and for the control of abuses, including the use of false weights, adulteration, misrepresentation, counterfeiting, profiteering and price fixing.

Sacrifice - *From the Latin roots 'sacer' meaning 'sacred' and 'facere' meaning 'to make'. The English word has two relevant meanings, 'to offer to a deity' and 'to give up for some higher purpose'. Both meanings are operable within these extracts (and sometimes these meanings merge).*

Sacrifice is established as part of the mechanism of creation.

The primary purpose of wealth is said to be for sacrifice (MhB, Santi 20). The Geeta goes on to note that it is sacrifice that produces rain, and that rain is required for the production of crops

etc (refer Bhagavad Geeta 3, 14) hence it is required for the production of wealth. Sacrifice is said to be the foremost duty of the Bronze Age (MhB, Santi 232), men devoted to sacrifice obtaining the fruition of all their desires by this means (MhB, Santi 263).

Other texts imply that in the performance of sacrifices, not all the wealth was destroyed. The remainder was distributed to the priests.

Philo observes (Special Laws 1) that the Hebrew taxation system was based on a sacrifice prescribed by the priests, so that the people did not think their wealth was being taken from them.

Salary - *Originally a payment made to Roman soldiers for the purchase of salt. The word has come to mean 'a fixed periodic payment, usually associated with non-manual labour (and typically being paid less frequently)'.* See wages below.

Savings - *Derived from a Latin word with the same meaning, the principle meaning being 'to protect', 'to rescue' or 'to guard against damage or loss'.*

The Sukra Niti makes two references to savings at the level of government. Firstly (4, 2, 25) that the treasury should be sufficient to maintain the subjects and the army for a period of twenty years (without further revenues). Secondly, that in times of danger the king should lodge his wealth with rich persons (4, 2, 45), but going on to add how the various forms of this wealth should be stored. It requires that the stock should be replenished continually, and details those items which should be retained in the accumulation. The text notes that maintenance of the accumulated wealth is more difficult than the acquisition of it and that care is needed for this endeavour.

Service - *From the word 'serve', coming into English from a French word of the same meaning, but ultimately from the Latin 'seruīre' meaning 'to serve', and akin to both the Latin* '*seruus*' - '*a servant or slave*' and, '*seruāre*' - '*to keep and protect*'. *The implication being that service is due to the one who keeps and protects the servant.* See also 'duty' above, for which there are many references.

All creatures are created for the service of all other creatures (MhB, Santi 142), and hence provide for the happiness of all other creatures. It should therefore be our incessant endeavour to seek the happiness of all creatures by service. Shantanand Saraswati (1974) notes that proper execution of the trade that men engage in services both society and the Lord, but that profiteering from this disrupts society and leads to misery and tension.

Slavery - *Derived from the Latin 'Sclavus', being the name of the now Slavic people, who were used by the Romans as 'slaves'. In practice it is simply 'one who is the property of another'.*

Aristotle is the only classical source amongst Scriptural and Philosophical material that mentions slavery explicitly (he accepts and justifies the situation). It is mentioned later by Justinian (Institutes 1, 3, 2), who says 'Slavery is an institution of the law of nations whereby one man is made the property of another, contrary to natural right.' Among the texts included herein, the Bible and Hammurabi's code acknowledge the right of creditors to take debtors (and also in some cases the debtor's family) as slaves, but in all these situations the law provided measures to limit the creditor's power by limiting the period during which this power could be exercised.

Specialisation - *The process of becoming specialised or particular, and in economics relating to the propensity for people to engage in a single trade; or merely part of the process of producing goods; or for regions to supply only those goods which can be produced efficiently in that region.*

See also 'Division of Labour' above.

Regional specialisation did not exist in the Golden Age because the earth yielded all that was required at the place it was required (Hesiod 225-237). Regional specialisation then represents a diminishment in the prosperity of the earth as a whole.

Two extensive examples of regional specialisation are provided in these texts, the Bible (Ezekiel 27), and in the Shu King.

Supply - *From a Latin word meaning 'to fill up', but in modern economics 'the availability of goods and services'.*

Two oblique references are made, firstly suggesting that the ease or difficultly of acquisition of goods is a determining factor in establishing the price (Sukra 2, 718), and secondly a rejection of monopoly (Bible, Isaiah 5, 8-10).

Tariff - *From an Arabic word meaning to 'make known', introduced to English as a table of rates applicable to different goods at customs posts. Most commonly used these days as a rate to be paid for importing goods, and usually established to discourage the import.*

A number of references are made to tariffs as forms of government revenue. Sukra suggests that light tariffs will not have an effect on prices (4, 2, 217), and the Laws of Manu, instructs that even the rate of tariffs should be set after considering the costs and difficultly of delivering the goods (L of M 7, 127) so that it does not discourage the trader.

Tax - *Derived originally from the Latin - 'taxare' meaning 'to touch sharply', 'to feel', or 'to handle', (from the Latin root 'tactum' - 'to touch'). In modern usage a charge imposed on (almost anything) by authorities for government revenue.*

The Sanskrit equivalent kara (कर:) carries the meanings both of a ray of light, sunbeam, moonbeam; and royal revenue, toll, tax, duty, tribute.

'Tax' should be taken here in its widest possible context, as any government revenue extracted from the citizens, including rents from land, tolls, tributes and all other forms. Acquisition of wealth by conquest, and tributes demanded from defeated nations are considered legitimate sources of revenue in the Vedic tradition (MhB, Santi 130 & 133) - and, indeed, are practised in various forms to this day.

The primary objective of taxation is to support the army (Sukra 4, 2, 5-6). Using this model, the requirements for taxation would be much less than those of most contemporary western societies. Mencius however acknowledges that more sophisticated societies require greater revenues (Book 6, B, 10).

From all production there is a portion due to the producer and a portion due to the king (L of M 7, 128). The King's right to a share arises from the protection he affords (the prosperity of the kingdom is entirely dependant on the virtuous behaviour of the monarch - MhB, Sabha 32).

The first principle of taxation is that the collection should be done in such a way as not to harm those being taxed - as the leech, the calf, and the bee take their food little by little. Excessive taxation on the other hand is said, in due course, to destroy the source of the revenue (MhB, Santi 72 & 88).

In times of distress however, the king may extract greater amounts of taxation - or compel the wealthy to donate or lend money to the crown (MhB, Santi 130 & 133). The burden of tax may be increased, with care, so that either the subjects do not become aware of it, or are induced by some means to support it (MhB, Santi 88). An example of this is provided in the Bible, where the Hebrew nation was asked to pay money as an atonement for their sins (Bible, Exodus 30, 11-15). Modest taxation, says the Sukra Niti, will not affect the price (4, 2, 217). In normal times however, taxation should be

levied on the net profit, bearing in mind the risks taken (L of M 7, 127). Everyone should pay some tax - even a trifle (L of M 7, 137).

A variety of sources of taxation are mentioned, including: rent on land (Sukra 4, 2, 222); land tax, including tax on retail premises (4, 2, 257); tax on profits from the sale of goods (L of M 7, 127); tax on interest (Sukra 4, 2, 245); a portion of the growth in herds (L of M 7, 130); and, royalties paid on mines (Sukra 4, 5, 643). Mencius has a discussion on the suitability of various forms of tax operational in China (3, A, 3).

Taxation should not be taken from new ventures until profits of at least twice the original investment have been accrued (Sukra 4, 2, 242), and no tax should be introduced without ascertaining the effect and the labour required to produce it (MhB, Santi 87).

Trade - *The English word is derived from the old Saxon, 'trada' meaning 'footstep' or 'path'. The current usage can range from meanings as diverse as 'a course of action'; 'the practice of a particular occupation'; 'commercial dealings (especially, but not exclusively exchange)'; and 'a generic name for a specific business or industry (such as the liquor trade)'. Generally in other languages the concept is mostly associated with words translated as 'merchant'.*

Although ultimately the same, these extracts acknowledge two classes of trade: retail trade (the trade of the shop keeper); and wholesale trade (traditionally perhaps the trade of the travelling merchant).

The function of trade is described as 'nourishing the state and the trader with true faith and diligence with the good things from abroad' (Ficino, Letters 2, 53). Retail trade is 'to collect useful commodities, keep them in good order, place them before his customers, and charge a reasonable profit' (Shantanand Saraswati 1974). Plato, looking at the totality of trade, describes its function as the re-distribution of goods where they are distributed disproportionately (Laws 918).

Trade did not exist during the golden age (MHB, Vana 148), due both to the lack of existence of the concept of property (see 'property' above), and to the abundance that made regional specialisation unnecessary (Hesiod, Works & Days 225).

In the Vedantic tradition, trade was conducted by the Vaisya class which included farmers. This class, by its nature, does not possess the degree of virtue held by the Brahmana and Kṣatriya classes. Trade is described in the Srimad as Satyānṛta - a mixture of truth and falsehood (7, 11,19). The word used for merchant in the Bible (Canaan) is also largely associated with improper dealing (Leviticus 18, 3). Merchants are therefore extolled to practise virtuous behaviour, such as fully disclosing the condition of the property being sold (eg Cicero, Offices 3, 16). Yagnavalkya (2, 244) describes a number of measures for the regulation of trade and for the control of abuses (including the use of false weights, adulteration, misrepresentation, counterfeiting, profiteering and price fixing). The Srimad states that trade will be carried on almost entirely by fraud in the Iron age (12, 3, 34).

Trade is also taxed. The Laws of Manu and Sukra Niti both recommend taxation after consideration of the difficulty of bringing goods to the market (L of M 7, 127), although it is clear from the Sukra Niti (4, 2, 213) that this especially applies where value is increased by exchange 'on the streets and in market places' where land tax cannot be applied (note that the Sukra Niti also provides that taxation can only be taken from a merchant who profits). Solomon, also collected taxes from traders (Bible, 1 Kings 10, 14) and these traders came to him to give him taxation.

See also 'Retail Trade'.

Treasure - *From the same Greek root as the word 'thesis' literally meaning 'a store laid up', but in general usage means, valuables stored or accumulated, especially in the form of precious metals.*

Defined in the Sukra Niti as a collection of wealth by one person (4, 2, 1) but in this context referring to the king. It's function, for a king, is maintenance of the army and subjects, as well as for performance of sacrifices.

Tyranny - *From the Greek τύραννος which was originally 'an absolute sovereign', but later used to describe a severe or cruel ruler. In Greek usage, it is more inclined to reflect the irregular way in which a ruler came to power (especially in those states which had been traditionally hereditary monarchies). In modern usage it means, 'government by a tyrant' or 'a state where the ruler(s) uses power to oppress the subjects' or 'where authority is exercised in an unlawful manner; one where taxation, injustice, or cruel punishment, or the demand of unreasonable services, imposes burdens and hardships on the subjects which law and morality do not authorize'.*

In the older traditions, Tyranny is said to arise where the king is weak and does not protect the people. Plato states that Tyranny arises when people in a democracy have drunk too deeply the draft of freedom and will not accept authority and become subject to their worst and unrestrained desires (Republic 562 c).

Usury - *from the Latin 'usura' meaning 'use', 'usury' or 'interest', arising from the root 'usus' - 'to use'. Usury is a 'premium' or 'increase paid', or 'interest stipulated to be paid for a loan'. The Sanskrit word for this - kusidam (कुसीद) is akin to a word which carries the meaning lazy, inert. The old testament Hebrew word ('neh'-shek' from 'naw-shak'') means literally 'to strike with a sting in the tail' and figuratively 'to oppress with interest'.*

The practice was originally only permitted to the merchant and farming classes (L of M 10,115). It was considered a lawful way of acquiring wealth and part of the science of Varta (Sukra 1, 311). Indeed Jesus endorses the practise in the parable of the talents (Bible, Matthew 25, 14), generally interpreted as an injunction to make full use of all available resources.

Some limitations are recommended on the practice. The Jews were not permitted to charge interest to each other (Bible, Deut 23, 19) but were permitted to charge usury to non Jews (which is consistent with other measures such as the Jubilee Year, preventing substantial disparities of wealth within the community). Plato cautioned that not much money should be made from interest (Laws 743).

The Sukra Niti states that interest should be taxed (4, 2, 255) and imposes a limit on the amount of interest that can accrue against a debt (4, 5, 631).

Value - *Derived from the Latin 'valēre' meaning 'to be worth'. In economics, it means 'the amount of some commodity, medium of exchange, etc., which is considered to be an equivalent for something else'.*

What men value determines what is produced within the community. The Mahabharata explains that men's values fall into three categories, the desire for virtue, the desire for wealth and the desire for pleasure. The interplay of these is illustrated by Plato (Republic 543a-575b) as the nature of men change.

These values then come into operation in exchange where value is related to price. The value of any item is all that is paid for it (Sukra 2, 717).

Virtue - *From a common root found in many European languages meaning 'I grow'. The English words 'wax' and 'virile' are both from the same root. The English word has been received from the Latin uirtūs meaning 'manly excellence' (uir, 'a man'). Within these translations, the word is used to translate the Greek 'arete' meaning 'manliness, in the sense of valour' or 'excellence' (or refer to Plato on this subject) and in some contexts the Sanskrit 'dharma' (see Non English Terms).*

Virtue is described in the Vedic tradition as one of the three possible objectives of action, the other being wealth and pleasure (the relationship between these is described in MhB, Santi 123). All traditions describe Virtue as the source of wealth (eg Plato, Apology 30b). In some traditions the duty of work is highlighted, but in the larger context, the virtue is the work undertaken, and, wealth the result of this. On the other hand, the practice of 'virtue' requires wealth (MhB, Santi 8).

Wages - *Arriving in English from the old French word 'wage' meaning, 'a gage' (pledge or guarantee), 'a pledge', 'a stake' as well as 'payment for service'. Originally from the Latin 'wadium' - meaning 'a pledge'. Hence in due course it came to mean 'a guaranteed payment for service'. In economics, 'that for which one labours', and 'the price of labour hired and employed by an entrepreneur' (labour being the commodity offered for sale by a worker).*

The Sukra Niti contains quite a long section on wages (2, 788). Sukra defines wages as being paid by time (so much per day), or by work (so much per bucket of apples picked). Wages should be enough to support the worker and all those dependent on him, and provision should be made for holidays. The employer should also support the employee and or the family if the employee is no longer able to work. Rates of wages will vary largely depending on the skill of the employee (but Plato also notes that the skill in attending to a trade and the skill of obtaining a high salary are different skills (Republic 345c). Sukra also notes that wages are a contract (see also Bible, Matthew 20, 1-15), and rates are by agreement.

The general impression given is that wages do not leave any surplus for the employee or his family. In fact the amassing of surplus by the working class (Sudra's) is expressly prohibited in the Vedantic tradition (MhB, Santi 60). Not withstanding this, Sukra notes that low wages make enemies of the workers (2, 836). The importance of wages being paid promptly is stressed in a number of texts (Rama 1, 52; Sukra 2, 788 & Bible, Leviticus 19, 13). and given that the wages earner invariably has no surplus, the protection afforded by such laws is vital for the protection of the people.

Wealth - *Meaning variously, 'welfare', 'prosperity', or, more generally, 'a comparative abundance of things which are the objects of human desire'. The word is derived from the Anglo Saxon word 'wela' meaning 'opulence' or 'prosperity'.*

The Sanskrit word for the same is 'dhanam' (धन) which translates literally as both 'the prize in a contest', and 'any valued object'.

Wealth is one of the three principles objectives of human life, the others being Virtue and Pleasure (MhB, Santi 123). Further, wealth is required for the pursuit of these other objectives (MhB, Santi 176). It's principle function in creation is for sacrifice (virtuous behaviour) and the result of such sacrifice is pleasure (MhB, Santi 20). Not withstanding this, it is required, for the pursuit of a virtuous life and for pleasure (MhB, Santi 167), for the support and sustenance of life itself (MhB, Udyoga 114) for a man's sense of dignity and honour (MhB, Santi 8) & for government - especially for maintenance of the army (MhB, Santi 130). Wealth is not enjoyed by hoarding but in passing it on (MhB, Vana 199).

All the references in this collection are explicit that Wealth arises from virtue (eg Plato, Apology 30b).

The earth (land) is the source of all wealth

(Sukra 1, 357) and effort is required to extract it from the land. The Sukra Niti goes on to add that no amount of wealth is sufficient to satisfy all our desires and the effort required is continuous and woe betides the man who extracts wealth without protecting the land (1, 349).

People are devoted to the wealthy (MhB, Santi 322) & and the wealthy should be honoured by the King (MhB, Santi 88).

The accumulation of wealth however causes division in society (Plato, Republic 543). Government should move strongly to ensure that the distribution of wealth does not become lopsided (Bible. Leviticus 25, 8-17 & Plato, Laws 741). Once wealth has become mal-distributed, re-distribution becomes extremely painful (Plato, Laws 736). Pre-occupation with it causes the ruination of all the interests of man (Srimad 4, 22). The most favourable distribution is for all wealth to be shared equally among the community, but this is only possible among a strong and disciplined people (Note with Ficino, Letters 1, 73). Law is subsequently required to clearly identify for each man what is his, and what another's.

Work - *Meaning 'to exert one's self for a purpose' or 'to put forth an effort for the attainment of an objective'. The word or variations of it are found in many languages and have virtually identical meanings. The word is akin to 'wright', 'a workman' and 'wrought'. Sankara in his Commentary on Brihadaranyaka Upanishad defines it thus, 'Production, attainment, modification and purification are the functions of work. In other words, work can produce, or bring within reach, or modify, or purify something; it has no other function besides these'.*

All wealth is the result of work (Philo, Abel & Cain). The Bhagavad Geeta recommends that our attention should always remain with the work, and not the result of the work (MhB, Bishma 109). Plato expanding on this theme, uses the art of keeping sheep to demonstrate that the work is not for the worker, but the benefit of the work itself - say for the benefit of the sheep (Republic 345c).

All these extracts encourage engagement in work (Hesiod, Works & Days 293) so that mans natural attributes can be exercised. See also Labour above.

The Texts

Atharva Veda 1

Holy Bible - Old Testament
    Genesis 5
    Exodus 10
    Leviticus 12
    Numbers 15
    Deuteronomy 15
    Joshua 17
    1 Samuel 18
    2 Samuel 19
    1 Kings 19
    1 Chronicles 21
    Ezra 21
    Nehemiah 22
    Job 22
    Psalms 23
    Proverbs 23
    Ecclesiastes 23
    Isaiah 24
    Ezekiel 24
    Zechariah 26

Holy Bible - New Testament
    Matthew 29
    Mark 31
    Luke 32
    Romans 32
    Galatians 33

Gospel According to Thomas 34

Bṛhadāraṇyaka Upaniṣad 35

Brihaspati Smriti 39

Cicero
    The Offices 41
    On Laws 46

Confucius
    The Analects 47
    The Great Learning 48

Marsilio Ficino 49

Hammurabi's Code of Laws 53

Hesiod
    Works and Days 57

Lao Tsze
    Tao Te Ching 63

Laws of Manu 65

Mahabharata
    Adi Parva 75
    Sabha Parva 76
    Vana Parva 77
    Udyoga Parva 84
    Bishma Parva 86
    Santi Parva 88
    Anusasana Parva 105
    Aswamedha Parva 107
    Swargarohanika Parva 107

Mencius 109

Narada Smriti 120

Philo
    The Sacrifices of Able & Cain . . . 121
    On The Virtues 121
    Every Good Man Is Free 122
    The Special Laws 122

Plato
    Apology 127
    The Statesman 127
    The Republic 129
    The Laws 138

Ramayana 143

Shantanand Saraswati
    Conversations 149
    Man Who Wanted To Meet God . . . 153

The Shû King
    The Tribute of Yu 155

Śrīmad Bhāgavata 161

Sukra-Niti 167

Yajnawalkya Smriti 187

Zarathushtra 191

Atharva Veda

1. Truth, greatness, universal order (rita), strength, consecration, creative fervour (tapas), spiritual exaltation (Brahma), the sacrifice, support the earth. May this earth, the mistress of that which was and shall be, prepare for us a broad domain!

2. The earth that has heights, and slopes, and great plains, that supports the plants of manifold virtue, free from the pressure that comes from the midst of men, she shall spread out for us, and fit herself for us!

3. The earth upon which the sea, and the rivers and the waters, upon which food and the tribes of men have arisen, upon which this breathing, moving life exists, shall afford us precedence in drinking!

4. The earth whose are the four regions of space, upon which food and the tribes of men have arisen, which supports the manifold breathing, moving things, shall afford us cattle and other possessions also!

5. The earth upon which of old the first men unfolded themselves, upon which the gods overcame the Asuras, shall procure for us (all) kinds of cattle, horses, and fowls, good fortune, and glory!

6. The earth that supports all, furnishes wealth, the foundation, the golden-breasted resting-place of all living creatures, she..., shall furnish us with property!

7. The broad earth, which the sleepless gods ever attentively guard, shall milk for us precious honey, and, moreover, besprinkle us with glory!

8. That earth which formerly was water upon the ocean (of space), which the wise (seers) found out by their skilful devices; whose heart is in the highest heaven, immortal, surrounded by truth, shall bestow upon us brilliancy and strength, (and place us) in supreme sovereignty!

9. That earth upon which the attendant waters jointly flow by day and night unceasingly, shall pour out milk for us in rich streams, and, moreover, besprinkle us with glory!

11. Thy snowy mountain heights, and thy forests, O earth, shall be kind to us! The brown, the black, the red, the multi-coloured, the firm earth, that is protected by *Indra*, I have

---

XII, 1. Hymn to goddess Earth.

In praise of the Earth, *but also exemplifying the importance function of the earth in relationship to man.*

1. Note that these also relate to the nine stages of creation.

3. All life is dependant on the earth. See also verse 15 below.

4. All possessions are derived from earth (see also 6 below).

5. Asuras = Demons. Not only is the wealth from the earth, but the opportunity for man to express himself requires the earth.

6. See MhB, Bishma 4 (page 85) & Sukra 1, 357 (page 168).

8. Refer Old Testament, Genesis 1, 6.

11. No harm is to be done to the earth.

1

settled upon, not suppressed, not slain, not wounded.

12. Into thy middle set us, O earth, and into thy navel, into the nourishing strength that has grown up from thy body; purify thyself for us! The earth is the mother, and I the son of the earth; Parjanya is the father; he, too, shall save us!

13. The earth upon which they (the priests) in-close the alter (vedi) upon which they, devoted to all (holy) works, unfold the sacrifice, upon which are set up, in front of the sacrifice, the sacrificial posts, erect and brilliant, that earth shall prosper us, herself prospering !...

15, The mortals born of thee live on thee, thou supportest both bipeds and quadrupeds. Thine, O earth, are these five races of men, the mortals, upon whom the rising sun sheds undying light with his rays.

16. These creatures all together shall yield milk for us;...

17. Upon the firm, broad earth, the all-begetting mother of the plants, that is supported by (divine) law, upon her, propitious and kind, may we ever pass our lives!

18. A great gathering-place thou, great (earth), hast become; great haste, commotion, and agitation are upon thee. Great *Indra* protects thee unceasingly. Do thou, O earth, cause us to brighten as if at the sight of gold: not any one shall hate us!...

22. Upon the earth men give to the gods the sacrifice, the prepared oblation; upon the earth mortal men live pleasantly by food. May this earth give us breath and life, may she cause me to reach old age!

23 The fragrance, O earth, that has arisen upon thee, which the plants and the waters hold, which the Gandharvas and the Apsaras have partaken of, with that make me fragrant: not any one shall hate us!

24. That fragrance of thine which has entered into the lotus, that fragrance, O earth, which the immortals of yore gathered up at the marriage of Surya, with that make me fragrant: not any one shall hate us!

25. That fragrance of thine which is in men, the loveliness and charm that is in male and female, that which is in steeds and heroes, that which is in the wild animals with trunks (elephants), the lustre that is in the maiden, O earth, with that do thou blend us; not any one shall hate us!...

27. The earth, upon whom the forest-sprung trees ever stand firm, the all-nourishing, compact earth, do we invoke. ...

29. To the pure earth I speak, to the ground, the soil that has

12. Parjanya, the god of rain (usually shown as rain clouds), whose milk rains down as blessings, husband of the god earth.

13. Even sacrifice requires the earth. - see 22 below.

17. See MhB, Santi 190 (page 101) & Bible, Genesis 2, 19 (page 6).

18. Presumably as result of man's activities.

22. See also 13 above & 38 below.

23. Gandharvas = celestial singers & possessors of the secrets of soma (the divine nectar), Apsaras = Nymphs (wives of Gandharvas). NB Fragrance is the property associated with earth, like sweetness with water, brilliance with fire, strength with air, & sound with space.

24. Surya = deity of the sun

25. Thus the substance of all these is the same, vis earth.

grown through the Brahma (spiritual exaltation). Upon thee, that holdest nourishment, prosperity, food, and ghee, we would settle down, O earth!

30. Purified the waters shall flow for our bodies; what flows off from us that do we deposit upon him we dislike: with a purifier, O earth, do I purify myself! ...

32. Do not drive us from the west, nor from the east; not from the north, and not from the south! Security be thou for us, O earth: waylayers shall not find us, hold far away (their) murderous weapon!...

35. What, O earth, I dig out of thee, quickly shall that grow again: may I not, O pure one, pierce thy vital spot, (and) not thy heart!

36. Thy summer, O earth, thy rainy season, thy autumn, winter, early spring, and spring; thy decreed yearly seasons, thy days and nights shall yield us milk!...

38. Upon whom rests the sacrificial hut (sadas) and the (two) vehicles that hold the soma, in whom the sacrificial post is fixed, upon whom the *Brahmanas* praise (the gods) with riks and samans, knowing (also) the yagur-formulas; upon whom the serving-priests are employed so that *Indra* shall drink the soma;
...

40. May this earth point out to us the wealth that we crave; may Bhaga (fortune) add his help, may *Indra* come here as (our) champion!

41. The earth upon whom the noisy mortals sing and dance, upon whom they fight, upon whom resounds the roaring drum, shall drive forth our enemies, shall make us free from rivals! ...

44. The earth that holds treasures manifold in secret places, wealth, jewels, and gold shall she give to me; she that bestows wealth liberally, the kindly goddess, wealth shall she bestow upon us!

45. The earth that holds people of manifold varied speech, of different customs, according to their habitations, as a reliable milch-cow that does not kick, shall she milk for me a thousand streams of wealth!...

47. Thy many paths upon which people go, thy tracks for chariots and wagons to advance, upon which both good and evil men proceed, this road free from enemies, and free from thieves, may we gain: with what is auspicious (on thee) be gracious to us!

48. The earth holds the fool and holds the wise, endures that

30. The sense here is that it is the earth that purifies. Rivers & streams were always regarded as sacred, & not to be defiled by waste & impurity.

32. Thus allowing stability for the development & accumulation of wealth. See also Leviticus 18, 25 (page 12).

38. See 22 above. Riks, samans, yagurs = prayers etc from the Veda.

40. The verse acknowledges that man desires the product of the earth.

41. All activities including recreation & conflict require space on the surface of the earth.

45. The earth supports diversity.

good and bad dwell (upon her); she keeps company with the boar, gives herself up to the wild hog...

56. In the villages and in the wilderness, in the assembly-halls that are upon the earth; in the gatherings, and in the meetings, may we hold forth agreeably to thee!

57. As dust a steed did she, as soon as she was born, scatter these people, that dwelt upon the earth, she the lovely one, the leader, the guardian of the world, that holds the trees and plants...

58. The words I speak, honeyed do I speak them: the things I see they furnish me with. Brilliant I am and alert: the others that rush (against me) do I beat down.

59. Gentle, fragrant, kindly, with the sweet drink in her udder, rich in milk, the broad earth together with (her) milk shall give us courage! ...

61. Thou art the scatterer of men, the broadly expanding Aditi that yields milk according to wish. What is wanting in thee Pragapati, first-born of the divine order (rita), shall supply for thee!

61. See Bible, Leviticus 18, 25 (page 12).

62. Thy laps, O earth, free from ailment, free from disease, shall be produced for us! May we attentively, through our long lives, be bearers of bali offerings to thee!

62. Bali = an offering or oblation, & in other contexts a tax, impost or royal revenue.

63. O mother earth, kindly set me down upon a well-founded place! With (father) heaven cooperating, O thou wise one, do thou place me into happiness and prosperity!

Holy Bible - Old Testament

1. In the beginning God created the heaven and the earth.

Genesis 1:1 Origin

24. And God said, Let the earth bring forth the living creature after his kind, cattle, and creeping thing, and beast of the earth after his kind: and it was so.
25. And God made the beast of the earth after his kind, and cattle after their kind, and every thing that creepeth upon the earth after his kind: and God saw that it was good.

Genesis 1:24-25
God Created Creatures
see also Genesis 2, 19 (page 6) & MhB, Santi 190 (page 102)

26. And God said, Let us make man in our image, after our likeness: and let them have dominion over the fish of the sea, and over the fowl of the air, and over the cattle, and over all the earth, and over every creeping thing that creepeth upon the earth.
27. So God created man in his own image, in the image of God created he him; male and female created he them.
28. And God blessed them, and God said unto them, Be fruitful, and multiply, and replenish the earth, and subdue it: and have dominion over the fish of the sea, and over the fowl of the air, and over every living thing that moveth upon the earth.
29. And God said, Behold, I have given you every herb bearing seed, which is upon the face of all the earth, and every tree, in the which is the fruit of a tree yielding seed; to you it shall be for meat.
30. And to every beast of the earth, and to every fowl of the air, and to every thing that creepeth upon the earth, wherein there is life, I have given every green herb for meat: and it was so.

Genesis 1:26-30
Authority of Man
26. See Cicero, Offices 1, 7 (page 41).

27. Origen notes that male & female here, refers to 'soul & mind'.
28. See Zarathushtra, 3 (page 191). See similar Genesis 9, 7 below.
29. 'Meat' in NIV & NAS is translated as 'food'. With this diet no other creature is harmed. Note the change in Genesis 9, 3 below. See also MhB, Bhishma 9 (page 86) for description of the abundance given.

8. And the LORD God planted a garden eastward in Eden; and there he put the man whom he had formed.
9. And out of the ground made the LORD God to grow every tree that is pleasant to the sight, and good for food; the tree of life also in the midst of the garden, and the tree of knowledge of good and evil.
10. And a river went out of Eden to water the garden; and from thence it was parted, and became into four heads.

Genesis 2:8-24 The Garden of Eden
8.Jerome's notes show for this 'Moreover the Lord God had planted, from the beginning, a paradise in Eden (pleasure or bliss)'. It can also be read 'The Lord created a universe...'

11. The name of the first is Pison: that is it which compasseth the whole land of Havilah, where there is gold;
12. And the gold of that land is good: there is bdellium and the onyx stone.
13. And the name of the second river is Gihon: the same is it that compasseth the whole land of Ethiopia.
14. And the name of the third river is Hiddekel: that is it which goeth toward the east of Assyria. And the fourth river is Euphrates.
15. And the LORD God took the man, and put him into the garden of Eden to dress it and to keep it.
16. And the LORD God commanded the man, saying, Of every tree of the garden thou mayest freely eat:
17. But of the tree of the knowledge of good and evil, thou shalt not eat of it: for in the day that thou eatest thereof thou shalt surely die.
18. And the LORD God said, It is not good that the man should be alone; I will make him an help meet for him.
19. And out of the ground the LORD God formed every beast of the field, and every fowl of the air; and brought them unto Adam to see what he would call them: and whatsoever Adam called every living creature, that was the name thereof.
20. And Adam gave names to all cattle, and to the fowl of the air, and to every beast of the field; but for Adam there was not found an help meet for him.
21. And the LORD God caused a deep sleep to fall upon Adam, and he slept: and he took one of his ribs, and closed up the flesh instead thereof;
22. And the rib, which the LORD God had taken from man, made he a woman, and brought her unto the man.
23. And Adam said, This is now bone of my bones, and flesh of my flesh: she shall be called Woman, because she was taken out of Man.
24. Therefore shall a man leave his father and his mother, and shall cleave unto his wife: and they shall be one flesh.

11. Pison = increase, havilah = circle.
12. Meanings are obscure.
13. Gihon = bursting forth, Ethopia = black. 14. Hiddekel = rapid, Assyria = success, Euphrates = fruitfulness. Refer also Gospel of Bartholomew 63 'Thou that .. named the 4 rivers: to the 1st Phison, because of the faith (pistis) .. thou didst appear in the world to preach; to the 2nd Geon, for the man was of earth; to the 3rd Tigris, because by thee was revealed unto us the con-substantial Trinity; to the 4th Euphrates,.. by thy presence in the world thou madest every soul rejoice...
15. NIV ' to work it and take care of it'. See also Sukra 1, 357-360 (page 168).
17. The Hebrew implies good & evil as an object rather than a concept. The meanings include 'prosperity & adversity'.
19. See Genesis 1, 24 (page 5), MhB, Santi 190 (page 102) & Atharveda 12, 1 (page 1). Refer also Geeta 3, 14 'all creatures are the product of food'.
20. Other references to the Golden Age say man only had to think of things to satisfy desire. See eg MhB, Vana 148 (page 78).

18.Thorns also and thistles shall it bring forth to thee; and thou shalt eat the herb of the field;
19. In the sweat of thy face shalt thou eat bread, till thou return unto the ground; for out of it wast thou taken: for dust thou art,

Genesis 3:18-23 On expulsion from the Garden of Eden. *See MhB, Adi 68 (page 75) & MhB, Vana 148 (page 78), No*

and unto dust shalt thou return.

20. And Adam called his wife's name Eve; because she was the mother of all living.

21. Unto Adam also and to his wife did the LORD God make coats of skins, and clothed them.

22. And the LORD God said, Behold, the man is become as one of us, to know good and evil: and now, lest he put forth his hand, and take also of the tree of life, and eat, and live for ever:

23. Therefore the LORD God sent him forth from the garden of Eden, to till the ground from whence he was taken.

effort was required until after the end of the Golden Age.

19. See also Hesiod on the 'race of iron' (page 59).

20. 'Eve' literally= 'life giver'.

22. Meanings of Good & Evil here include prosperity & adversity.

23. The end of 'Golden Age', see Srimad 12, 3 (page 164).

1. And God blessed Noah and his sons, and said unto them, Be fruitful, and multiply, and replenish the earth.

2. And the fear of you and the dread of you shall be upon every beast of the earth, and upon every fowl of the air, upon all that moveth upon the earth, and upon all the fishes of the sea; into your hand are they delivered.

3. Every moving thing that liveth shall be meat for you; even as the green herb have I given you all things.

4. But flesh with the life thereof, which is the blood thereof, shall ye not eat.

5. And surely your blood of your lives will I require; at the hand of every beast will I require it, and at the hand of man; at the hand of every man's brother will I require the life of man.

6. Whoso sheddeth man's blood, by man shall his blood be shed: for in the image of God made he man.

7. And you, be ye fruitful, and multiply; bring forth abundantly in the earth, and multiply therein.

8. And God spake unto Noah, and to his sons with him, saying,

9. And I, behold, I establish my covenant with you, and with your seed after you;

10. And with every living creature that is with you, of the fowl, of the cattle, and of every beast of the earth with you; from all that go out of the ark, to every beast of the earth.

11. And I will establish my covenant with you; neither shall all flesh be cut off any more by the waters of a flood; neither shall there any more be a flood to destroy the earth.

12. And God said, This is the token of the covenant which I make between me and you and every living creature that is with you, for perpetual generations:

Genesis 9:1-12 God's instructions after the flood

1. Refer Plato Laws 676 & after for more on relevance of the flood. See also Shu King (page 155) for further references to the period after the flood.

3. Note the difference from Genesis 1, 29 above

7. See Genesis 1, 28 above. Expressed as a commandment, especially in relationship to the previous verse.

14. ¶ And the LORD said unto Abram, after that Lot was

Genesis 13:14-18 The Land

separated from him, Lift up now thine eyes, and look from the place where thou art northward, and southward, and eastward, and westward:

15. For all the land which thou seest, to thee will I give it, and to thy seed for ever.

16. And I will make thy seed as the dust of the earth: so that if a man can number the dust of the earth, then shall thy seed also be numbered.

17. Arise, walk through the land in the length of it and in the breadth of it; for I will give it unto thee.

18. Then Abram removed his tent, and came and dwelt in the plain of Mamre, which is in *Hebron*, and built there an altar unto the LORD.

is a gift from the Lord, to all generations (forebears & successors). *This is oft repeated in the Old Testament (see eg Lev 25, 23-34 page 14, Num 27, 6-11 page 15, Josh 24, 1-3 page ?, 1 Kings 21, 1-4 page 21) and other texts, (see eg Plato, Laws 923 page 142).*

14. 'Lot' = 'ignorance'.

18. Alternate Translation - 'Then Abram removed his tent, & came & dwelt in prosperity which is unity..'

7. And he said unto him, I *am* the LORD that brought thee out of Ur of the *Chaldees*, to give thee this land to inherit it.

Genesis 15:7 Gift of Land from the Lord. *Literally 'out of the light'*

28. This is the thing which I have spoken unto Pharaoh: What God is about to do he sheweth unto Pharaoh.

29. Behold, there come seven years of great plenty throughout all the land of *Egypt*:

30. And there shall arise after them seven years of famine; and all the plenty shall be forgotten in the land of *Egypt*; and the famine shall consume the land;

31. And the plenty shall not be known in the land by reason of that famine following; for it shall be very grievous...

33. Now therefore let Pharaoh look out a man discreet and wise, and set him over the land of *Egypt*.

34. Let Pharaoh do this, and let him appoint officers over the land, and take up the fifth part of the land of *Egypt* in the seven plentcous years.

35. And let them gather all the food of those good years that come, and lay up corn under the hand of Pharaoh, and let them keep food in the cities.

36. And that food shall be for store to the land against the seven years of famine, which shall be in the land of *Egypt*; that the land perish not through the famine...

41. And Pharaoh said unto Joseph, See, I have set thee over all the land of *Egypt*...

46. ... And Joseph went out from the presence of Pharaoh, and

Genesis 41:28-57 Joseph's management of the economy during famine (approximately 1800 B.C.).

Joseph = 'let him add (future)'.

28. see Srimad 7, 11 (page 161) for similar principle.

34. See L of M 10, 118 (page 73)

High taxation is appropriate in times of distress. See also MhB, Santi 87 (page 93) on organisation of a kingdom.

went throughout all the land of *Egypt*.

47. And in the seven plenteous years the earth brought forth by handfuls.

48. And he gathered up all the food of the seven years, which were in the land of *Egypt*, and laid up the food in the cities: the food of the field, which was round about every city, laid he up in the same.

49. And Joseph gathered corn as the sand of the sea, very much, until he left numbering; for it was without number...

53. And the seven years of plenteousness, that was in the land of *Egypt*, were ended.

54. And the seven years of dearth began to come, according as Joseph had said: and the dearth was in all lands; but in all the land of *Egypt* there was bread.

54. Bread = literally food, but sometimes bread.

55. And when all the land of *Egypt* was famished, the people cried to Pharaoh for bread: and Pharaoh said unto all the Egyptians, Go unto Joseph; what he saith to you, do.

56. And the famine was over all the face of the earth: and Joseph opened all the storehouses, and sold unto the Egyptians; and the famine waxed sore in the land of *Egypt*.

56. Sold = literally, to deal in grain.

57. And all countries came into *Egypt* to Joseph for to buy corn; because that the famine was so sore in all lands.

57. Buy corn = same word translated as 'sold' above.

6. And Joseph was the governor over the land, and he it was that sold to all the people of the land:...

Genesis 42:6
Joseph governs Egypt

13. And there was no bread in all the land; for the famine was very sore, so that the land of *Egypt* and all the land of *Canaan* fainted by reason of the famine.

Genesis 47:13-26
Joseph sells the corn
13. Figurative translation could read 'so that the land of bondage and the land of humiliation fainted by reason of hunger...'

14. And Joseph gathered up all the money that was found in the land of *Egypt*, and in the land of *Canaan*, for the corn which they bought: and Joseph brought the money into Pharaoh's house.

14. Money = literally, silver

15. And when money failed in the land of *Egypt*, and in the land of *Canaan*, all the Egyptians came unto Joseph, and said, Give us bread: for why should we die in thy presence? for the money faileth.

16. And Joseph said, Give your cattle; and I will give you for your cattle, if money fail.

17. And they brought their cattle unto Joseph: and Joseph gave them bread in exchange for horses, and for the flocks, and for the cattle of the herds, and for the asses: and he fed them with

bread for all their cattle for that year.

18. When that year was ended, they came unto him the second year, and said unto him, We will not hide it from my lord, how that our money is spent; my lord also hath our herds of cattle; there is not ought left in the sight of my lord, but our bodies, and our lands:

19. Wherefore shall we die before thine eyes, both we and our land? buy us and our land for bread, and we and our land will be servants unto Pharaoh: and give us seed, that we may live, and not die, that the land be not desolate.

Joseph bought the land

20. And Joseph bought all the land of *Egypt* for Pharaoh; for the Egyptians sold every man his field, because the famine prevailed over them: so the land became Pharaoh's.

21. And as for the people, he removed them to cities from one end of the borders of *Egypt* even to the other end thereof.

22. Only the land of the priests bought he not; for the priests had a portion assigned them of Pharaoh, and did eat their portion which Pharaoh gave them: wherefore they sold not their lands.

23. Then Joseph said unto the people, Behold, I have bought you this day and your land for Pharaoh: lo, here is seed for you, and ye shall sow the land.

24. And it shall come to pass in the increase, that ye shall give the fifth part unto Pharaoh, and four parts shall be your own, for seed of the field, and for your food, and for them of your households, and for food for your little ones.

25. And they said, Thou hast saved our lives: let us find grace in the sight of my lord, and we will be Pharaoh's servants.

26. And Joseph made it a law over the land of *Egypt* unto this day, that Pharaoh should have the fifth part; except the land of the priests only, which became not Pharaoh's.

21. N.I.V. translates as 'and Joseph reduced the people to servitude'

22. See Leviticus 25, 32 (page 14), Srimad 7, 11 (page 162) for similar provisions for priests. L of M prohibit a king acquiring the property of a priest, refer L of M 9, 189 & see Rama 1, 7 (page 145).

25 N.I.V & N.A.S. translations emphasise 'bondage to pharaoh' & 'slaves'

26. Priest are exempt from tax, see Leviticus 25, 33 (page 14).

1. And God spake all these words, saying,

2. I am the LORD thy God, which have brought thee out of the land of *Egypt*, out of the house of bondage.

3. Thou shalt have no other gods before me.

4. Thou shalt not make unto thee any graven image, or any likeness of any thing that is in heaven above, or that is in the earth beneath, or that is in the water under the earth:

5. Thou shalt not bow down thyself to them, nor serve them: for I the LORD thy God am a jealous God, visiting the iniquity of the fathers upon the children unto the third and fourth genera-

Exodus 20:1-17
The 10 Commandments (Approximately 1500 B.C.)
Refer Philo's 'The Decalogue' for a complete commentary on these commandments.

tion of them that hate me;

6. And shewing mercy unto thousands of them that love me, and keep my commandments.

7. Thou shalt not take the name of the LORD thy God in vain; for the LORD will not hold him guiltless that taketh his name in vain.

8. Remember the Sabbath day, to keep it holy.

9. Six days shalt thou labour, and do all thy work:

10. But the seventh day is the Sabbath of the LORD thy God: in it thou shalt not do any work, thou, nor thy son, nor thy daughter, thy manservant, nor thy maidservant, nor thy cattle, nor thy stranger that is within thy gates:

11. For in six days the LORD made heaven and earth, the sea, and all that in them is, and rested the seventh day: wherefore the LORD blessed the Sabbath day, and hallowed it.

12. Honour thy father and thy mother: that thy days may be long upon the land which the LORD thy God giveth thee.

13. Thou shalt not kill.

14. Thou shalt not commit adultery.

15. Thou shalt not steal.

16. Thou shalt not bear false witness against thy neighbour.

17. Thou shalt not covet thy neighbour's house, thou shalt not covet thy neighbour's wife, nor his manservant, nor his maidservant, nor his ox, nor his ass, nor any thing that is thy neighbour's.

10. Sabbath translates literally as 'desist from activity'.

12. See also Mencius 4, A, 5 (page 117).

14. The Hebrew word also means to apostatize (renounce totally a religious belief). Adultery and adulterate have the same root. The full context therefore covers pollution.

17. The Hebrew translates literally as 'Thou shall not delight in..."

25. If thou lend money to any of my people that is poor by thee, thou shalt not be to him as an usurer, neither shalt thou lay upon him usury.

Exodus 22:25 Usury forbidden among Jews. *See L of M 10, 115 (page 73). The same applies for the release from debt, see Deut 15, 3 (page 15) & 23, 19-20 (page 17).*

11. And the LORD spake unto Moses, saying,

12. When thou takest the sum of the children of Israel after their number, then shall they give every man a ransom for his soul unto the LORD, when thou numberest them; that there be no plague among them, when thou numberest them.

13. This they shall give, every one that passeth among them that are numbered, half a shekel after the shekel of the sanctuary: (a shekel is twenty gerahs:) an half shekel shall be the offering of the LORD.

Exodus 30:11-15 Taxation

12. The same Hebrew word is translated as 'ransom' (verse 12) and 'atonement' (verse 15).

13. 'Shekel' and 'gerah' are both weights. The effect is the same as a poll tax, but note the nature of the implementation. See Deut 18, 4 (page 16).

14. Every one that passeth among them that are numbered, from twenty years old and above, shall give an offering unto the LORD.

15. The rich shall not give more, and the poor shall not give less than half a shekel, when they give an offering unto the LORD, to make an atonement for your souls.

1. And the LORD spake unto Moses, saying,

2. Speak unto the children of Israel, and say unto them, I am the LORD your God.

3. After the doings of the land of *Egypt*, wherein ye dwelt, shall ye not do: and after the doings of the land of *Canaan*, whither I bring you, shall ye not do: neither shall ye walk in their ordinances.

4. Ye shall do my judgments, and keep mine ordinances, to walk therein: I am the LORD your God.

5. Ye shall therefore keep my statutes, and my judgments: which if a man do, he shall live in them: I am the LORD ...

24. Defile not ye yourselves in any of these things: for in all these the nations are defiled which I cast out before you:

25. And the land is defiled: therefore I do visit the iniquity thereof upon it, and the land itself vomiteth out her inhabitants.

26. Ye shall therefore keep my statutes and my judgments, and shall not commit any of these abominations; neither any of your own nation, nor any stranger that sojourneth among you:

27. (For all these abominations have the men of the land done, which were before you, and the land is defiled;)

28. That the land spue not you out also, when ye defile it, as it spued out the nations that were before you.

29. For whosoever shall commit any of these abominations, even the souls that commit them shall be cut off from among their people.

30. Therefore shall ye keep mine ordinance, that ye commit not any one of these abominable customs, which were committed before you, and that ye defile not yourselves therein: I am the LORD your God.

9. And when ye reap the harvest of your land, thou shalt not wholly reap the corners of thy field, neither shalt thou gather the gleanings of thy harvest.

10. And thou shalt not glean thy vineyard, neither shalt thou gather every grape of thy vineyard; thou shalt leave them for

Leviticus 18:1-30
The land ejects the unrighteous
3. Canaan = merchant, largely associated with improper dealings in the old testament. Refer Hosea 12, 7 'He is a merchant, the balances of deceit are in his hand: he loveth to oppress', & see Srimad 12, 3, 34 for nature of a merchant in this age (page 164).

25. See Atharva Veda 12, 1, 61 (page 1), Plato, Laws 740 (page 139) & MhB, Santi 97 (page 97) on the power of the land to expel its unrighteous inhabitants.

Leviticus 19:9-19 Provision for Priests.
9. For expansion see Philo, On Virtues (page 121). See also Srimad 7, 11, 15 (page 162),

the poor and stranger: I am the LORD your God.

11. Ye shall not steal, neither deal falsely, neither lie one to another.

12. And ye shall not swear by my name falsely, neither shalt thou profane the name of thy God: I am the LORD.

13. Thou shalt not defraud thy neighbour, neither rob him: the wages of him that is hired shall not abide with thee all night until the morning.

14. Thou shalt not curse the deaf, nor put a stumbling block before the blind, but shalt fear thy God: I am the LORD.

15. Ye shall do no unrighteousness in judgment: thou shalt not respect the person of the poor, nor honour the person of the mighty: but in righteousness shalt thou judge thy neighbour.

16. Thou shalt not go up and down as a talebearer among thy people: neither shalt thou stand against the blood of thy neighbour: I am the LORD.

17. Thou shalt not hate thy brother in thine heart: thou shalt in any wise rebuke thy neighbour, and not suffer sin upon him.

18. Thou shalt not avenge, nor bear any grudge against the children of thy people, but thou shalt love thy neighbour as thyself: I am the LORD.

19. Ye shall keep my statutes.

MhB, Santi 89 (page 96) & L of M 10, 125 (page 73) for proper livelihood of priest. See also Mencius 3, A (page 111) for similar provisions.

11. See Plato on the requirement for unity, Laws 739 (page 139)

13. See Sukra 2,799 (page 174) & Refer L of M 8, 215 for Law of Wages. Note the Hebrew language uses the same word for both 'work' and 'wages'.

14. See MhB, Santi 68 for protection of the weak (page 90).

18. See also Matthew 22, 36 (page 30)

1 And the LORD spake unto Moses in mount Sinai, saying,

2 Speak unto the children of Israel, and say unto them, When ye come into the land which I give you, then shall the land keep a sabbath unto the LORD.

3 Six years thou shalt sow thy field, and six years thou shalt prune thy vineyard, and gather in the fruit thereof;

4 But in the seventh year shall be a sabbath of rest unto the land, a sabbath for the LORD: thou shalt neither sow thy field, nor prune thy vineyard.

5 That which groweth of its own accord of thy harvest thou shalt not reap, neither gather the grapes of thy vine undressed: for it is a year of rest unto the land.

6 And the sabbath of the land shall be meat for you; for thee, and for thy servant, and for thy maid, and for thy hired servant, and for thy stranger that sojourneth with thee,

7 And for thy cattle, and for the beast that are in thy land, shall all the increase thereof be meat.

Leviticus 25:1-7 Seventh Year[1].

8. ¶ And thou shalt number seven Sabbaths of years unto thee, **Leviticus 25:8-17**

seven times seven years; and the space of the seven Sabbaths of years shall be unto thee forty and nine years.

9. Then shalt thou cause the trumpet of the jubilee to sound on the tenth day of the seventh month, in the day of atonement shall ye make the trumpet sound throughout all your land.

10. And ye shall hallow the fiftieth year, and proclaim liberty throughout all the land unto all the inhabitants thereof: it shall be a jubilee unto you; and ye shall return every man unto his possession, and ye shall return every man unto his family.

11. A jubilee shall that fiftieth year be unto you: ye shall not sow, neither reap that which groweth of itself in it, nor gather the grapes in it of thy vine undressed.

12. For it is the jubilee; it shall be holy unto you: ye shall eat the increase thereof out of the field.

13. In the year of this jubilee ye shall return every man unto his possession.

14. And if thou sell ought unto thy neighbour, or buyest ought of thy neighbour's hand, ye shall not oppress one another:

15. According to the number of years after the jubilee thou shalt buy of thy neighbour, and according unto the number of years of the fruits he shall sell unto thee:

16. According to the multitude of years thou shalt increase the price thereof, and according to the fewness of years thou shalt diminish the price of it: for according to the number of the years of the fruits doth he sell unto thee.

17. Ye shall not therefore oppress one another; but thou shalt fear thy God: for I am the LORD your God.

Jubilee Year *See also Deut 15, 1-11 (page 15). Refer also Philo 'On the Virtues' 99 & Special Laws 2, 110).*
10. Not withstanding any other significance of the number 50, note that it is both within a human life time & it is the period of major economic cycles (eg recessions of 1840's, 1890's 1930's & 1990's).
Note:- The principles of being sold into slavery for recovery of debt have been omitted here but proceed on the same lines. Hammurabi 117 limits such servitude to 3 years (page 57). 15. One effect of the Jubilee is to prevent the disproportionate accumulation of wealth. A prime requirement for unity & happiness within the state according to Plato, see Laws 729 (page 138). The commercial effect is the same as buying a 100 year lease on property. 17. Note: the principle for all commercial dealings.

23. ¶ The land shall not be sold for ever: for the land is mine; for ye are strangers and sojourners with me.

24. And in all the land of your possession ye shall grant a redemption for the land.

25. ¶ If thy brother be waxen poor, and hath sold away some of his possession, and if any of his kin come to redeem it, then shall he redeem that which his brother sold.

26. And if the man have none to redeem it, and himself be able to redeem it;

27. Then let him count the years of the sale thereof, and restore the overplus unto the man to whom he sold it; that he may return unto his possession .

28. But if he be not able to restore it to him, then that which is

Leviticus 25:23-34 Land is not to be sold
23. (NIV) 'you are but aliens and my tenants' ... aliens/- strangers can also be guests. See also Plato, Laws 740 (page 139) & Psalms 24, 1 (page 23). 27. Refer also L of M 8, 222 'If anybody in this (world), after buying or selling anything repent (of his bargain), he may return or take (back) that chattel within ten days'

sold shall remain in the hand of him that hath bought it until the year of jubilee: and in the jubilee it shall go out, and he shall return unto his possession.

29. And if a man sell a dwelling house in a walled city, then he may redeem it within a whole year after it is sold; within a full year may he redeem it.

30. And if it be not redeemed within the space of a full year, then the house that is in the walled city shall be established for ever to him that bought it throughout his generations: it shall not go out in the jubilee.

31. But the houses of the villages which have no wall round about them shall be counted as the fields of the country: they may be redeemed, and they shall go out in the jubilee.

32. Notwithstanding the cities of the Levites, and the houses of the cities of their possession, may the Levites redeem at any time.

33. And if a man purchase of the Levites, then the house that was sold, and the city of his possession, shall go out in the year of jubilee: for the houses of the cities of the Levites are their possession among the children of Israel.

34. But the field of the suburbs of their cities may not be sold; for it is their perpetual possession.

29. Note the distinction between income earning and residential property. This distinction is not made in the Sukra-Niti.

32. Note: Cities were allocated specifically for the Levites.

33. See also Genesis 47, 26 (page 9) for similar provisions for the priests.

34. In the word translated as 'suburb' can also be translated as; 'common', 'common land', 'open land'. NBD says this is a place or area to which the city livestock could be driven. Refer Numb 35, 1-5 for size of Common Land & Ezekiel 48, 15. Similar laws were provided by the Assyrians - see Ham 58 (page 55), & Vedic tradition see L of M 8, 237 (page 71) & Yaj 2,166 (page 188).

6. ¶ And the LORD spake unto Moses, saying,

7. The daughters of Zelophehad speak right: thou shalt surely give them a possession of an inheritance among their father's brethren; and thou shalt cause the inheritance of their father to pass unto them.

8. And thou shalt speak unto the children of Israel, saying, If a man die, and have no son, then ye shall cause his inheritance to pass unto his daughter.

9. And if he have no daughter, then ye shall give his inheritance unto his brethren.

10. And if he have no brethren, then ye shall give his inheritance unto his father's brethren.

11. And if his father have no brethren, then ye shall give his inheritance unto his kinsman that is next to him of his family, and he shall possess it: and it shall be unto the children of Israel a statute of judgment, as the LORD commanded Moses.

Numbers 27:6-11 Women can inherit

8. See Plato, Laws 923 (page 142), 1 Kings 21, 1-4 (page 21) for similar provisions. The import of this provision is that land will be available (in this agricultural community) by virtue of inheritance (see also 1 Kings 21, 1-4). There cannot be a market for land (see Leviticus 25, 23-34 above), and control of land cannot be accumulated into a few hands. The Platonic provisions are similar.

1. At the end of every seven years thou shalt make a release.

Deuteronomy 15:1-11

2. And this is the manner of the release: Every creditor that lendeth ought unto his neighbour shall release it; he shall not exact it of his neighbour, or of his brother; because it is called the LORD's release.

3. Of a foreigner thou mayest exact it again: but that which is thine with thy brother thine hand shall release;

4. Save when there shall be no poor among you; for the LORD shall greatly bless thee in the land which the LORD thy God giveth thee for an inheritance to possess it:

5. Only if thou carefully hearken unto the voice of the LORD thy God, to observe to do all these commandments which I command thee this day.

6. For the LORD thy God blesseth thee, as he promised thee: and thou shalt lend unto many nations, but thou shalt not borrow; and thou shalt reign over many nations, but they shall not reign over thee.

7. If there be among you a poor man of one of thy brethren within any of thy gates in thy land which the LORD thy God giveth thee, thou shalt not harden thine heart, nor shut thine hand from thy poor brother:

8. But thou shalt open thine hand wide unto him, and shalt surely lend him sufficient for his need, in that which he wanteth.

9. Beware that there be not a thought in thy wicked heart, saying, The seventh year, the year of release, is at hand; and thine eye be evil against thy poor brother, and thou givest him nought; and he cry unto the LORD against thee, and it be sin unto thee.

10. Thou shalt surely give him, and thine heart shall not be grieved when thou givest unto him: because that for this thing the LORD thy God shall bless thee in all thy works, and in all that thou puttest thine hand unto.

11. For the poor shall never cease out of the land: therefore I command thee, saying, Thou shalt open thine hand wide unto thy brother, to thy poor, and to thy needy, in thy land.

1. The priests the Levites, and all the tribe of Levi, shall have no part nor inheritance with Israel: they shall eat the offerings of the LORD made by fire, and his inheritance.

2. Therefore shall they have no inheritance among their brethren: the LORD is their inheritance, as he hath said unto them.

Care of the Poor Note the aspects of unity here as referred to by Plato eg. See also Ficino, Letters 1, 78 (page 49).

3. See also Exodus 22, 25 (page 11).

4. Note:- The implication being that man's activities are only blessed when all members of the community are provided for.

5. Lending is permitted but borrowing discouraged.

11. See also Matthew 26, 11 below.

Deuteronomy 18:1-5
Support of Priests
Note:- Priests were effectively the governing class, and in some contexts this could also be seen as taxation.

3. And this shall be the priest's due from the people, from them that offer a sacrifice, whether it be ox or sheep; and they shall give unto the priest the shoulder, and the two cheeks, and the maw.

4. The first fruit also of thy corn, of thy wine, and of thine oil, and the first of the fleece of thy sheep, shalt thou give him.

5. For the LORD thy God hath chosen him out of all thy tribes, to stand to minister in the name of the LORD, him and his sons for ever.

4. Expanded & explained by Philo, On Virtues 17 & 18 (page 121).

14. Thou shalt not remove thy neighbour's landmark, which they of old time have set in thine inheritance, which thou shalt inherit in the land that the LORD thy God giveth thee to possess it.

Deuteronomy 19:14 Bound- *aries See Plato Laws 843 (page 141) & L of M 8 245-265, (page 71) NB Manu only acknowledges boundaries of villages. See also Mencius 3, A, 3 (page 111) for effects of ignoring boundaries. Refer also Deut 27, 11, Prov 22, 28; 23, 10; Hosea 5, 10.*

19. Thou shalt not lend upon usury to thy brother; usury of money, usury of victuals, usury of any thing that is lent upon usury:

20. Unto a stranger thou mayest lend upon usury; but unto thy brother thou shalt not lend upon usury: that the LORD thy God may bless thee in all that thou settest thine hand to in the land whither thou goest to possess it.

Deuteronomy 23:19-20 *Money is not to be lent for interest i.e. to fellow Israelites, see also Exodus (page 11). For further on Usury See L of M 10, 115 (page 73). The Hebrew word here means literally 'to strike with a sting'.*

24. When thou comest into thy neighbour's vineyard, then thou mayest eat grapes thy fill at thine own pleasure; but thou shalt not put any in thy vessel.

25. When thou comest into the standing corn of thy neighbour, then thou mayest pluck the ears with thine hand; but thou shalt not move a sickle unto thy neighbour's standing corn.

Deuteronomy 23:24-25 Private Property

6. No man shall take the nether or the upper millstone to pledge: for he taketh a man's life to pledge.

Deuteronomy 24:6 No man can pledge his livelihood.

1. And Joshua gathered all the tribes of Israel to Shechem, and called for the elders of Israel, and for their heads, and for their

Joshua 24:1-13 Land is a gift of God

judges, and for their officers; and they presented themselves before God.

2. And Joshua said unto all the people, Thus saith the LORD God of Israel, Your fathers dwelt on the other side of the flood in old time, even Terah, the father of Abraham, and the father of Nachor: and they served other gods.

3. And I took your father Abraham from the other side of the flood, and led him throughout all the land of *Canaan*, and multiplied his seed, and gave him Isaac.

4. And I gave unto Isaac Jacob and Esau: and I gave unto Esau mount Seir, to possess it; but Jacob and his children went down into *Egypt*.

5. I sent Moses also and Aaron, and I plagued *Egypt*, according to that which I did among them: and afterward I brought you out...

8. And I brought you into the land of the Amorites, which dwelt on the other side Jordan; and they fought with you: and I gave them into your hand, that ye might possess their land; and I destroyed them from before you...

11. And ye went over Jordan, and came unto Jericho: and the men of Jericho fought against you, the Amorites, and the Perizzites, and the *Canaanites*, and the Hittites, and the Girgashites, the *Hivites*, and the Jebusites; and I delivered them into your hand.

12. And I sent the hornet before you, which drave them out from before you, even the two kings of the Amorites; but not with thy sword, nor with thy bow.

13. And I have given you a land for which ye did not labour, and cities which ye built not, and ye dwell in them; of the vineyards and oliveyards which ye planted not do ye eat.

See Genesis 13, 14-18 (page 7).

3. Canaan = 'merchants' or 'traffickers'.

11. Perizzites = 'belonging to a village'. Girgashites = 'dwelling on clayey soil'. Hivites = 'villagers'. Jebusites, 'an early name for Jerusalem, meaning threshing place'.
13. Note:- Olives are always planted for succeeding generations because of the period of time required before they bear fruit. Each generation lives by virtue of the previous generation or as in this case the previous inhabitants of the land.

10. And Samuel told all the words of the LORD unto the people that asked of him a king.

11. And he said, This will be the manner of the king that shall reign over you: He will take your sons, and appoint them for himself, for his chariots, and to be his horsemen; and some shall run before his chariots.

12. And he will appoint him captains over thousands, and captains over fifties; and will set them to ear his ground, and to reap his harvest, and to make his instruments of war, and instruments of his chariots.

1 Samuel 8:10-18 A king will oppress the people (Approx 1000 BC). *In the context of the Vedantic tradition quoted here, the Virtue of the king to protect the people is not available in this age. See Srimad 12, 3 (page 164), Plato Republic from 543a (page 131), and Tao Te Ching 17 (page 63). See 1*

13. And he will take your daughters to be confectionaries, and to be cooks, and to be bakers.

14. And he will take your fields, and your vineyards, and your oliveyards, even the best of them, and give them to his servants.

15. And he will take the tenth of your seed, and of your vineyards, and give to his officers, and to his servants.

16. And he will take your menservants, and your maidservants, and your goodliest young men, and your asses, and put them to his work.

17. He will take the tenth of your sheep: and ye shall be his servants.

18. And ye shall cry out in that day because of your king which ye shall have chosen you; and the LORD will not hear you in that day.

Kings 21 for another occurrence of this (page 21).

18. See 1 Kings 12, 3-19 (page 20) & 1 Kings 21, 1-4 (page 21) for a vindication of this prophecy.

6. Then David put garrisons in Syria of Damascus: and the Syrians became servants to David, and brought gifts. And the LORD preserved David whithersoever he went.

7. And David took the shields of gold that were on the servants of Hadadezer, and brought them to Jerusalem.

8. And from Betah, and from Berothai, cities of Hadadezer, king David took exceeding much brass.

9. When Toi king of Hamath heard that David had smitten all the host of Hadadezer,

10. Then Toi sent Joram his son unto king David, to salute him, and to bless him, because he had fought against Hadadezer, and smitten him: for Hadadezer had wars with Toi. And Joram brought with him vessels of silver, and vessels of gold, and vessels of brass:

11. Which also king David did dedicate unto the LORD, with the silver and gold that he had dedicated of all nations which he subdued;

2 Samuel 8:6-11 David collected tribute. *See L of M (page 73) & Srimad 7, 11 (page 162) for proper sources of revenue for the King.*

8. Abstract sense from the Hebrew is 'from security & from Cypress Groves, places of watch, mighty help, king David took...'

14. Now the weight of gold that came to Solomon in one year was six hundred threescore and six talents of gold,

15. Beside that he had of the merchantmen, and of the traffick of the spice merchants, and of all the kings of Arabia, and of the governors of the country.

I Kings 10:14-15 Taxation taken by Solomon

15. Note:- Merchants were taxed and tribute paid.

3. That they sent and called him. And Jeroboam and all the congregation of Israel came, and spake unto Rehoboam, saying,

4. Thy father made our yoke grievous: now therefore make thou

1 Kings 12:3-19 Oppressive taxation causes revolution (around 930 B.C.) *See 1 Sam-*

the grievous service of thy father, and his heavy yoke which he put upon us, lighter, and we will serve thee.

5. And he said unto them, Depart yet for three days, then come again to me. And the people departed.

6. And king Rehoboam consulted with the old men, that stood before Solomon his father while he yet lived, and said, How do ye advise that I may answer this people?

7. And they spake unto him, saying, If thou wilt be a servant unto this people this day, and wilt serve them, and answer them, and speak good words to them, then they will be thy servants for ever.

8. But he forsook the counsel of the old men, which they had given him, and consulted with the young men that were grown up with him, and which stood before him...

10. And the young men that were grown up with him spake unto him, saying, Thus shalt thou speak unto this people that spake unto thee, saying, Thy father made our yoke heavy, but make thou it lighter unto us; thus shalt thou say unto them, My little finger shall be thicker than my father's loins.

11. And now whereas my father did lade you with a heavy yoke, I will add to your yoke: my father hath chastised you with whips, but I will chastise you with scorpions.

12. So Jeroboam and all the people came to Rehoboam the third day, as the king had appointed, saying, Come to me again the third day.

13. And the king answered the people roughly, and forsook the old men's counsel that they gave him;

14. And spake to them after the counsel of the young men, ...

15. Wherefore the king hearkened not unto the people; ...

16. So when all Israel saw that the king hearkened not unto them, the people answered the king, saying, What portion have we in David? neither have we inheritance in the son of Jesse: to your tents, O Israel: now see to thine own house, David. So Israel departed unto their tents.

17. But as for the children of Israel which dwelt in the cities of Judah, Rehoboam reigned over them.

18. Then king Rehoboam sent Adoram, who was over the tribute; and all Israel stoned him with stones, that he died. Therefore king Rehoboam made speed to get him up to his chariot, to flee to Jerusalem.

19. So Israel rebelled against the house of David unto this day.

uel 8, 10-18 above, Sukra 2, 836 (page 176) & Srimad 12, 2, 7-9 (page 164).

1. Jeroboam = 'the people will contend', Rehoboam = 'a people enlarged'.

7. Note the King is expected to be the servant of the people. See Sukra 2, 838 (page 176).

10. See Confucius, Analects 12 (page 47).

1. ¶ And it came to pass after these things, that Naboth the Jezreelite had a vineyard, which was in Jezreel, hard by the palace of Ahab king of Samaria.

2. And Ahab spake unto Naboth, saying, Give me thy vineyard, that I may have it for a garden of herbs, because it is near unto my house: and I will give thee for it a better vineyard than it; or, if it seem good to thee, I will give thee the worth of it in money.

3. And Naboth said to Ahab, The LORD forbid it me, that I should give the inheritance of my fathers unto thee.

4. And Ahab came into his house heavy and displeased because of the word which Naboth the Jezreelite had spoken to him: for he had said, I will not give thee the inheritance of my fathers.

1 Kings 21:1-4 A man's inheritance cannot be sold *See also Leviticus 25, 23 (page 14).*

1. The abstract sense derived from the translation of the names is of the fruit of God's efforts being next to the might of Ahab, Naboth's (figurative) brother.

3. See Plato, Laws 923 (page 142) and Numbers 27, 6 (page 15) for similar injunctions.

1. Now the children of Israel after their number, to wit, the chief fathers and captains of thousands and hundreds, and their officers that served the king in any matter of the courses, which came in and went out month by month throughout all the months of the year, of every course were twenty and four thousand.

2. Over the first course for the first month was Jashobeam the son of Zabdiel: and in his course were twenty and four thousand.

3. Of the children of Perez was the chief of all the captains of the host for the first month.

1 Chronicles 27:1-3 Military Service as tax *Note: The service by month was presumably to allow attention to the land they held. Service of this kind has historically created problems for land-holders during harvest.*

21. And I, even I Artaxerxes the king, do make a decree to all the treasurers which are beyond the river, that whatsoever Ezra the priest, the scribe of the law of the God of heaven, shall require of you, it be done speedily,...

24. Also we certify you, that touching any of the priests and Levites, singers, porters, Nethinims, or ministers of this house of God, it shall not be lawful to impose toll, tribute, or custom, upon them.

25. And thou, Ezra, after the wisdom of thy God, that is in thine hand, set magistrates and judges, which may judge all the people that are beyond the river, all such as know the laws of thy God; and teach ye them that know them not.

26. And whosoever will not do the law of thy God, and the law of the king, let judgment be executed speedily upon him, whether it be unto death, or to banishment, or to confiscation of goods, or to imprisonment.

Ezra 7:21-26 Taxation

24. Taxation of priest forbidden see Leviticus 19, 9 (page 12). See also Srimad 7, 11 (page 162), MhB, Santi 89 (page 96) & L of M 10, 115 (page 73) for proper livelihood of priest. Nethinims - Temple Slaves.

26. Refer to MhB, Santi on punishment, and L of M.

1. And there was a great cry of the people and of their wives against their brethren the Jews.

2. For there were that said, We, our sons, and our daughters, are many: therefore we take up corn for them, that we may eat, and live.

3. Some also there were that said, We have mortgaged our lands, vineyards, and houses, that we might buy corn, because of the dearth.

4. There were also that said, We have borrowed money for the king's tribute, and that upon our lands and vineyards.

5. Yet now our flesh is as the flesh of our brethren, our children as their children: and, lo, we bring into bondage our sons and our daughters to be servants, and some of our daughters are brought unto bondage already: neither is it in our power to redeem them; for other men have our lands and vineyards.

6. And I was very angry when I heard their cry and these words.

7. Then I consulted with myself, and I rebuked the nobles, and the rulers, and said unto them, Ye exact usury, every one of his brother. And I set a great assembly against them.

8. And I said unto them, We after our ability have redeemed our brethren the Jews, which were sold unto the heathen; and will ye even sell your brethren? or shall they be sold unto us?

Nehemiah 5:1-8
Oppressive Taxation (approximately 430 B.C.)

4. some translations imply the money was borrowed with land as security, and others that the tax was calculated on the land. The former seems more consistent with the consequences described.

3. Doth God pervert judgment? or doth the Almighty pervert justice?

4. If thy children have sinned against him, and he have cast them away for their transgression;

5. If thou wouldest seek unto God betimes, and make thy supplication to the Almighty;

6. If thou wert pure and upright; surely now he would awake for thee, and make the habitation of thy righteousness prosperous.

Job 8:3-6
Righteousness produces prosperity
See MhB, Varna 31 (page 77).

8. And if they be bound in fetters, and be holden in cords of affliction;

9. Then he sheweth them their work, and their transgressions that they have exceeded.

10. He openeth also their ear to discipline, and commandeth that they return from iniquity.

11. If they obey and serve him, they shall spend their days in prosperity, and their years in pleasures.

Job 36:8-12
Prosperity arises from righteousness
The same principle is stated in every tradition used within these extracts. The operation of this law is described in the MhB, Santi 123 (page 97).

12. But if they obey not, thcy shall perish by the sword, and they shall die without knowledge.

1. The earth is the LORD's, and the fulness thereof; the world, and they that dwell therein.

Psalms 24:1 Earth is the Lord's
See Leviticus 25, 23 (page 14).

6. Go to the ant, thou sluggard; consider her ways, and be wise:
7. Which having no guide, overseer, or ruler,
8. Provideth her meat in the summer, and gathereth her food in the harvest.
9. How long wilt thou sleep, O sluggard? when wilt thou arise out of thy sleep?
10. Yet a little sleep, a little slumber, a little folding of the hands to sleep:
11.So shall thy poverty come as one that travelleth, and thy want as an armed man.

Proverbs 6:6-11 Idleness produces poverty

1. To every thing there is a season, and a time to every purpose under the heaven:
2. A time to be born, and a time to die; a time to plant, and a time to pluck up that which is planted;...
6. A time to get, and a time to lose; a time to keep, and a time to cast away;
7. A time to rend, and a time to sew; a time to keep silence, and a time to speak;
8. A time to love, and a time to hate; a time of war, and a time of peace.
9. What profit hath he that worketh in that wherein he labour-eth?
10. I have seen the travail, which God hath given to the sons of men to be exercised in it.
11. He hath made every thing beautiful in his time: also he hath set the world in their heart, so that no man can find out the work that God maketh from the beginning to the end.
12. I know that there is no good in them, but for a man to rejoice, and to do good in his life.
13. And also that every man should eat and drink, and enjoy the good of all his labour, it is the gift of God.
14. I know that, whatsoever God doeth, it shall be for ever: nothing can be put to it, nor any thing taken from it: and God doeth it, that men should fear before him.

Ecclesiastes 3:1-15 Time and Measure *See also Plato, Republic 2, 370 (page 129) & Mencius 3, A, 3 (page 111).*
1. 'It is time that does every act. Acts are of diverse kinds, and all proceed from Time. Who, therefore, injures whom? Birth and death happen in the same way...' MhB, Santi 139. See also MhB, Santi 224 (page 102).
11. With attention on the mani-festation, man does not see the cause.
13. The fruit of man's labour belongs to the man.
15. Refer Geeta Chap 2, 16 'That which is not shall never

15. That which hath been is now; and that which is to be hath already been; and God requireth that which is past. *be; that which is, shall never cease to be'.*

8. ¶ Woe unto them that join house to house, that lay field to field, till there be no place, that they may be placed alone in the midst of the earth!

Isaiah 5:8-10
Injunction against monopoly
(740 B.C.)

9. In mine ears said the LORD of hosts, Of a truth many houses shall be desolate, even great and fair, without inhabitant.
10. Yea, ten acres of vineyard shall yield one bath, and the seed of an homer shall yield an ephah.

10. Bath = approx 40 litres, ephah is the same but a dry measure.

1. The word of the LORD came again unto me, saying,...
3. And say unto Tyrus, O thou that art situate at the entry of the sea, which art a merchant of the people for many isles, Thus saith the Lord GOD; O Tyrus, thou hast said, I am of perfect beauty.

Ezekiel 27:1-33 (590 B.C.)
Picture of a Trading Port
(Tyrus a city in Phoenicia. Note the extent of trade at the time.)

4. Thy borders are in the midst of the seas, thy builders have perfected thy beauty.
5. They have made all thy ship boards of fir trees of Senir: they have taken cedars from Lebanon to make masts for thee.

5. Senir - Mt Hemon Lebanon

6. Of the oaks of Bashan have they made thine oars; the company of the Ashurites have made thy benches of ivory, brought out of the isles of Chittim.

6. Bashan - East of sea of Galilea, Ashurites - from Assyria, Chittim - on Cyprus.

7. Fine linen with broidered work from *Egypt* was that which thou spreadest forth to be thy sail; blue and purple from the isles of Elishah was that which covered thee.

7. Elishah - Cyprus.

8. The inhabitants of Zidon and Arvad were thy mariners: thy wise men, O Tyrus, that were in thee, were thy pilots.

8. Zidon - in Lebanon, Arvad - in Palestine.

9. The ancients of Gebal and the wise men thereof were in thee thy calkers: all the ships of the sea with their mariners were in thee to occupy thy merchandise.

9. Gebal - in Phoenicia - now the Syrian coast.

10. They of Persia and of Lud and of Phut were in thine army, thy men of war: they hanged the shield and helmet in thee; they set forth thy comeliness.

10. Lud - near Persia, Phut - Libya.

11. The men of Arvad with thine army were upon thy walls round about, and the Gammadims were in thy towers: they hanged their shields upon thy walls round about; they have made thy beauty perfect.

11. Arvad - Phoenicia.

12. Tarshish was thy merchant by reason of the multitude of all kind of riches; with silver, iron, tin, and lead, they traded in thy fairs.

12. Tarshish - Turkey

13. Javan, Tubal, and Meshech, they were thy merchants: they

13. Javan - Greece, Tubal -

24

traded the persons of men and vessels of brass in thy market.

14. They of the house of Togarmah traded in thy fairs with horses and horsemen and mules.

15. The men of Dedan were thy merchants; many isles were the merchandise of thine hand: they brought thee for a present horns of ivory and ebony.

16. Syria was thy merchant by reason of the multitude of the wares of thy making: they occupied in thy fairs with emeralds, purple, and broidered work, and fine linen, and coral, and agate.

17. Judah, and the land of Israel, they were thy merchants: they traded in thy market wheat of Minnith, and Pannag, and honey, and oil, and balm.

18. Damascus was thy merchant in the multitude of the wares of thy making, for the multitude of all riches; in the wine of Helbon, and white wool.

19. Dan also and Javan going to and fro occupied in thy fairs: bright iron, cassia, and calamus, were in thy market.

20. Dedan was thy merchant in precious clothes for chariots.

21. Arabia, and all the princes of Kedar, they occupied with thee in lambs, and rams, and goats: in these were they thy merchants.

22. The merchants of Sheba and Raamah, they were thy merchants: they occupied in thy fairs with chief of all spices, and with all precious stones, and gold.

23. Haran, and Canneh, and Eden, the merchants of Sheba, Asshur, and Chilmad, were thy merchants.

24. These were thy merchants in all sorts of things, in blue clothes, and broidered work, and in chests of rich apparel, bound with cords, and made of cedar, among thy merchandise.

25. The ships of Tarshish did sing of thee in thy market: and thou wast replenished, and made very glorious in the midst of the seas.

26. Thy rowers have brought thee into great waters: the east wind hath broken thee in the midst of the seas.

27. Thy riches, and thy fairs, thy merchandise, thy mariners, and thy pilots, thy calkers, and the occupiers of thy merchandise, and all thy men of war, that are in thee, and in all thy company which is in the midst of thee, shall fall into the midst of the seas in the day of thy ruin.

28. The suburbs shall shake at the sound of the cry of thy pilots...

Asia Minor, Meshech - on the border of Armenia.

14. Togarmah - Near Armenia

15. Dedan - probably Ethiopia

17. Minnith - probably part of Armenia, Pannang - probably pastry.

18. Helbon - a place in Syria

19. Dan - Palestine, Javan - Greece Cassia - a bark, Calamus- a reed or rod.

20. Dedan - Ethiopia.

21. Kedar - Nomads of Arabia.

22. Sheba - Ethiopia

23. Haran - probably near the Persian Gulf, Canneh etc - near the Tigris river.

25. Dictionaries give a variety of locations for this city.

28. Suburbs - translated as pasture lands NAS and shore lands NIV. See Leviticus 25, 34 (page 14).

33. When thy wares went forth out of the seas, thou filledst many people; thou didst enrich the kings of the earth with the multitude of thy riches and of thy merchandise.

33. See Plato, Laws 918 (page 141) On the proper function of a merchant.

1. And it came to pass in the fourth year of king Darius, that the word of the LORD came unto Zechariah...

5. Speak unto all the people of the land, and to the priests, saying, When ye fasted and mourned in the fifth and seventh month, even those seventy years, did ye at all fast unto me, even to me?

6. And when ye did eat, and when ye did drink, did not ye eat for yourselves, and drink for yourselves?

7. Should ye not hear the words which the LORD hath cried by the former prophets, when Jerusalem was inhabited and in prosperity, and the cities thereof round about her, when men inhabited the south and the plain?

8. And the word of the LORD came unto Zechariah, saying,

9. Thus speaketh the LORD of hosts, saying, Execute true judgment, and shew mercy and compassions every man to his brother:

10. And oppress not the widow, nor the fatherless, the stranger, nor the poor; and let none of you imagine evil against his brother in your heart.

11. But they refused to hearken, and pulled away the shoulder, and stopped their ears, that they should not hear.

12. Yea, they made their hearts as an adamant stone, lest they should hear the law, and the words which the LORD of hosts hath sent in his spirit by the former prophets: therefore came a great wrath from the LORD of hosts.

13. Therefore it is come to pass, that as he cried, and they would not hear; so they cried, and I would not hear, saith the LORD of hosts:

14. But I scattered them with a whirlwind among all the nations whom they knew not. Thus the land was desolate after them, that no man passed through nor returned: for they laid the pleasant land desolate.

Zechariah 7:1-14
Failure to obey the law of God will result in poverty. *i.e to act Virtuously.*
5-6. So that the act was selfish, See MhB, Varna 31 (page 77).

14. See Leviticus 18, 25 (page 12).

26

Supplementary Notes

1. *On Leviticus 25, 1-7* Philo comments 'Again. Are not the enactments about the seventh year so formally established, enjoining the people to leave all the land that year fallow and uncultivated, and allowing the poor to go with impunity over the fields of the rich to gather the fruits which that year grow spontaneously as the gift of nature, most merciful and humane ordinances? (98) The law says,"Six years let the inhabitants of the land enjoy the fruits as a reward for the acquisitions which they have made and for the labours which they have undergone in cultivating the land; but for one year, namely, the seventh, let the poor and needy enjoy it, as no work pertaining the agriculture has been done in that year."For, if any work had been done, it would have been absurd for one man to labour and for another to reap the fruit of his labours. But this ordinances was given in order that, the lands being left this year in some manner without any owners, no cultivation of the land contributing to its fertility, the produce, although full and complete, might be seen to proceed wholly from the bounty of God, coming forth as it were to meet and relieve the necessitous.'

Holy Bible - New Testament

1. For the kingdom of heaven is like unto a man that is an householder, which went out early in the morning to hire labourers into his vineyard.

2. And when he had agreed with the labourers for a penny a day, he sent them into his vineyard.

3. And he went out about the third hour, and saw others standing idle in the marketplace,

4. And said unto them; Go ye also into the vineyard, and whatsoever is right I will give you. And they went their way.

5. Again he went out about the sixth and ninth hour, and did likewise.

6. And about the eleventh hour he went out, and found others standing idle, and saith unto them, Why stand ye here all the day idle?

7. They say unto him, Because no man hath hired us. He saith unto them, Go ye also into the vineyard; and whatsoever is right, that shall ye receive.

8. So when even was come, the lord of the vineyard saith unto his steward, Call the labourers, and give them their hire, beginning from the last unto the first.

9. And when they came that were hired about the eleventh hour, they received every man a penny.

10. But when the first came, they supposed that they should have received more; and they likewise received every man a penny.

11. And when they had received it, they murmured against the good man of the house,

12. Saying, These last have wrought but one hour, and thou hast made them equal unto us, which have borne the burden and heat of the day.

13. But he answered one of them, and said, Friend, I do thee no wrong: didst not thou agree with me for a penny?

14. Take that thine is, and go thy way: I will give unto this last, even as unto thee.

15. Is it not lawful for me to do what I will with mine own? Is thine eye evil, because I am good?

Matthew 20:1-15 Contracts

1. 'Hire' -from Μτσθοσ - payment for service. Penny - using the Greek word 'denarias', a silver coin.

3. The Greek for Market Place 'Agora' can also mean activity. it is akin 'Egeiro' meaning to arise from sleep. Hence there is a double emphasis.

6. Note the abhorrence of idleness.

7. 'Right', here is used to translate 'dikaios'. More frequently within the New testament this is translated as 'righteous', 'virtuous' or 'observing divine laws'.

10. Note that the rate was agreed only with the first labourers. This technically is more in the area of gift. See also the definition of wages in Sukra Niti 2, 788 (page 174).

15. Evil here is from 'poneros' which is literally 'full of labors, or full of difficulties'.

17. Tell us therefore, What thinkest thou? Is it lawful to give tribute unto Caesar, or not?

18. But Jesus perceived their wickedness, and said, Why tempt ye me, *ye* hypocrites?

19. Shew me the tribute money. And they brought unto him a penny.

20. And he saith unto them, Whose *is* this image and superscription?

21. They say unto him, Caesar's. Then saith he unto them,

Matthew 22:17
Render unto Caesar

Note, the Hebrew tradition of 'sacrificing the first fruit made taxation a religious act. The Roman imposition would therefore have been even more vexatious.

36. Master, which is the great commandment in the law?

37. Jesus said unto him, Thou shalt love the Lord thy God with all thy heart, and with all thy soul, and with all thy mind.

38. This is the first and great commandment.

39. And the second is like unto it, Thou shalt love thy neighbour as thyself.

40. On these two commandments hang all the law and the prophets.

Matthew 22:36-40 Love thy neighbour as thyself

39. see also Leviticus 19, 18 (page 13). This verse is the basis of modern consumer protection law as cited in the Donahue vs Stevenson case.

14. For the kingdom of heaven is as a man travelling into a far country, who called his own servants, and delivered unto them his goods.

15. And unto one he gave five talents, to another two, and to another one; to every man according to his several ability; and straightway took his journey.

16. Then he that had received the five talents went and traded with the same, and made them other five talents.

17. And likewise he that had received two, he also gained other two.

18. But he that had received one went and digged in the earth, and hid his lord's money.

19. After a long time the lord of those servants cometh, and reckoneth with them.

20. And so he that had received five talents came and brought other five talents, saying, Lord, thou deliveredst unto me five talents: behold, I have gained beside them five talents more.

21. His lord said unto him, Well done, thou good and faithful servant: thou hast been faithful over a few things, I will make thee ruler over many things: enter thou into the joy of thy lord.

22. He also that had received two talents came and said, Lord, thou deliveredst unto me two talents: behold, I have gained two other talents beside them.

Matthew 25:14-30
Parable of the Talents *Refer also Luke 19, 11-26.*

15. A talent of Silver is approximately 45 kilograms. A substantials sum.

Note:- The substance of the parable can be taken as both an abhorance of idleness, and an expectation that wealth should be used to create more wealth, see Mark 4, 25-29 below.

23. His lord said unto him, Well done, good and faithful servant; thou hast been faithful over a few things, I will make thee ruler over many things: enter thou into the joy of thy lord.
24. Then he which had received the one talent came and said, Lord, I knew thee that thou art an hard man, reaping where thou hast not sown, and gathering where thou hast not strawed:
25. And I was afraid, and went and hid thy talent in the earth: lo, there thou hast that is thine.
26. His lord answered and said to him, Thou wicked and slothful servant, thou knewest that I reap where I soweth not not, and gather where I have not strawed:
27. Thou oughtest therefore to have put my money to the exchangers, and then at my coming I should have received mine own with usury.
28. Take therefore the talent from him, and give it unto him which hath ten talents.
29. For unto every one that hath shall be given, and he shall have abundance: but from him that hath not shall be taken away even that which he hath.
30. And cast ye the unprofitable servant into outer darkness: there shall be weeping and gnashing of teeth.

26. See Hammurabi 43 (page 54) & Zarathushtra 3 (page 191).

27. The first mention of bankers in the bible. 'Exchangers' is from the word 'trapezites' the origin being from the word for 'table' (the table which the money changers sat at and counted on). Similar origins for the Renaissance bankers and concepts such as 'cheque'.

29. See also MhB, Santi 8 (page 87).

11. For ye have the poor always with you; but me ye have not always.

Matthew 26:11 Poor always with you *See also Deut 15, 11 (page 15).*

25. For he that hath, to him shall be given: and he that hath not, from him shall be taken even that which he hath.
26. And he said, So is the kingdom of God, as if a man should cast seed into the ground;
27. And should sleep, and rise night and day, and the seed should spring and grow up, he knoweth not how.
28. For the earth bringeth forth fruit of herself; first the blade, then the ear, after that the full corn in the ear.
29. But when the fruit is brought forth, immediately he putteth in the sickle, because the harvest is come.

Mark 4:25-29 He that hath *25. See also MhB, Santi 8 (page 87).*

28-29. Note that it is nature which produces 'of itself' and in its own time, but the man is required to exert himself and collect the wealth immediately it is available.

10. And the people asked him, saying, What shall we do then?
1.1 He answereth and saith unto them, He that hath two coats, let him impart to him that hath none; and he that hath meat, let him do likewise.
12. Then came also publicans to be baptized, and said unto

Luke 3:10-14 Giving

12. Publicans = in the original

him, Master, what shall we do?

13. And he said unto them, Exact no more than that which is appointed you.

14. And the soldiers likewise demanded of him, saying, And what shall we do? And he said unto them, Do violence to no man, neither accuse any falsely; and be content with your wages.

Greek, 'a renter or farmer of taxes'. It was customary for the government to lease the right to collect taxes to individuals who then profited as they collected more.

6. He spake also this parable; A certain man had a fig tree planted in his vineyard; and he came and sought fruit thereon, and found none.

7. Then said he unto the dresser of his vineyard, Behold, these three years I come seeking fruit on this fig tree, and find none: cut it down; why cumbereth it the ground?

8. And he answering said unto him, Lord, let it alone this year also, till I shall dig about it, and dung it:

9. And if it bear fruit, well: and if not, then after that thou shalt cut it down.

Luke 13:6-9 Patience

7. Cumbereth - the Greek translates literally as 'to render idle, unemployed, or inactive'.

22. Is it lawful for us to give tribute unto Caesar, or no?

23. But he perceived their craftiness, and said unto them, Why tempt ye me?

24. Shew me a penny. Whose image and superscription hath it? They answered and said, Caesar's.

25. And he said unto them, Render therefore unto Caesar the things which be Caesar's, and unto God the things which be God's.

Luke 20:22-25 Render unto Caesar
Repeated Matthew 22, 17-21 & Mark 12, 14-17.
25. The Greek original for render can imply to 'deliver, sell discharge a debt, pay wages, tax or tribute'.

1. Let every soul be subject unto the higher powers. For there is no power but of God: the powers that be are ordained of God.

2. Whosoever therefore resisteth the power, resisteth the ordinance of God: and they that resist shall receive to themselves damnation.

3. For rulers are not a terror to good works, but to the evil. Wilt thou then not be afraid of the power? do that which is good, and thou shalt have praise of the same:

4. For he is the minister of God to thee for good. But if thou do that which is evil, be afraid; for he beareth not the sword in vain: for he is the minister of God, a revenger to execute wrath upon him that doeth evil.

5. Wherefore ye must needs be subject, not only for wrath, but also for conscience sake.

Romans 13:1-8 Authority
NAS Translation reads as follows:-1. Let every person be in subjection to the governing authorities. For there is no authority except from God,... 2. Therefore he who resists authority has opposed the ordinance of God; ... 6. For because of this you also pay taxes, For rulers are servants of God, devoting themselves to this very thing. 7. Render to all what is due them: tax to whom

6. For this cause pay ye tribute also: For they are God's ministers, attending continually upon this very thing.

7. Render therefore to all their dues: tribute to whom tribute is due; custom to whom custom; fear to whom fear; honour to whom honour.

8. Owe no man any thing, but to love one another: For he that loveth another hath fulfilled the law.

tax is due; custom to whom custom; fear to whom fear; honour to whom honour.

6. Tribute = the annual levy upon land houses and persons (from the Greek word meaning to carry or to bear).

7. ... For whatsoever a man soweth, that shall he also reap.

Galatians 6:7 Production

8. Neither did we eat any man's bread for nought; but wrought with labour and travail night and day, that we might not be chargeable to any of you:

9 Not because we have not power, but to make ourselves an ensample unto you to follow us.

10 For even when we were with you, this we commanded you, that if any would not work, neither should he eat.

11 For we hear that there are some which walk among you disorderly, working not at all, but are busybodies.

12 Now them that are such we command and exhort by our Lord Jesus Christ, that with quietness they work, and eat their own bread.

2 Thessalonians 3:8-12 Encouragement to work

Other Biblical Writings

And He said: The man is like a wise fisherman who cast his net into the sea, he drew it up from the sea full of small fish; among them he found a large (and) good fish, that wise fisherman, he threw all the small fish down into the sea, he chose the large fish without regret.

Gospel According to Thomas
81, 28
Ecology

[A man said] to him: Tell my brethren to divide my father's possessions with me. He said to him: O man, who made me a divider? He turned to his disciples, he said to them: I am not a divider, am I?

Gospel According to Thomas
94, 1

Brihadaranyaka Upanisad

11. In the beginning this (the *Ksatriya* and other castes) was indeed *Brahman*, one only. Being one, he did not flourish. He specially projected an excellent form, the *Ksatriya* - those who are *Ksatriyas* among the gods: *Indra*, Varuna, the moon, Rudra, Parjanya, Yama, Death, and Isana. Therefore there is no higher than the *Ksatriya*. Hence the *Brahmana* worships the *Ksatriya* from a lower position in the Rajasuya sacrifice. He imparts that glory to the *Ksatriya*. The *Brahmana* is the source of the *Ksatriya*. Therefore, although the king attains supremacy (in the sacrifice), and at the end of it he resorts to the *Brahmana* his source...

Sankara's Commentary:- *In the beginning this,* the Ksatriya and other castes, *was indeed Brahman,* identical with that Brahman[1] (Viraj) who after manifesting Fire assumed the form of that. He is called Brahman because he identified himself with the Brahmana caste. *One only:* Then there was no differentiation into other castes such as Ksatriya[2]. *Being one.* i.e. without any protector etc. such as Ksatriya, *he did not flourish,* i.e. could not do his work properly, Hence *he,* Viraj, thinking, 'I am a Brahmana, and these are my duties[3],' in order to create duties pertaining to a Brahmana by birth - to glorify himself as a performer of rites--*specially,* pre-eminently, *projected an excellent form.* What is that? The caste called Ksatriya. This is being pointed out by a reference to its individuals. -*Those who* are well known in the world as *Ksatriyas among the gods...* Who are they? This the text answers by mentioning particularly the anointed ones: *Indra,* the King of gods; *Varuna,* of the aquatic animals: *the moon,* of the Brahmanas; *Rudra,* of the beasts; *Parjanya,* of lightning etc.; *Yama,* of the Manes; *Death,* of disease etc.; and *Isana,* of luminaries[4]. These are some of the Ksatriyas, among the gods[5]. It should be understood that after them the human Ksatriyas, Pururavas and others belonging to the Lunar and Solar dynasties, presided over by the Ksatriya gods, Indra and the rest, were also created. For the creation of the gods is mentioned for this very purpose. Because Viraj created the Ksatriyas with some special eminence attached to them,

Book 1 iv 11
The origins of the castes (orders of society).
The substance here being that differentiation and specialisation is required to manifest the full glory, ie to flourish.

[1] *Ie originally men were not identified by caste. See also MhB, Santi 319 (page 104).*
[2] *See also Sukra 1, 375 (page 169) & MhB, Bishma 109 (page 87).*
[3] *The duties of a Brahmana are, teaching, studying the scriptures, performing sacrifices for others, and accepting alms, see L of M 1, 88 (page 65).*

[4] *Indra, also the power of the senses; Varuna, also the god of health.. All of these are associated with powers of nature (including death) & reflected in the nature of men.*
[5] *And these powers are reflected in earthly kings, See also MhB, Santi (page 90), Sukra 1, 141-*

therefore there is none higher than the Ksatriya, who is the controller of the Brahmana caste even. *Hence the Brahmana,* although he is the source of him, *worships the Ksatriya, who has a higher seat, from a lower position. Where? In the Rajasuya sacrifice. He imparts that glory* or fame which belongs to him, viz the title of Brahman, to the *Ksatriya. That* is to say, when the king, anointed for the Rajasuya sacrifice, addresses the priest from his chair as 'Brahman,' the latter replies to him, 'You, O King, are Brahman,' This is referred to in the sentence, 'He imparts that glory to the Ksatriya.' *The Brahmana who is the topic under consideration, is indeed the source* of the Ksatriya. *Therefore although the attains suprem-acy, viz- the distinction of being anointed for the Rajasuya sacrifice[6], at the end of it, when the ceremony is over, he resorts to the Brahmana, his source,-* i.e. puts the priest forward. *But he who* proud of his strength, *slights* or looks down upon the *Brahmana his own source, strikes at or destroys his own source. He becomes more wicked by doing* this. The Ksatriya is already wicked on account of his cruelty[7], and he is more so by hurting his own source *as in life one is more wicked by slighting one's superior.*

[6] *The coronation of the king.*
[7] *In as much as his duty to fight & protect the kingdom causes harm to others & in his adminis-tration of punishment. See L of M 7, 13 (page 67). This cruelty is often referred to in the MhB, especially in the Santi Parva.*

12. Yet he did not flourish. He projected the Vaisya - those species of gods who are designated in groups; The Vasus, Rudras, Ādityas, Visvadevas and Maruts.
13. He did not still flourish. He projected the *Sudra* caste - Pusan. This (earth) is Pusan. For it nourishes all this that exists.
14. Yet he did not flourish. He specially projected that excellent form, righteousness (*Dharma*). This righteousness is the controller of the Ksatriya. Therefore there is nothing higher than that. (So) even a weak man hopes to defeat a stronger man though righteousness, as (one contending) with the king. That righteousness is verily truth. Therefore they say about a person speaking of truth, 'He speaks of righteousness,' or about a person speaking of righteousness, 'He speaks of truth,' for both of these are but righteousness.
Sankara's Commentary:- *Yet, even after projecting the four castes, he did not flourish, fearing that the Ksatriya, being fierce, might be unruly. He specially projected that excellent form. What is it ? Righteousness. This righteousness, the projected excellent form is the controller of even the Ksatriya,*

Book 1.iv 12
12. That is merchants & Farm-ers, those who create wealth. The Sanskrit translates literally as 'a man who settles on the soil' from the root 'Viś - a set-tlement, homestead, house dwelling.
13. That is, those who are to serve the former three.
14. Dharma - The concept in-cludes righteousness, virtues, law, justice & religion. It is translated (usually) as one of these depending on the context. Alternatively, 'He flourished, or became prosperous as a result of virtue'. See Confucius, The Great Learning, 10 (page 48) For further references.

fiercer than that fierce race even... *Therefore, since it is the controller of even the Ksatriya, there is nothing higher than that,* for it controls all. The text proceeds to explain how it is: *So even a weak man hopes to defeat a stronger man than himself through the strength of righteousness, as in life a* householder contending even *with the king[1],* who is the most powerful of all. *Therefore it goes without saying that righteousness, being stronger than everything else, is the controller of all. That righteousness, which is expressed as conduct,* being practised by people, *is verily truth.* 'Truth' is the fact of being in accordance with the scriptures. The same thing, when it is practised, is called righteousness, and when it is understood to be in accordance with the scriptures, is truth. Since it is so, *therefore* bystanders knowing the difference between them *say about person speaking of truth,* i.e. what is in accordance with the scriptures in dealing with another, '*He speaks of righteousness,*' or well-known conventional propriety. Conversely also, *about a person speaking of righteousness* or conventional conduct, they say, '*He speaks of truth,*' or what is in accordance with the scriptures. *For both these* that have been described, that which is known and that which is practised, *are but righteousness.* Therefore that righteousness in its double aspect of knowledge and practice controls those that know the scriptures as well as those that do not. Therefore it is the 'controller of the Ksatriya.' Hence an ignorant man identified with righteousness, in order to practise its particular forms, identifies himself with one or other of the castes, Brahmana, Ksatriya, Vaisya or Sudra, which is the pre-condition of that practice[2]; and these are naturally the means that qualify one for the performance of rites.

See also Cicero, Offices, 2, 4 for the requirement of law to facilitate this flourishing (page 43).
[1] *Or in a modern context, civil law protects individuals against the excesses of government. Note also Bractons famous observation 'it is the law that creates the king'.*

[2] *That is to say, a man ignorant of his true universal nature (as Brahman), identifies with one or other of the forms of Dharma and becomes Brahmana, Ksatriya, Vaisya or Sudra. The difference being the identification only. See note 1 in verse 11 above.*

Brihaspati Smriti

2. That which may not be given is declared to be of eight sorts, joint property, a son, a wife, a pledge, one's entire wealth, a deposit, what has been borrowed for use, and what has been promised to another.

3. What remains after defraying (the necessary expenses for the food and clothing of his family, may be given away by a man; otherwise (by giving more than that), the religious merit (supposed to be acquired by the giver) though tasting like honey at first, will change into poison in the end.

4. When any field (or house) is given away, belonging to a number of houses or fields acquired in one of the seven modes of (lawful) acquisition, it is ordained to be viewed as a valid gift, whether it have been inherited from the father or acquired by the donor himself.

5. Self-acquired property may be given away at pleasure (by its owner); a pledge may be disposed of according to the rules of mortgage; in the case of property received as a marriage portion, or inherited from an ancestor, the bestowal of the whole is not admitted.

6. When, however, a marriage gift, or inherited property, or what has been obtained by valour, is given with the assent of the wife, kinsmen, or supreme ruler, the gift acquires validity.

7. Co-heirs (or joint-tenants), whether divided in interests or not, have an equal claim to the immovable wealth; a single (parcener) has no power to give, mortgage, or sell the whole (wealth).

8. The following eight sorts of gifts are recognised as valid by persons acquainted with the law of gift, viz. wages, (what was given) for the pleasure (of hearing bards, or the like), the price of merchandise, the fee paid for (or to) a damsel, (and what was given) to a benefactor (as a return for his kindness), through reverence, kindness, or affection.

9. What has been given by one angry, or resenting an injury, or through inadvertence, or by one distressed, by a minor, a madman, one terrified, intoxicated, overaged, cast out from society, idiotic, or afflicted with grief or an illness,

10. Or what is given in jest; all such gifts are declared to be

XV The Law of Gifts
See also Narada (page 120).

4. See L of M 10, 115 (page 73) For the seven modes of lawful acquisition of wealth.

6. See L of M 4, 227 for the virtue of a gift (page 67).

void gifts.

11. When anything has been given through desire of a reward, or to an unworthy man mistaken for a worthy person, or for an immoral purpose, the owner may resume the gift.

Cicero

.. Now, though this be a subject which all philosophers have employed themselves about (for, who ever dared to assume that name without laying down some instructions about duty?), yet have some sects of them given such accounts of man's happiness and misery, as destroy the very being of virtue and honesty: For he that makes any thing his chiefest good, wherein justice or virtue does not bear a part, and sets up profit, not honesty, for the measure of his happiness; as long as he acts in conformity with his own principles, and is not overruled by the mere dictates of reason and humanity, can never do the offices of friendship, justice, or liberality: nor can he ever be a man of courage, who thinks that pain is the greatest evil; or he of temperance, who imagines pleasure to be the sovereign good.

The Offices, Book I, II
Three pursuits of man, virtue, profit and pleasure *See also MhB, Santi, 123 (page 97) and 167 (page 100).*

Of the other remaining three [virtues], that which consists in upholding society, and keeping up mutual love and good nature amongst mankind, seems of the largest and most diffusive extent. It comprehends under it these two parts: first, justice, which is much the most glorious and splendid of all virtues, and alone entitles us to the name and appellation of good men; and, secondly, beneficence, which may also be called either bounty or liberality. Now the first thing that justice requires of us is this; that no one should do any hurt to another, unless by way of reasonable and just retribution for some injury received from him: and whatever belongs either to all in common, or particular persons as their own property, should not be altered, but made use of accordingly. Now no man can say that he has anything his own by a right of nature[1]; but either by an ancient immemorial seizure, as those who first planted uninhabited countries; or, secondly, by conquest, as those who have got things by the right of the sword; or else by some law compact, agreement, or lot... However, since at present, by some of these ways, each particular man has his personal possessions, out of that which by nature was common to all, it is but just that each should hold what is now his own; which, if any one endeavour to take away from him, he directly breaks in on common justice, and violates the rights of human society. "But seeing (as is excellently said by Plato) we are not born for ourselves

The Offices, Book I, VII
Property in Land
Justice and beneficence required to uphold society.

Charity upholds Society.

No-one is to be harmed.

[1]*Property does not exist by right of nature, see Plato, Republic 8, 543 (page 131) & Laws 739 (page 139) and in fact is only an appearance - MhB, Santi 321 (page 104), Shantanand Saraswati, The Man Who Wanted to Meet God (page 153) & Sukra 4, 5, 581 (page 182).*

[2] *'Now I...regard you & your*

alone; but that our native country, our friends and relations[2], have a just claim and title to some part of us;" and seeing whatsoever is created on earth was merely designed (as the Stoics will have it) for the service of men[3]; and men themselves for the service, good, and assistance of one another; we certainly in this should be followers of Nature, and second her intentions; and by producing all that lies within the reach of our power for the general interest, by mutually giving and receiving good turns, by our knowledge, industry, riches, or other means, should endeavour to keep up that love and society, that should be amongst men. Now the great foundation of justice is faithfulness, which consists in being constantly firm to your word, and a conscientious performance of all compacts and bargains.

possessions, not as belonging to yourselves, but as belonging to your whole family, both past & future, & yet more do regard both family & possessions as belonging to the state' - Plato, Laws Book 9. See also Plato Laws 923 (page 142).
[3] The Earth is for the use of man, see Bible, Genesis 1, 26 (page 5).

Riches then are most commonly desired, either to supply us with the necessaries of life, or furnish us with the pleasures and conveniences of it; or else, as it often is observed to happen in persons of great and aspiring minds, as a means of obtaining an interest in the public, and a power of obliging and gratifying one's friends[1]; to which purpose was that saying of the late Marcus Crassus, that whoever designed to be a leading man in the commonwealth, ought never to think he had estate enough, till he could maintain an army with its yearly revenue[2]. Others take pleasure in splendour and magnificence, in a handsome, noble, and plentiful way of living: all which things have begot an insatiable greediness after money, without which they can never be supported and maintained. Not but that a moderate desire of riches, and bettering a man's estate, so long as it abstains from oppressing of others, is allowable enough[3]; but a very great care ought always to be taken that we be not drawn to any injustice by it.

The Offices, Book I, VII
Wealth, for pleasure or public interest *See MhB, Santi 167 (page 101).*

[1] See also Sukra 4, 2, 5-8 (page 177).

[2] A statesman should have enough wealth to support an army. See Sukra, 1, 359 (page 168).

[3] See also MhB, Santi 8 (page 87).

But here it is observable, that the limits of justice are not so fixed, but that they may be altered by an alteration of circumstances; so that what at one time appears to be the duty of an honest and good man, at another is altered and becomes the quite contrary; to deliver up a trust, for example, or perform a promise, and other things relating to truth and faithfulness, are duties which justice itself will allow as, in several cases, to neglect or omit: for respect must be had to those general rules we before laid down, as the ground and foundation of all justice

The Offices, Book I, X
Justice cannot be fixed *See Plato, Statesman 294b (page 127). See also Shantanand Saraswati, 1978 (page 150).*

first, that no injury be done to another; and, secondly, that we make it our earnest endeavour to promote the good and interest of all mankind: so that our duty is not always the same, but various, according to a variety of circumstances[1]. There may be a contract or promise, for instance, the performance of which would bring very great damage, either to the person himself that made it, or the other party to whom it was made.

[1] See Also Ficino, Letters 1, 78 (page 49) & 2, 53 (page 50) For examples of how duty changes with different roles in the society.

Those who design to be partakers in the government should be sure to remember those two precepts of Plato; first, to make the safety and interest of their citizens the great aim and design of all their thoughts and endeavours, without ever considering their own personal advantage[1]; and, secondly, so to take care of the whole collective body of the republic, as not to serve the interest of any one party[2], to the prejudice or neglect of all the rest: for the government of a state is much like the office of a guardian or trustee; which should always be managed for the good of the pupil, and not of the persons to whom he is entrusted[3]; and those men who, whilst they take care of one, neglect or disregard another part of the citizens, do but occasion sedition and discord, the most destructive things in the world to a state: whence it comes to pass, that while some take part with the popular faction, and others make their court to every great one, there are but very few left who are concerned for the benefit and good of the whole[4].

The Offices, Book I, XXV
Rules to be observed in the government of the state and the administration of justice.
[1] See MhB, Bhishma 109 (page 87).
[2] See Ficino, Letters 1, 78 (page 49).

[3] As cited by Plato, Republic 554.

[4] See Plato on Oligarchy, Republic 550c onwards (page 132).

So houses, which serve to defend us from the extremities of heat and cold could neither at first have been made by mankind, or afterwards, if by earthquake, tempest, or length of days, they had fallen to decay, have been repaired or rebuilt, had not men joined together in one common society, and learned to borrow help and assistance of one another[1]. To this industry of men we are also indebted for conveyances of water, for making new channels and arms to rivers, and for turning the streams after such a manner, as thereby to water and fatten our grounds[2]; for throwing up banks to defend us from the waves, and making of new harbours in convenient places. From all which instances, and a great many others, that might easily be produced, it is abundantly manifest that the fruits and advantages reaped from those things which are called inanimate, are entirely owing to men's labour and industry[3]: secondly, those we receive from unreasonable animals, how

The Offices, Book II, IV
The advantages arising from men's joining in society.

[1] See L of M 7, 55 (page 68).

[2] For example see Shu King 3, 1, 2 (page 158)

[3] Wealth is the product of men's endeavours applied to nature.

very little and inconsiderable would they be if they were not augmented by the same people's industry? for who was it but men that first discovered the uses to which beasts in their several kinds might be serviceable? and how at this time could we feed or break them? How could we keep them, and get the most profit and advantage by them, without the endeavours and assistance of the same men? It is they that destroy us those creatures which are hurtful, and procure for us those which may be serviceable to us. Why need I mention a multitude of arts, which are absolutely necessary to our well-being here? for what help or succour could those that are sick, or what pleasure those that are healthy, find? how could mankind be supplied with victuals, and other conveniences or comforts of life, if it were not for that number of callings in the world[4], which are wholly designed to provide them of such things[5]; by means of which men have improved their way of living, and are raised to a condition so far above that of unreasonable animals? Again, cities could neither have been built nor frequented without a community and society of men: hence have arisen all laws and customs[6]; the bounds of equity and justice have been settled; and a certain and regular method laid down for the conduct of men's lives. This has brought modesty into request, and filed off the natural roughness of men's tempers; has contributed to the greater security of their lives[7], and established such a commerce and correspondence among them, as by mutual giving and receiving of benefits, by bartering and changing one commodity for another, one convenience for another, supplies them to the full with whatever they stand in need of.

But the principal thing for a governor to take care of is, that each individual be secured in the quiet enjoyment of his own[1], and that private men be not dispossessed of what they have, under a pretence of serving and taking care of the public: for nothing is more destructive to the peace of any nation than to bring in a new distribution of estates[2], which was attempted by Philip, in the time of his tribuneship: however, he quickly gave over his design, and did not persist stubbornly in defence of it, as soon as he found it was so vigorously opposed; but in his public speeches and harangues to the people, among a great many things to obtain their favour, he was heard to say one of very dangerous consequence;- That the whole city had not two

See also MhB, Vana 32 (page 78).

[4] *See Also Plato, Republic 2, 370 (page 129) & Mencius 3, A, 4 (page 113).*
[5] *As illustrated in the Brihad (page 35).*

[6] *The Brihad turns this around and states that the law comes first (page 35).*

[7] *Which is the first duty of government. See L of M 7, 2 (page 67).*

The Offices, Book II, XXI
Principal duty of Government
[1] *That person should be able to quietly enjoy his own property requires protection against robbers and hostile kings, see MhB, Santi 58 (page 88).*
[2] *See also Plato, Laws 736 (page 138) & Mencius 3, A (page 111).*

thousand men in it that were masters of estates: a very pernicious and desperate saying, directly tending to bring all things
to a level; which is the greatest misfortune that can befall any
people: for to what end were cities and commonwealths
established, but only that every one might be safer and securer
in the enjoyment of his own? For though men are by nature
sociable creatures, yet it was the design of preserving what they
had that first put them on building of cities for a refuge. It is a
second duty of the governors of a state to see that the people be
not forced to pay taxes[3], as they often were in our forefathers'
time, partly because they were always in war, and partly by
reason of the lowness of the treasury. This is an inconvenience,
which ought, as far as possible, to be provided against beforehand: but if any state should be under such circumstances, as
that it must be forced to make use of this expedient... care must
be taken to let the people know that it is absolutely necessary[4],
as affairs now stand; and that otherwise they must needs be
inevitably ruined.

[3] *The people should not be taxed. It is not clear whether he is
speaking of the common people
(wage earners) or all people.
The former is more consistent
with other extracts.*
[4] *See MhB, Santi 87 (page 93).*

Care ought therefore to be taken beforehand, which it is easy to
do by a great many ways, to keep people from running so much
into debt[1], as may bring any damage or inconvenience to the
public; and not, when they are in, to oblige the creditors to lose
what is their own, and let the debtors gain what in justice is
another's; for nothing so cements and holds together in union
all the parts of a society, as faith or credit; which can never be
kept up, unless men are under some force and necessity[2] of
honestly paying what they owe to one another...

The Offices, Book II, XXIV
To much debt is to be avoided
*See MhB, Santi 140 (page
100).*
[1] *The object of the Jubilee Year
& provisions in Hammurabi.*
[2] *That force being ultimately
punishment under law, see L of
M 7, 13 (page 67).*

The interest of individuals inseparable from that of the whole
community. The rule of not wronging another for our own
advantage extends to all mankind[1].
We should all of us therefore propose the same end, and every
one think his own interest, in particular, to be the same with
that of the community in general: which, if each one endeavour
to draw solely to himself, all union and agreement amongst
men will be dissolved. And if Nature enjoin us, that every man
should desire and procure the advantage of another, whoever he
be, though for no other reason than because he is a man, it
necessarily follows that all men are joined by the self-same
nature in one common interest; which, if it be true, then all
men are subject to, and live equally under, the same law of

The Offices, Book III, VI
Individual interest is not different from that of society
[1] *See Ficino, Letters 1, 78
(page 49), Plato, Republic 4,
423 (page 130), L of M 9, 296
(page 73).*

nature[2]: and if this be true, too, then certainly they are forbid, by that same law of nature, any ways to injure or wrong one another; but the first of these is undoubtedly certain, therefore the last must needs be so likewise: for as to what is usually said by some men, that they would not take anything away from a father or brother for their own advantage, but that there is not the same reason for their ordinary citizens, it is foolish and absurd: for they thrust themselves out from partaking of any privileges, and from joining in common with the rest of their citizens, for the public good; an opinion that strikes at the very root and foundation of all civil societies.

[2] *all men live under the same law of nature.*

The care taken by the Romans to make the seller tell the Faults of the thing to be sold.

In the matter of buying and selling estates, it is provided amongst us by the civil constitutions, that he who is the seller should tell all the faults that he knows of to the purchaser: for the twelve tables ordering no more than this, that the seller should be bound to make good those faults which were expressly mentioned by word of mouth in the bargain, and which whoever denied was to pay double damages, the lawyers have appointed a punishment for those who themselves do not discover the defects of what they sell: for they have so decreed, that if the seller of an estate, when he made the bargain, did not tell all the faults in particular that he knew of it, he should afterwards be bound to make them good to the purchaser.

The Offices, Book III, XVI
Morality in the sale of goods
See Plato, Laws 918 (page 141), and Ficino 1, 78 (page 49).
Note:- The propensity for immorality to be practised by traders must have been high due to the number of references extolling virtue. See also MhB, Udyoga 187 (page 85), & the note associated with Leviticus 18, 1-30 (page 12).

...Besides, government is something supremely in accordance with the prescriptions of justice and with nature; by which I mean that it is supremely in accordance with the law. For without government, no household can exist at all, and no community, and no nation, and not the human race itself, or the world of nature, or for that matter the entire universe. For the universe obeys God, and is obeyed by the seas and lands, so that human life is governed by the law which is universally valid.

On Laws (III) 1 - 4
Everything is governed by law
See Shantanand Saraswati 1978 (page 150).

And there shall be lesser officials assigned to particular functions, with authority in their fields. ... They shall issue bronze, silver and gold coinage on behalf of the state.

On Laws (III) 5 - 7 Issue of money. *A virtue Aristotle attributes to Solon was reform of weights, measures & coins. See Plato, Laws 741 (page 139).*

Confucius

The Master said, 'To rule a country of a thousand chariots, there must be reverent attention to business, and sincerity; economy in expenditure, and love for men; and the employment of the people at the proper seasons.'

Analects Bk I Chap V *Tf:-* *'this means people should not be taken from their husbandry for military service or public works at improper seasons'.*

1. The Master said, 'Ts'ze, you think, I suppose, that I am one who learns many things and keeps them in memory ?'
2. Tsze-kung replied, 'Yes,--but perhaps it is not so?'
3 ' No,' was the answer; 'I seek a unity all-pervading.'

Analects Bk X. Chap. II
Authority of Confucius

1. The duke Âi inquired of Yû Zo, saying, 'The year is one of scarcity, and *the returns for* expenditure are not sufficient;- what is to be done ? '
2. Yû Zo replied to him, 'Why not *simply* tithe the people?'
3.'With two-tenths,' said the duke, 'I find them not enough; - how could I do with that system of one tenth? '
4. Yû Zo answered, 'If the people have plenty, their prince not be left to want alone. If the people are in want, their prince cannot enjoy plenty alone'...

Analects Bk XII Ch. IX.
Light taxation is preferable[1]
2. Commentary from text below. See 1 Kings 12, 7 (page 20), L of M 10, 115-131 (page 73) & L of M 7, 127 (page 67) 4. See Plato, Laws 739 (page 139) & MhB, Santi 87 (page 93).

1. The duke of Sheh asked about government.
2. The Master said, *'Good government obtains, when* those who are near are made happy, and those who are far off are attracted.'

Analects Bk XIII Ch. XVI.
see MhB, Adi 109 (page 76) & Mencius 2, A (page 111).

10. 'I have heard that rulers of States and chiefs of families are not troubled lest their people should be few, but are troubled lest they should not keep their several places; that they are not troubled with fears of poverty, but are troubled with fears of a want of contented repose *among the people in their several places.* For when people keep their several places, there will be no poverty; when harmony prevails, there will be no scarcity of people; and when there is such a *contented* repose, there will be no rebellious upsettings'.
11. 'So it is, -- therefore, if remoter people are not submissive, all the influences of civil culture and virtue are to be cultivated attract them to be so; and when they have been so attracted,

Analects Bk, XVI Ch.1.
See MhB, Adi 49 (page 75), Santi 295 (page 103) & Srimad 4, 21 (page 161). The Duty of the King is to ensure each class attends to its 'proper' duty.

11. See Notes on Shu King (page 160).

they must be made contented and tranquil.

5. Book of Poetry, it is said, 'Before the sovereigns of the *dynasty* had lost the *hearts of the* people, they could appear before God. Take warning from the *house of* Yin. The great decree is not easily *preserved*.' This shows that, by gaining the people, the Kingdom is gained, and, by losing the people, the kingdom is lost.

The Great Learning Ch. X.
Virtue should be placed first
See Sukra 1, 133 (page 167).
Around 1400 BC.

6. On this account, the ruler will first take pains about *his own* virtue. Possessing virtue will give him the people. Possessing the people will give him the territory. Possessing the territory will give him its wealth. Possessing the wealth, he will have resources for expenditure.

7. Virtue is the root; wealth is the result.

7. See Plato, Apology 30 (page 127), explained at length in MhB, Santi 123 (page 97).

8. If he make the root his secondary object, and the result his primary, he will *only* wrangle with his people, and teach them rapine.

8. 'Virtue's dross is desire for reward...' See MhB, Santi 123 (page 97).

9. Hence, the accumulation of wealth is the way to scatter the people; and the letting it be scattered among them is the way to collect the people.

9 See also Plato on Oligarchy, Republic 550c onwards (page 132).

10. And hence, the ruler's words going forth contrary to right, will come back to him in the same way, and wealth, gotten by improper ways, will take its departure by the same...

19. From the perspective of both monopoly and frugality.

19. There is a great course *also* for the production of wealth. Let the producers be many and the consumers few. Let there be activity in the production, and economy in the expenditure. Then the wealth will always be sufficient.

20. The virtuous *ruler*, by means of his wealth, makes himself more distinguished. The vicious ruler accumulates wealth, at the expense of his life.

Supplemenary Notes:-

1. Re Analects Bk XII Chapter II. Commentary in Text - *By the law of the Chau dynasty (1765 - 249 B.C.), the land was divided into allotments cultivated in common by the families located upon them. 9/10 of the produce divided equally by the farmers, & 1/10 being a contribution to the State... 3. A former duke of Lû, Hsüan (B.C. 609-591) had imposed additional tax of 1/10 from each family's share. 4. The translator explains this is literally rendered, as,- 'The people having plenty, the prince-with whom not plenty? The people not having plenty, with whom can the prince have plenty?' Yû Zo wished to impress on the duke that a sympathy & common condition should unite him & his people. If he lightened his taxation to the regular tithe then they would cultivate their allotments with so much vigour, that his receipts would be abundant. They would be able, moreover to help their kind ruler in any emergency.*

Marsilio Ficino

Marsilio Ficino to Angelo Poliziano, the Homeric Poet: greetings.

GOD ordained all the waters of the world to be in common for creatures of the water, and all the earth for creatures of the earth. Only that unhappy being, man, divided what God had united[1].

He confined his dominion, which was vast by nature, to narrow limits. He introduced into the world 'mine' and 'yours', the origin of all strife and evil. Thus it was to good purpose that Pythagoras directed that everything should be held in common among friends[2], and that Plato directed the same among citizens. Therefore, those who are rich are regarded as most unjust if, because of their pride, they forget God, the bountiful giver of all riches. They make themselves masters over the poor, and call themselves possessors of wealth, when it is they who are possessed by their wealth. On the other hand, they are just and happy men who, endowed with great riches, regard themselves as servants of God, protecting the poor and distributing their wealth...

Letters, Volume 1, letter 73
"The rich man who is unjust, and the one who is just"
[1] See Shantanand Saraswati 'The man who wanted to see God' (page 153)
[2] Iamblichus 'Life of Pythagoras' Chptr 18 & Plato, Laws 739 (page 139). Pythagoras had an inner circle who shared everything in common and an outer circle (for those not strong enough to participate) who had private property.

Marsilio Ficino to Piero del Nero: greetings.

...It is the duty of a citizen to consider the state as a single being formed of its citizens who are the parts; and that the parts should serve the whole, not the whole the parts; For when the profit of the part alone is sought, there is no profit at all for either part or whole. When, however, the good of the whole is sought, the good of both is assured. Therefore because of this connection the citizen ought to remember that nothing good or bad can touch one limb of the state, without affecting the others and indeed the state as a whole. And again, nothing can happen to the whole body of the state without soon affecting each limb.

Let no one, then, in this household of city say, 'This is mine', and 'That is yours', for everything in this vast organism belongs in a way to everyone in common[1]. Rather let him say, 'Both this and that are mine', not because they are his personal property, but because he loves and cares for them. Let each

The Letters, Volume 1, Letter 78
"On the duty of a citizen"
See Plato, Republic 4, 423 (page 131) & L of M 9, 296 (page 73), Cicero, Offices 3, 4 (page 46).

[1] See Plato, Republic 5, 462 b (page 130).

man love and reverence his country as he would the founder of his family. Let the ordinary citizen obey the ancient, well-tried laws[2], just as he would obey God, for such laws are not established without God. Let the magistrate remember that he is subject to the laws in just the same way as the ordinary citizen is subject to the magistrate. Let him understand that when he passes judgement he is himself being judged by God. Let him always have before him the injunction of Plato, to have regard not for himself, but the state; and not just some part of the state but the whole. In short, he should know that Heaven's highest place is reserved for the man who has done his best to model his earthly country on the heavenly one. For nothing pleases the universal ruler of the world more than the universal good.

[2] Principle provided by the Common Law in the English Legal Tradition..

The virtue and duty of the priest are a wisdom that glows with piety, and a piety that shines with wisdom. The duty of the prince is to watch over all; mercy in justice, humility in greatness and greatness in humility. The duty of the magistrate is to remember that he is not the master but the servant of the law, and the public guardian of the state; furthermore, that while he is judging men he is being judged by God. The duty of the private individual is to obey the magistrates' commands so willingly that he seems not to be compelled by the necessity of the law but to be led by his own will. The duty of the citizen, whether he be a magistrate or private individual, is to care as greatly for the public interest as he greatly cherishes his own. The duty of the knight is bravery in war and noble action in peace; of the merchant, with true faith and diligence to nourish both the state and himself with good things from abroad; of the tradesman, honestly to distribute the provisions received from the merchant to each member of the state[1]. Merchants, craftsmen and others should so seek wealth that they harm no one. For whatever arises from evil in the end falls back into evil. Let them keep their wealth in such a way that they do not seem to have acquired it in vain, nor just for the sake of keeping it. Let them so spend that they may long be able to spend, and may prove to have spent honestly and usefully. The duty of the farmer is to consider the weather, and to consult older farmers on when to cultivate the land, and also to offer the fruits of the farm to his guests with trust and liberality equal to that of the farm which yielded those fruit with interest.

The duty of the master is to serve law and reason, so that he

The Letters, Volume 2, Letter 53 "Concerning Duties" *See also MhB, Sahbha 13 (page 76) & Santi 58 (page 88) For these requirements of both prince & magistrate embodied in the King. Note also this lack of humility in the prologue to Hammurabi's Code.*

[1] See Cicero, Offices 3, 4 (page 46).

can rule his servants lawfully and reasonably[2]; to consider the servant to be a man as much as the master, and always to combine humanity with authority. The servant's duty is to regard his own life as his master's, and his master's interest as his own; the husband's to love his wife as his own body and faculty of perception, and most carefully to lead her; the wife's to honour her prudent husband as if he were her mind and reason, and to follow him most willingly. The duty of the father is to cherish his sons as branches of his own life which have taken root, and to keep them upright by his own best example as if they were parts of himself; of the sons, to follow their father as their root and head, and to revere him as a second God; of a brother, to be disposed towards his brother as to a second self; of blood relatives, mutually to love each other as members of the same body; of those related by marriage, to remember that they have been joined by law as if it were by nature, and that they should share their possessions and labours...

[2] *See Sukra 2, 523 (page 171) & Srimad 7, 11, 13 (page 162).*

Hammurabi's Code of Laws

When Anu the Sublime. King of the Anunaki, and Bel, the lord of Heaven and earth, who decreed the fate of the land, assigned to Marduk, the over-ruling son of Ea, God of righteousness, dominion over earthly man, and made him great among the Igigi, they called Babylon by his illustrious name, made it great on earth, and founded an everlasting kingdom in it, whose foundations are laid so solidly as those of heaven and earth; then Anu and Bel called by name me, Hammurabi, the exalted prince, who feared God, to bring about the rule of righteousness in the land, to destroy the wicked and the evil-doers; so that the strong should not harm the weak; so that I should rule over the black-headed people like Shamash, and enlighten the land, to further the well-being of mankind. Hammurabi, the prince, called of Bel am I, making riches and increase, enriching Nippur and Dur-ilu beyond compare, sublime patron of E-kur; who reestablished Eridu and purified the worship of E-apsu; ..., who brought plenteous water to its inhabitants,...; shield of the land, who reunited the scattered inhabitants of Isin;... who firmly founded the farms of Kish,... who broadened the fields of Dilbat, who heaped up the harvests for Urash;... the White, Potent, who penetrated the secret cave of the bandits, saved the inhabitants of Malka from misfortune, and fixed their home fast in wealth; who established pure sacrificial gifts for Ea and Dam-gal-nun-na,... the shepherd of the oppressed and of the slaves;... who recognizes the right, who rules by law; who gave back to the city of Ashur its protecting god; who let the name of Ishtar of Nineveh remain in E-mish-mish; the Sublime, who humbles himself before the great gods... When Marduk sent me to rule over men, to give the protection of right to the land, I did right and righteousness in .., and brought about the well-being of the oppressed.

36. The field, garden, and house of a chieftain, of a man, or of one subject to quit-rent, can not be sold.

37. If any one buy the field, garden, and house of a chieftain, man, or one subject to quit-rent, his contract tablet of sale shall be broken (declared invalid) and he loses his money. The field, garden, and house return to their owners.

38. A chieftain, man, or one subject to quit-rent can not assign his tenure of field, house, and garden to his wife or daughter, nor can he assign it for a debt.

39. He may, however, assign a field, garden, or house which he has bought, and holds as property, to his wife or daughter or give it for debt.

40. He may sell field, garden, and house to a merchant (royal agents) or to any other public official, the buyer holding field, house, and garden for its usufruct.

41. If any one fence in the field, garden, and house of a

Hammurabi's Code 36-41

Property in Land The god of a city originally owned it's land, including an inner ring of irrigable arable land & an outer fringe of pasture. The citizens were his tenants, the king his vice-regent. Land tenure had devolved into a variety forms & kings were content with fixed dues in naturalia, stock, money or service. Many tablets found contain grants by the king removing the obligation of tenants & successors to pay revenues to the king (usually as a chieftain, man, or one subject to quit-rent, furnishing the palings therefor; if the chieftain, man, or one subject to quit-rent return to field, garden, and house, the palings which were given to him become his property.

favour for services rendered).
36. 'Subject to a quit rent' is
literally 'A bearer of dues'.
39. Holds as property is owned
in 'fee simple'.

42. If any one take over a field to till it, and obtain no harvest therefrom, it must be proved that he did no work on the field, and he must deliver grain, just as his neighbour raised, to the owner of the field.

Hammurabi's Code 42-44
Rent of Land *Note these mea-*
sures limit speculation.

43. If he do not till the field, but let it lie fallow, he shall give grain like his neighbour's to the owner of the field, and the field which he let lie fallow he must plow and sow and return to its owner.

43. see Bible, Matthew 25, 26
(page 30).

44. If any one take over a waste-lying field to make it arable, but is lazy, and does not make it arable, he shall plow the fallow field in the fourth year, harrow it and till it, and give it back to its owner, and for each ten gan (a measure of area) ten gur of grain shall be paid.

45. If a man rent his field for tillage for a fixed rental, and receive the rent of his field, but bad weather come and destroy the harvest, the injury falls upon the tiller of the soil.

Hammurabi's Code 45-52
Rent & Wages

46. If he do not receive a fixed rental for his field, but lets it on half or third shares of the harvest, the grain on the field shall be divided proportionately between the tiller and the owner.

47. If the tiller, because he did not succeed in the first year, has had the soil tilled by others, the owner may raise no objection; the field has been cultivated and he receives the harvest according to agreement.

48. If any one owe a debt for a loan, and a storm prostrates the grain, or the harvest fail, or the grain does not grow for lack of water; in that year he need not give his creditor any grain, he washes his debt-tablet in water and pays no rent for this year.

48. Other translations say - no
interest is paid.

49. If any one take money from a merchant, and give the merchant a field tillable for corn or sesame and order him to plant corn or sesame in the field, and to harvest the crop; if the cultivator plant corn or sesame in the field, at the harvest the corn or sesame that is in the field shall belong to the owner of the field and he shall pay corn as rent, for the money he received from the merchant, and the livelihood of the cultivator shall he give to the merchant.

49. Note here the difference
between Rent & Wages. See
also L of M 9, 48-56 (page 72).

50. If he give a cultivated corn-field or a cultivated sesame-field, the corn or sesame in the field shall belong to the owner of the field, and he shall return the money to the merchant as rent.

51. If he have no money to repay, then he shall pay in corn or sesame in place of the money as rent for what he received from the merchant, according to the royal tariff.

52. If the cultivator do not plant corn or sesame in the field, the debtor's contract is not weakened.

51. Especially where the stock of money is limited, this measure prevents the abuse of the debtor by the creditor, when the debtor cannot obtain coins to satisfy the debt.

53. If any one be too lazy to keep his dam in proper condition, and does not so keep it; if then the dam break and all the fields be flooded, then shall he in whose dam the break occurred be sold for money, and the money shall replace the corn which he has caused to be ruined.

54. If he be not able to replace the corn, then he and his possessions shall be divided among the farmers whose corn he has flooded.

55. If any one open his ditches to water his crop, but is careless, and the water flood the field of his neighbour, then he shall pay his neighbour corn for his loss.

56. If a man let in the water, and the water overflow the plantation of his neighbour, he shall pay ten gur of corn for every ten gan of land.

57. If a shepherd, without the permission of the owner of the field, and without the knowledge of the owner of the sheep, lets the sheep into a field to graze, then the owner of the field shall harvest his crop, and the shepherd, who had pastured his flock there without permission of the owner of the field, shall pay to the owner twenty gur of corn for every ten gan.

58. If after the flocks have left the pasture and been shut up in the common fold at the city gate, any shepherd let them into a field and they graze there, this shepherd shall take possession of the field which he has allowed to be grazed on, and at the harvest he must pay sixty gur of corn for every ten gan.

59. If any man, without the knowledge of the owner of a garden, fell a tree in a garden he shall pay half a mina in money.

60. If any one give over a field to a gardener, for him to plant it as a garden, if he work at it, and care for it for four years, in the fifth year the owner and the gardener shall divide it, the owner taking his part in charge.

Hammurabi's Code 53-65
Liability for Damage
The same provisions are found in other legal codes of the Middle East. Refer to 'Ancient & Near East Texts' relating to extracts from the Assyrian legal code. ...

58. See Bible, Leviticus 25, 34 (page 14). Note the concept of common land around villages towns and cities is also found in Yajnavalya and others. See Yaj 2, 166 (page 188) & L of M 8, 237 (page 71).

61. If the gardener has not completed the planting of the field, leaving one part unused, this shall be assigned to him as his.

62. If he do not plant the field that was given over to him as a garden, if it be arable land (for corn or sesame) the gardener shall pay the owner the produce of the field for the years that he let it lie fallow, according to the product of neighbouring fields, put the field in arable condition and return it to its owner. *62. Rent is payable by the productiveness of the land, not for the product.*

63. If he transform waste land into arable fields and return it to its owner, the latter shall pay him for one year ten gur for ten gan.

64. If any one hand over his garden to a gardener to work, the gardener shall pay to its owner two-thirds of the produce of the garden, for so long as he has it in possession, and the other third shall he keep.

65. If the gardener do not work in the garden and the product fall off, the gardener shall pay in proportion to other neighbouring gardens. *[Here a portion of the text is missing, apparently comprising 34 paragraphs.]*

100. ... interest for the money, as much as he has received, he shall give a note therefor, and on the day, when they settle, pay to the merchant. **Hammurabi's Code 100-119 Loans, Merchants and Debts**

101. If there are no mercantile arrangements in the place whither he went, he shall leave the entire amount of money which he received with the broker to give to the merchant.

102. If a merchant entrust money to an agent (broker) for some investment, and the broker suffer a loss in the place to which he goes, he shall make good the capital to the merchant.

103. If, while on the journey, an enemy take away from him anything that he had, the broker shall swear by God and be free of obligation.

104. If a merchant give an agent corn, wool, oil, or any other goods to transport, the agent shall give a receipt for the amount, and compensate the merchant therefor. Then he shall obtain a receipt form the merchant for the money that he gives the merchant.

105. If the agent is careless, and does not take a receipt for the money which he gave the merchant, he can not consider the unreceipted money as his own.

106. If the agent accept money from the merchant, but have a quarrel with the merchant (denying the receipt), then shall the merchant swear before God and witnesses that he has given this

money to the agent, and the agent shall pay him three times the sum.

107. If the merchant cheat the agent, in that as the latter has returned to him all that had been given him, but the merchant denies the receipt of what had been returned to him, then shall this agent convict the merchant before God and the judges, and if he still deny receiving what the agent had given him shall pay six times the sum to the agent...

112. If any one be on a journey and entrust silver, gold, precious stones, or any movable property to another, and wish to recover it from him; if the latter do not bring all of the property to the appointed place, but appropriate it to his own use, then shall this man, who did not bring the property to hand it over, be convicted, and he shall pay fivefold for all that had been entrusted to him.

117. If any one fail to meet a claim for debt, and sell himself, his wife, his son, and daughter for money or give them away to forced labour: they shall work for three years in the house of the man who bought them, or the proprietor, and in the fourth year they shall be set free.

117. The concept of the Jubilee Year provided this for the Hebrews. See Bible, Leviticus 25 (page 13). Yaj also provides for indenture for debts unpaid. See Yaj 2, 43 (page 187).

118. If he give a male or female slave away for forced labour, and the merchant sublease them, or sell them for money, no objection can be raised.

119. If any one fail to meet a claim for debt, and he sell the maid servant who has borne him children, for money, the money which the merchant has paid shall be repaid to him by the owner of the slave and she shall be freed.

120. If any one store corn for safe keeping in another person's house, and any harm happen to the corn in storage, or if the owner of the house open the granary and take some of the corn, or if especially he deny that the corn was stored in his house: then the owner of the corn shall claim his corn before God (on oath), and the owner of the house shall pay its owner for all of the corn that he took.

Hammurabi's Code 120-125 Other People's Property

Similar Provisions are described in the Laws of Manu, refer Book 8).

121. If any one store corn in another man's house he shall pay him storage at the rate of one gur for every five ka of corn per year.

122. If any one give another silver, gold, or anything else to keep, he shall show everything to some witness, draw up a contract, and then hand it over for safe keeping.

123. If he turn it over for safe keeping without witness or

contract, and if he to whom it was given deny it, then he has no legitimate claim.

124. If any one deliver silver, gold, or anything else to another for safe keeping, before a witness, but he deny it, he shall be brought before a judge, and all that he has denied he shall pay in full.

125. If any one place his property with another for safe keeping, and there, either through thieves or robbers, his property and the property of the other man be lost, the owner of the house, through whose neglect the loss took place, shall compensate the owner for all that was given to him in charge. But the owner of the house shall try to follow up and recover his property, and take it away from the thief.

Hesiod

(106) Or if you will, I will sum you up another tale well and skilfully -- and do you lay it up in your heart, -- how the gods and mortal men sprang from one source.

(109) First of all the deathless gods who dwell on Olympus made a golden race of mortal men And they lived like gods without sorrow of heart, remote and free from toil and grief: miserable age rested not on them; but with legs and arms never failing they made merry with feasting beyond the reach of all evils. Vile old age[1].

When they died, it was as though they were overcome with sleep, and they had all good things; for the fruitful earth unforced bare them fruit abundantly and without stint [2].

They dwelt in ease and peace upon their lands with many good things, rich in flocks and loved by the blessed gods.

(121) But after earth had covered this generation -- they are called pure spirits dwelling on the earth, and are kindly, delivering from harm, and guardians of mortal men; for they roam everywhere over the earth, clothed in mist and keep watch on judgements and cruel deeds, givers of wealth; for this royal right also they received; -- then they who dwell on Olympus made a second generation which was of silver and less noble by far. [3]: It was like the golden race neither in body nor in spirit. ...[4]

(170) ... would that I were not among the men of the fifth generation, but either had died before or been born afterwards. For now truly is a race of iron, [5] and men never rest from labour and sorrow by day[6]; and from perishing by night; and the gods shall lay sore trouble upon them. But, notwithstanding, even these shall have some good mingled with their evils. when they come to have grey hair on the temples at their birth The father will not agree with his children, nor the children with their father, nor guest with his host, nor comrade with comrade; nor will brother be dear to brother as aforetime. Men will dishonour their parents as they grow quickly old... They will not repay their aged parents the cost their nurture, for might shall be their right: and one man will sack another's city. There will be no favour for the man who keeps his oath or for the just or for the good; but rather men will praise the evil-doer

Hesiod, Works and Days 106-201

The Ages in the Greek Tradition

This story is similar to those found in the Vedantic tradition both in structure & substance. Each age has a finite beginning & end. The change is based on a diminution of virtue. See eg Srimad 12, 3 (page 164). Refer also a similar story from Virgil.

[1] *The Vedantic tradition also provides that the span of life is diminished with each successive age. It is reflected in places in the bible (and .. Begat .. and he live for ..years etc).*

[2] *See MhB, Adi 68 (page 75).*

[3] *Refer also Plato, Republic 8, 543 for these differences.*

[4] *The descriptions of the intervening ages have been omitted. They largely follow the Vedantic tradition except that a fifth has been added and some of the qualities of men in each age are not represented in the same sequence.*

[5] *See Srimad 12, 2 (page 164) and the end of 12, 3 (page 164) for similar descriptions of the qualities of this age.*

[6] *See also Bible, Genesis 3, 19 & 3, 23 (page 6).*

[7] *See also Plato, Republic 573d (page 137).*

and his violent dealing. Strength will be right and reverence will cease to be[8]. ...

[8] *See also MhB, Udyoga 187 (page 85).*

(225) But they who give straight judgements to strangers and to the men of the land, and go not aside from what is just, their city flourishes, and the people prosper in it: Peace, the nurse of children, is abroad in their land, and all-seeing Zeus never decrees cruel war against them. Neither famine nor disaster ever haunt men who do true justice; but light-heartedly they tend the fields which are all their care. The earth bears them victual in plenty [1], and on the mountains the oak bears acorns upon the top and bees in the midst. Their woolly sheep are laden with fleeces; their women bear children like their parents. They flourish continually with good things, and do not travel on ships, for the grain-giving earth bears them fruit. The plenty-bringing land gives them her fruit[2].

Hesiod Works and Days 225-- 237 In virtuous situations the earth is abundant and trade is not required. *The substance of this verse is almost identical to MbB, Adi 109 (page 76).*
[1] *See also MhB, Vana 148 (page 78).*
[2] *The implication read here is that trade (eg especially between nations or regions) is only required if the region cannot satisfy all it needs.*

(293) But do you at any rate, always remembering my charge, work, high-born Perses, that Hunger may hate you, and venerable Demeter [1] richly crowned may love you and fill your barn with food[2]; for Hunger is altogether a meet comrade for the sluggard. Both gods and men are angry with a man who lives idle, for in nature he is like the stingless drones who waste the labour of the bees, eating without working; but let it be your care to order your work properly, that in the right season your barns may be full of victual. Through work men grow rich in flocks and substance, and working they are much better loved by the immortals. Work is no disgrace: it is idleness which is a disgrace. But if you work, the idle will soon envy you as you grow rich, for fame and renown attend on wealth[3]. And whatever be your lot, work is best for you, if you turn your misguided mind away from other men's property to your work and attend to your livelihood as I bid you. An evil shame is the needy man's companion, shame which both greatly harms and prospers men: shame is with poverty, but confidence with wealth.

Hesiod Works and Days 293-320
An encouragement to work
[1] *Demeter = the goddess of grain and fertility.*
[2] *Note both here and below that it is the gods that provide the wealth, not the work of men.*

[3] *People admire and respect the wealthy. See also MhB, Santi 322 (page 105)*

(352) Do not get base gain: base gain is as bad as ruin. Be friends with the friendly, and visit him who visits you. Give to one who gives, but do not give to one who does not give. A man gives to the free-handed, but no one gives to the close-- fisted. Give is a good girl, but Take is bad and she brings death.

Hesiod Works and Days 353-370
On Gift *Note:- Gift is said to be the singular duty of this age, see Laws of Manu 1, 86*

For the man who gives willingly, even though he gives a great *(page 65).* thing, rejoices in his gift and is glad in heart; but whoever gives way to shamelessness and takes something himself, even though it be a small thing, it freezes his heart. He who adds to what he has, will keep off bright-eyed hunger; for it you add only a little to a little and do this often, soon that little will become great. What a man has by him at home does not trouble him: it is better to have your stuff at home, for whatever is abroad may mean loss. It is a good thing to draw on what you have; but it grieves your heart to need something and not to have it, and I bid you mark this. Take your fill when the cask is first opened and when it is nearly spent, but midways be sparing: it is poor saving when you come to the lees.

Lao Tsze

In the first age men knew not that there were rulers.
In the next age men loved and praised the rulers.
In the third age men of their rulers were afraid.
In the next age those who ruled men were despised.
For verily it is said: "If your faith be lacking, no confidence will
you inspire."
But how cautious is the Master; how sparing in his words! For
with his task accomplished, and the affairs of men well-
ordered, he hears the people say: " We have become so of
ourselves[1]. "

Tao Te Ching XVII
The periods of history *This is a succinct exposition of the 4 ages. See Srimad 12, 3 (page 164), L of M 1, 81 (page 65) & Plato, Republic 8 (page 131).*

[1] Note MhB, Santi 69 (page 92) - 'The King makes the age'.

'Kingdoms can only be governed if rules are kept;
Battles can only be won if rules are broken.'
But the adherence of all under heaven can only be won by
letting-alone.
How do I know that it is so?
By this.
The more prohibitions there are, the more ritual avoidances[1],
The poorer the people will be.
The more 'sharp weapons' there are,
The more benighted will the whole land grow.
The more cunning craftsmen there are,
The more pernicious contrivances will be invented.
The more laws are promulgated,
The more thieves and bandits there will be.
Therefore- a sage has said:
So long as I 'do nothing' the people will of themselves be
transformed.
So long as I love quietude, the people will of themselves go
straight.
So long as I act only by inactivity the people will of themselves
become prosperous.
So long as I have no wants the people will of themselves return
to the 'state of the Uncarved Block'.

Tao Te Ching LVII
The Kingdom Requires Law
See also L of M 7, 17 (page 67) & Cicero, Offices 2, 4 (page 43).

[1] The multitude of Laws arises when virtue is not practised - See Ficino, Letters 1, 78 (page 49) - 'Let them obey the ancient ...law'. Note also Plato 'But when intemperance and disease multiply in a State, halls of justice and medicine are always being opened; and the arts of the doctor and the lawyer give themselves airs, finding how keen is the interest which not only the slaves but the freemen of a city take about them.' Republic 405.

The people are in want because those who receive from them
demand more than is their due[1].

Tao Te Ching LXXV
Principles of Government

This is the cause of their need.

The people are difficult to govern because those who are placed over them fail in their duties.

This is the cause of the trouble.

The people make light of death because of their excessive labour to provide the means of life.

This is the cause of their indifference.

It is only those who are selfless who esteem life at its right value.

[1] *This sentence is variously translated 'The people are in want because they are taxed too much' and 'The people are in want because too much Tax Grain is taken'. The later appears to be the most literal translation.*

Laws of Manu

81. In the Krita age *Dharma* is four-footed and entire, and (so is) Truth; nor does any gain accrue to men by unrighteousness.

82. In the other (three ages), by reason of (unjust) gains (agama), *Dharma* is deprived successively of one foot, and through (the prevalence of) theft, falsehood, and fraud the merit (gained by men) is diminished by one fourth (in each).

83. Men are free from disease, accomplish all their aims, and live four hundred years in the Krita age, but in the Treta and (in each of) the succeeding (ages) their life is lessened by one quarter.

84. The life of mortals, mentioned in the Veda, the desired results of sacrificial rites and the (super-natural) power of embodied (spirits) are the fruits proportioned among men according to (the character of) the age.

85. One set of duties (is prescribed) for men in the Krita age, different ones in the Treta and in the Dwapara and (again) and (set) in the Kali, in proportion as those ages decrease in length.

86. In the Krita age the chief (virtue) is declared to be (the performance of) austerities, in the Treta (divine) knowledge, in the Dwapara (the performance of) sacrifices, in the Kali liberality alone.

87. But in order to protect this universe He, the most resplendent one, assigned separate (duties and) occupations to those who sprang from his mouth, arms, thighs and feet.

88. To *Brahmanas* he assigned teaching and studying (the Veda), sacrificing for their own benefit and for others, giving and accepting (of alms).

89. The *Kshatriya* he commanded to protect the people, to bestow gifts, to offer sacrifices, to study (the Veda), and to abstain from attaching himself to sensual pleasures;

90. The Vaisya to tend cattle, to bestow gifts, to offer sacrifices, the study (the Veda), to trade, to lend money, and to cultivate land.

91. One occupation only the lord prescribed to the *Sudra*, to serve meekly even these (other) three castes.

100. Whatever exists in the world is the property of the *Brah-*

Chapter 1, 81

The four ages of man

See Srimad 11, 17 (page 163), 12, 2 & 3 (page 164) & Hesiod (page 59).

83. The Burnell translation renders this as '...and with all sorts of prosperity, live for four hundred years ...'. This is reflected in Genesis chapter 5.

86. Respectively Tapas (inner heat), Jnāna (knowledge), Yajna (sacrifice) &, Dāna (giving).

87-91. ie from the mouth (Brahmanas) teachers, arms (Kshatriyas) rulers & soldiers, thighs (Vaisyas) farmers & merchants, feet (Sudras) servants. See also Srimad 7, 11 (page 162). Names of individuals should imply prosperity (brahman), safeguard (ksatriya), wealth (vaisya) & service (Sudra) - refer L of M 2, 31, and greetings should enquire of happiness, welfare, prosperity & health respectively, see L of M 2, 127 below.

91. But service to the Brahmanas is preferred - refer L of M 10, 123.

Chapter 1, 100 Whatever

mana; on account of the excellence of his origin the *Brahmana* is, indeed, entitled to it all.

101. The *Brahmana* eats but his own food, wears but his own apparel, bestows but his own alms; other mortals subsist through the benevolence of that *Brahmana*.

102. In order to clearly settle his duties and those of the other (castes) according to their order, wise Manu sprung from the Self-existent, composed these Institutes (of the sacred law).

exists is the property of the Brahmana *See MhB, Santi 136 (page 99) & Anusasana 62 (page 106).*

1. Learn that sacred law which is followed by men learned (in the Veda) and assented to in their hearts by the virtuous, who are ever exempt from hatred and inordinate affection.

2. To act solely from a desire for rewards is not laudable, yet exemption from that desire is not (to be found) in this (world): for on (that) desire is grounded the study of the Veda and the performance of the actions, prescribed by the Veda.

3. The desire (for rewards), indeed, has its root in the conception that an act can yield them, and in consequence of (that) conception sacrifices are performed; vows and the laws prescribing restraints are all stated to be kept through the idea that they will bear fruit.

4. No single act here (below) appears ever to be done by a man free from desire; for whatever (man) does, it is (the result of) the impulse of desire.

5. He who persists in discharging these (prescribed duties) in the right manner, reaches the deathless state and even in this (life) obtains (the fulfilment of) all the desires that he may have conceived.

Chapter 2, 1 Desire motivates all actions *See MhB, Santi 167 (page 101) & 138 (page 100), & the desire is for happiness, see Shantanand 1965 (page 149) & MhB, Santi 190 (page 101). Refer also Cicero 'To be devoid of desire is something that does not exist in this world'.*

2. *See MhB, Santi 123 (page 97) For result of desire for reward.*

3. *See MhB, Vana 32 (page 78).*

127. Let him ask a *Brâhmana* on meeting him, after (his health), with the word kusala, a *Kshatriya* (with the word) anâmaya, a Vaisya (with the word) kshema, and a Sûdra (with the word) anârogya...

155. The seniority of Brâhmanas is from (sacred) knowledge, that of *Kshatriyas* from Valour, that of Vaisyas from wealth in grain (and other goods), but that of Sûdras alone from age.

Chapter 2, 127 Different Castes

127. *Which is asking of health, welfare, prosperity & happiness respectively.*

224. (Some declare that) the chief good consists in (acquisition of) spiritual merit and wealth, (others place it) in (the gratification of) desire and (the acquisition of) wealth, (others) in (the acquisition of) spiritual merit alone, and (others say that acquisition of) wealth alone is the chief good here (below); but

Chapter 2, 224 Virtue wealth and pleasure. *Expanded at length in MhB, Santi 123 (page 97).*

the correct decision is that it consists of the aggregate of (those) three.

227. Let him always practise, according to his ability, with a cheerful heart, the duty of liberality both by sacrifices and by charitable works, if he finds a worthy recipient (for his gifts).
228. If he is asked, let him always give some-thing, be it ever so little, without grudging; for a worthy recipient will (perhaps) be found who saves him from all (guilt).
229. A giver of water obtains the satisfaction (of his hunger and thirst), a giver of food imperishable happiness, a giver of sesamum desirable offspring, a giver of a lamp a most excellent eyesight...
230. A giver of land obtains land...

Chapter 4, 227 - 230 Gift Rewards the Giver
227. See MhB, Vana 199 (page 79) Santi 191 (page 102), Sukra 1, 418 (page 169) & Bible, Luke 3, 11 (page 31). Note that gifts are only to be given to the worthy (MhB, Santi 191). Detailed in Brihaspati & Narada (pages 39 & 120).

1. I will declare the duties of kings, (and) show how a king should conduct himself, how he was created, and how (he can obtain) highest success.
2. A *Kshatriya*, who has received according to the rule the sacrament prescribed by the Veda, most duly protects this whole (world).

Chapter 7, 1 - 8 Source of King's Authority and Strength
2. See MhB, Santi 58 (page 88), 68 (page 90) & Sukra 1, 375 (page 169).

3. For, when these creatures, being without a king, through fear dispersed in all directions, the Lord created a king for the protection of this whole (creation).
4. Taking (for that purpose) eternal particles of *Indra*, of the Wind, of Yama, of the Sun, of Fire, of Varuna, of the Moon, and of the Lord of wealth (*Kubera*).
5. Because a king has been formed of particles of those lords of the gods, he therefore surpasses all created beings in lustre;
6. And, like the sun, he burns eyes and hearts; nor can anybody on earth even gaze on him.
7. Through his (supernatural) power he is Fire and Wind, he Sun and Moon, he the Lord of justice (Yama), he *Kubera*, he Varuna, he great *Indra*.
8. Even an infant king must not be despised, (from an idea) that he is mere mortal; for he is a great deity in human form.

4-8. Indra - when attacking enemies, Yama (death) - when handing out punishment, fire - when angry without cause, the moon - when the anger disappears, Kubera - when bestowing wealth. The same concept is included in the Sukra 1, 141 (page 167) & MhB, Santi 68 (page 90) & detailed in the Brihad (page 35).

13. Let no (man) therefore transgress that law which the king decrees with respect to favourites, nor (his orders) which inflict pain on those in disfavour.
14. For the (king's) sake the Lord formerly created his own son, Punishment, the protector of all creatures, (an incarnation) of

Chapter 7, 13 - 27 Punishment Protects all Creatures *(& his wife is morality).*
14. N.B. The nature of punishment varies; for a Brahmana,

the law, formed of Brahman's glory.

15. Through fear of him all created beings, both the immovable and the movable, allow themselves to be enjoyed and swerve not from their duties.

16. Having fully considered the time and the place (of the offence), the strength and the knowledge (of the offender), let him justly inflict that (punishment) on men who act unjustly...

17. Punishment is (in reality) the king (and) the male, that the manager of affairs, that the ruler, and that is called the surety for the four orders' obedience to the law.

18. Punishment alone governs all created beings, punishment alone protects them, punishment watches over them while they sleep; the wise declare punishment (to be identical with) the law. ...

19. If (punishment) is properly inflicted after (due) consideration, it makes all people happy; but inflicted without consideration, it destroys everything.

20. If the king did not, without tiring, inflict punishment on those worthy to be punished, the strong would roast the weaker, like fish on a spit; ...

22. The whole world is kept in order by punishment, for a guiltless man is hard to find; through fear of punishment the whole world yields the enjoyments (which it owes).....

24. All castes (varna) would be corrupted (by intermixture), all barriers would be broken through, and all men would rage (against each other) in consequence of mistakes with respect to punishment.

26. They declare that king to be a just inflicter of punishment, who is truthful, who acts after due consideration, who is wise, and who knows (the respective value of) virtue, pleasure, and wealth.

27. A king who properly inflicts (punishment), prospers with respect to (those) three (means of happiness); but he who is voluptuous, partial, and deceitful will be destroyed, even through the (unjust) punishment (which he inflicts). ...

54, Let him appointment seven or eight ministers whose ancestors have been royal servants, who are versed in the sciences, heroes skilled in the use of weapons and descended from (noble) families and who have been tried.

55. Even an undertaking easy (in itself) is (sometimes) hard to be accomplished by a single man; how much (harder is it for a

censure; for a Kshatriya, removal of property; a Vaisyas, forfeiture of possessions; and virtually impossible for Sudras.

17. See Srimad 4, 21 (page 161). Dealt with at length in MhB, Refer Santi 15 & 121.

20. See for example Srimad 12, 2 (page 164) & 12, 3 (page 164) verse 23 onwards, Plato, Republic from 550c onwards (page 132) & behaviour of king Rehoboan in Bible, 1 Kings 12, 3 (page 20).

24. See Confucius, Anelects 16, 1 (page 47) Re positions of people in society.The Coke Burnell translation replaces 'barriers' with 'landmarks' which gives the same intent as Mencius 'despotic & corrupt rulers always neglect the boundaries' - 3, A, 3.

27. See MhB, Santi 123 (page 97) & refer to Solomon's resolution of the dispute over the custody of a child.

Chapter 7, 54 - 56
The Requirement for Ministers
54. See Rama 1, 7 (page 145), and refer to Sukra 2.
55. See Cicero, Offices 2, 4 (page 43).

king), especially (if he has) no assistant, (to govern) a kingdom which yields great revenues.

56 Let him daily consider with them the ordinary (business, referring to) peace and war, (the four subjects called) sthana, the revenue, the (manner of) protecting (himself and his kingdom), and the sanctification of his gains (by pious gifts).

56. Sthana, in this context probably means the capital of the kingdom (but may imply the kingdom).

80. Let him cause annual revenue in his kingdom to be collected by trusty (officials), let him obey the sacred law in (his transactions with) the people and behave like a father towards all men.

Chapter 7, 80[1]
Duty of King

122. ...Let him properly explore their behaviour in their districts through spies (appointed to) each.
123. For the servants of the king, who are appointed to protect (the people), generally become knaves who seize the property of others; let him protect his subjects against such (men).

Chapter 7, 122 - 123 Tax collectors. *Refer also Sukra 1, 751 2. Note, the earliest recorded Egyptian laws ensure restraint on the king's servants collecting taxes.*

127. Having considered (the rates of) purchase and (of) sale, (the length of) the road, (the expense for) food and condiments, the charges for securing the goods, let the king make the traders pay duty.
128. After (due) consideration the king shall always fix in his realm the duties and taxes in such a manner that both he himself and the man who does the work receive (their due) reward.
129. As the leech, the calf, and the bee take their food little by little, even so must the king draw from his realm moderate annual taxes ...
130. A fiftieth part of (the increments on) cattle and gold may be taken by the king, and the eight, sixth, or twelfth part of the crops.
131. He may also take the sixth part of trees, meat, honey, clarified butter, perfumes, (medical) herbs, substances used for flavouring food, flowers, roots and fruit;
132. Of leaves, pot-herbs, grass, (objects) made of cane, skins, of earthen vessels, and all (articles) made of stone.
133. Though dying (with want), a king must not levy a tax on Srotriyas, and no Srotiya, residing in his kingdom, must perish from hunger. ...
137. Let the king make the common inhabitants of his realm

Chapter 7, 127 - 138 Taxation
127. See MhB, Santi 87 (page 93) Most commentators take the intent to be a tax on net profit, but some say the risk is to be taken into account.
128. The implication being that there is a due portion for the king & the man who works & this is not arbitrary.
129. See MhB, Santi 72, 87 & 120 (page 92, 93), Sukra 2, 345 (page 171), & 4, 2, 222 (page 180).
130.Different rates here are traditionally accepted as reflecting the variation in productivity of land.
131-132. Presumably where no exclusive use of land is required.
133. Srotiya = priest, brah-

who live by traffic, pay annually some trifle, which is called a tax.

138. Mechanics and artisans, as well as Sûdras who subsist by manual labour, he may cause to work (for himself) one (day) in each month.

139. Let him not cut up his own root (by levying no taxes), nor the root of other (men) by excessive greed; for by cutting up his own root (or theirs), he makes himself or them wretched.

man.
137. See also Sukra 4, 2, 241 (page 180) Which accords with Adam Smith's Principles of Taxation.
139. See also Tao Te Ching 75 (page 63); Conf, Anal 12 (page 47); Sukra 2, 345 (page 171) & Bible, 1 Kings 12, 3 for example of excessive tax (page 20).

97. Hear now in order, good man, how many in number the relatives are whom a false witness destroys, and in what cases (he destroys them).

98.By untruth in regard to small cattle (he destroys) five; ten by untruth in regard to cows; one hundred, by untruth in regard to horses; a thousand by untruth in regards men.

99. Speaking an untruth for the sake of gold, he destroys those born and those (yet) unborn. By an untruth in regard to land he destroys everything. Speak thou not then an untruth in regard to land.

Chapter 8, 97 - 99 The degree of importance of land.
99. Everything in this case is taken by some commentators to be mankind and others the entire creation. The degree of relevance of land is clear.

140. A money-lender may stipulate as an increase of his capital, for the interest, allowed by Vasishtha, and take monthly the eightieth part of a hundred.

141. Or, remembering the duty of good men, he may take two in the hundred (by the month), for he who takes two in the hundred becomes not a sinner for gain.

Just two in the hundred, three, four, and five (and not more), he may take as monthly interest according to the order of the castes (varna)...

151. In money transactions interest paid at one time (not by instalments) shall never exceed the double of the principle; on grain, fruit, wool or hair, (and) beasts of burden it must not be more than five times (the original amount)...

152. Stipulated interest beyond the legal rate, being against (the law), cannot be recovered; they call that a usurious way (of lending); (the lender) is (in no case) entitled to (more than) five in the hundred.

153. Let him not take interest beyond the year, not such as is unapproved, nor compound interest, stipulated interest, and corporal interest.

Chapter 8, 140 - 153 Interest. *See also Yaj 2, 37 (page 187).*
140. Classical commentators say differences between this & verse 141 are what, in contemporary terms is referred to as 'secured' & 'unsecured' loans.
141. The variation here presumably relates to the relative trustworthiness and hence risk.
151. i.e. when the capital & interest are repaid as a single amount.
152. Stipulated interest - ie greater than the approved rate.
153. Corporal interest - i.e. paid by bodily labour, use of a pledged animal or by a slave (Medhatithi). NB capital invested for interest is called

kusīda, the increase, vŗddhi,
periodical interest, Kāla-
vŗddhih, paid by bodily labour,
Kāyikā.

180. In whatever manner a person shall deposit anything in the hands of another, in the same manner ought the same thing to be received back (by the owner); as the delivery (was, so must be) the re-delivery.

Chapter 8, 180
General principles for commercial conduct.

200. Where possession is evident, but no title is percieved, there the title (shall be) a proof (of ownership), not possession; such is the settled rule.

203. One commodity mixed with another must not be sold (as pure), nor a bad one (as good), nor less (than the proper quantity or weight), nor anything that is not at hand or that is concealed.

215. A hired (servant or workman) who, without being ill, out of pride fails to perform his work according to the agreement, shall be fined eight krisnalas and no wages shall be paid to him.

Chapter 8, 215-217
On wages
See also MhB, Santi 60 (page 89).

216. But (if he is really) ill, (and), after recovery performs (his work) according to the original agreement, he shall receive his wages even after (the lapse of) a very long time.

217. But if he, whether sick or well, does not (perform or) cause to be performed (by others) his work according to his agreement, the wages for that work shall not be given to him, even (if it be only) slightly incomplete.

237. On all sides of a village a space, one hundred dhanus or three samyâ-throws (in breadth), shall be reserved (for pasture), and thrice (that space) around a town.

Chapter 8, 237 Common land
Burnell translates the distances '100 bows', & '3 castes of a staff'. See also Yaj 2 167 (page 188).

245. If a dispute has arisen between two villages concerning a boundary, the king shall settle the limits in the month of Gyaishtha, when the landmarks are most distinctly visible.

Chapter 8, 245 - 266
Boundaries.
See also Yaj 2, 150 (page 188).

246. Let him mark the boundaries (by) trees, (e.g.) Nyagrodhas, Asvatthas, Kimsukas, cotton - tree Salas, Palmyra palms, and trees with milky juice,

245. Commentators take this to include, boundaries between cities, fields and houses also.

247. By clustering shrubs, bamboos of different kinds, Samis,

This month is when grass has

creepers and raised mounds, reed thickets of Kubgaka; thus the boundary will not forgotten.

248. Tanks, wells, cisterns, and fountains should be built where boundaries meet, as well as temples,

249. And as he will see that through men's ignorance of the boundaries trespasses constantly occur in the world, let him cause to be made other hidden marks for boundaries ... The omited text details how boundaries are to be marked and disputes resolved...

265. If the boundary cannot be ascertained (by any evidence), let a righteous king with (the intention of) benefiting them (all), himself assign (his) land (to each); that is the settled rule.

266. Thus the law for deciding boundary (disputes) has been fully declared,

dried up & marks easily seen.
246. See also Bible, Deut 19, 14 (page 17), Men 3, A, 3 (page 111) & Plato, Laws 843 (page 141). Nyagrodhas & Asvatthas - trees of the fig family, Kimskas - trees from which are produced dye from flowers, oil from seeds & gum from sap. These being on the border, are shared.
248. See also MhB, Anusasana (page 105), & Sukra 4, 2, 242 (page 180).
265. Note: Ownership of land is the king's.

44. (Sages) who know the past call this earth (prithivi) even the wife of Prithu; they declare a field to belong to him who cleared away the timber, and a deer to him who (first) wounded it.

Chapter 9 44 Land ownership *Land belongs to the first occupant. See also Cicero, Offices 1, 7 (page 41).*

48. As with cows, mares, female camels, slave-girls, buffalo cows, she goats, and ewes, it is not the begetter (or his owner) who obtains the offspring, even thus (it is) with wifes of others.

49. Those who, having no property in a field, but possessing seed-corn, sow it in another's soil, do indeed not receive the grain of the crop which may spring up...

52. If no agreement with respect to the crop has been made between the owner of the field and the owner of the seed, the benefit clearly belongs to the owner of the field; the receptacle is more important than the seed.

53. But if by a special contract (a field) is made over (to another) for sowing, then the owner of the seed and the owner of the soil are both considered in this world as sharers of the (crop).

54. If seed be carried by water of wind into somebodies field and germinates (there), the (plant sprung from that) seed belongs even to the owner of the field, the owner of the seed does not receive the crop.

55. Know that such is the law concerning the offspring of cows, mares, slaves-girls, female camels, she goats, and ewes, as well

Chapter 9 48-56 Ownership of the Produce. *Note:- this and the previous quote are in a section primarily concerned with the relationship between man and wife. The relevance of the quotation is that the produce of the land, always goes to the 'owner' of the land, except in the instance where the owner has made a bargain with another (either the owner or the planter of the seed). The illustration follows well current practices with stud live-stock, where, the owner of the cow, usually pays the owner of the bull to have the cow serviced, and receives the progeny (if any) for himself.*

as of female birds and buffalo-cows.

56. Thus the comparative importance of the seed and of the womb has been declared to you; ...

53. See MhB, Santi 60 (page 89).

294. The king and his minister, his capital, his realm, his treasury, his army, and his ally are the seven constituent parts (of a kingdom); (hence) a kingdom is said to have seven limbs (anga).

295. But let him know (that) among these seven constituent parts of a kingdom (which have been enumerated) in due order, each earlier (named) is more important and (its destruction) the greater calamity.

296. Yet in a kingdom, containing constituent parts, which is upheld like the triple staff (of an ascetic), there is no (single part) more important (than the others), by reason of the importance of the qualities of each for the others.

297. For each part is particularly qualified for (the accomplishment of) certain objects, (and thus) each is declared to be the most important for that particular purpose which is effected by its means.

Chapter 9 294-297

Parts of the Kingdom

294. Note, the army includes the functions of the police. All these are required to exercise the kings authority. Where the king wields his authority (such as public works etc) is an another issue.

296. (see Ficino, Letters 1, 78, (page 49) & Cicero, The Offices 3, 4 (page 45).

115. There are seven lawful modes of acquiring property, (viz.) inheritance, finding or friendly donation, purchase, conquest, lending at interest, the performance of work, and the acceptance of gifts from virtuous men.

116. Learning, mechanical arts, work for wages, service, rearing cattle, traffic, agriculture, contentment (with little), alms, and receiving interest on money, are the ten modes of subsistence (permitted to all men in times of distress).

117. Neither a *Brahmana*, nor a *Kshatriya* must lend (money at) interest; but at his pleasure (either of them) may, in times of distress (when he requires money) for sacred purposes, lend to a very sinful man at a small interest.

118. A *Kshatriya* (king) who, in times of distress, takes even the fourth part (of the crops), is free from guilt, if he protects his subjects to the best of his ability.

119. His peculiar duty is conquest, and he must not turn back in danger; having protected the Vaisyas by his weapons, he may cause the legal tax to be collected;

120. (Viz.) from Vaisyas one-eighth as the tax on grain, one--twentieth (on the profits on gold and cattle), which amount at least to one Karshapana; *Sudras*, artisans, and mechanics

Chapter 10, 115-131 Income

115. See also MhB, Sahbha 32 (page 77) & Sukra 2, 641 (page 171). Various commentators add, the first 3 (Āyah, lābhah, purchase) are for all castes, 4th (Jayah) for Ksatriya, 5th & 6th (Prayogah, Karmayogah) for Vaisya, 7th for Brahman only. Some say the 4th is for all castes (eg law suites), the 5th includes teaching & the 6th, priest officiating at sacrifices

117. See Srimad 11, 7 (page 162) and Bible, Deut 23, 19-20 (page 17).

118. See MhB, Santi 130 (page 98) For justification.

119. Conquest if required to protect his subjects, & also to expand the kingdom.

(shall) -benefit (the king) by (doing) work (for him).

121. If a *Sudra*, (unable to subsist by serving *Brahmanas*,) seeks a livelihood, he may serve *Kshatriyas*, or he may also seek to maintain himself by attending on a wealthy Vaisya.

122. But let a (*Sudra*) serve *Brahmanas* either for the sake of heaven, or with a view to both (this life and the next); for he who is called the servant of a *Brahmana* thereby gains all his ends.

123. The service of *Brahmanas* alone is declared (to be) an excellent occupation for a *Sudra*; for who has acquired wealth, whatever else besides this he may perform will bear no fruit.

124. They must allot to him out of their own family (-property) a suitable maintenance, after considering his ability, his industry and the number of those whom he is bound to support.

125. The remnants of their food must be given to him, as well as their old clothes, the refuse of their grain, and their old household furniture.

126. A *Sudra* cannot commit an offence, causing loss of caste (pataka), and he is not worthy to receive the sacraments; he has no right to (fulfil) the sacred law (of the Aryans, yet) there is no prohibition against (his fulfilling certain portions of) the law.

127. (*Sudras*) who are desirous to gain merit, and know (their) duty commit no sin, but gain praise, if they imitate the practice of virtuous men without reciting sacred texts.

128. The more a (*Sudra*), keeping himself free from envy, imitates the behaviour of the virtuous, the more he gains, without being censured, (exaltation in) this world and the next.

129. No collection of wealth must be made by a *Sudra*, even though he be able (to do it);

130. The duties of the four castes (varna) in times of distress have thus been declared, and if they perform them well, they will reach the most blessed state.

131. Thus all the legal rules for the four castes have been proclaimed; ..

120. i.e. The tax falls on the landholder or business not on the wage earner, but even the wage earner contributes by way of labour.

123. Note, that on the other hand the other castes are duty bound to provide employment, see MhB, Santi 60 (page 89).

124. See Sukra 2, 788 (page 174) & MhB, Santi 60 (page 89) for expansion of this principle.

125. See Bible, Leviticus 19, 10 (page 12).

129. Nor in practice can he because wages do not permit any surplus. See Sukra 2, 788 (page 174).

Supplementry Notes

1. *Chapter 7, 80 The Commentator Kāmandaka notes:- Agriculture, communications to facilitate commercial traffic, entrenchment of strongholds for soldiers in the capital, construction of dams and bridges across rivers, erection of enclosures for elephants, working of mines and quarries, felling and selling of timber and the peopling of uninhabited tracts, these eightfold sources of revenue the king should ever enhance; his officers looking up to him for livelihood should also do so, for maintaining themselves.*

Mahabharata

Thy father was virtuous and high souled, and always protected his people... he ... virtuously protected the four orders, each engaged in the discharge of their specific duties[1]. ... he protected the goddess Earth[2]. ... Widows and orphans, the maimed and the poor, he maintained.

Adi Parva Section 49 Protection by king. [1] See Conf, Anal 16, 1 (page 47), Santi 295 below, Srimad 4, 21 (page 161).[2] See Arthaveda 12 (page 1) & Plato, Laws 740 (page 139).

The gods said 'O lord of the earth, thou shouldest take care so that virtue may not sustain a diminution on earth! Protected by thee, virtue itself will in turn protect the universe.' And Indra said, '... Dwell thou in that region on earth which is delightful, and aboundeth in animals, is sacred, full of wealth and corn, is well protected like heaven, which is of agreeable climate, graced with every object of enjoyment, and blessed with fertility. ... Sons never divide their wealth with their fathers and are ever mindful of the welfare of their parents[1].

Adi Parva Section 63 Virtue protects the universe See Bible, Genesis 13, 14-18 (page 7).

[1] See Mencius 1, A (page 109).

... the earth from the very coasts of the ocean, became filled with men that were all long-lived. The *Kshatriyas* performed great sacrifices bestowing much wealth[1]... The Vaisyas, with the help of bullocks, caused the earth to be tilled. And they never yolked the cattle themselves[2]. And they fed with care all cattle that were lean. And men never milked kine as long as the calves drank only milk of their dams (without having taken to grass and other food). And no merchant in those days ever sold his articles by false scales... And thus, O king, the *krita* age having duly set in, the whole earth was filled with numerous creatures.

Adi Parva Section 64 A description of a virtuous kingdom. [1] *That is the wealth collected by the king was returned to the worthy by way of gift during and after the ceremony.* [2] *Taken to mean that there was an abundance of Sudra for executing such tasks.*

And during his rule there were no men of mixed castes, no tillers of the soil (for the land, of itself, yielded produce), no workers of mines (for the surface of the earth yielded in abundance), and no sinful men. All were virtuous, and did everything from virtuous motives, O tiger among men. There was no fear of thieves, O dear one, no fear of famine, no fear of disease. And all four orders took pleasure in doing their respective duties and never performed religious acts for obtaining fruition of desires. And his subjects depending upon

Adi Parva Section 68 A description of Golden age, see MhB, Vana 148 (page 78) & Hesiod, Works & Days 225 (page 60) for more descriptions.

him, never entertained any fear. Parjanya (*Indra*[1]) poured showers at the proper time, and the produce of the fields was always pulpy and juicy. And the earth was full of all kinds of wealth and all kinds of animals...

[1] Indra, here as the god of rain.

And the wheel of virtue having been set in motion by Bishma, and the country became so contented that subjects of other kingdoms, quitting their homes, came to dwell there and increase its population.

Adi Parva Section 109 Attraction of Virtuous Land *See Santi 58 below, Conf Anal 13 (page 47), Men 2 A (page 111).*

... The earth began to yield abundant harvest, and the crops were also of good flavour. And the clouds began to pour rain in season and trees became full of fruits and flowers. And the draught cattle were all happy and the birds and other animals rejoiced exceedingly. And flowers became fragrant and the fruits became sweet; the cities and towns became filled with merchants, artisans, traders and artists of every description. And the people became brave, learned, honest and happy. And there were no robbers then nor anybody who was sinful. And it seemed that the golden age had come upon every part of the kingdom. And the people devoted to virtuous acts, sacrifices and truth, and regarding one another with love and affection grew in prosperity. And free from pride, wrath and covetousness, they rejoiced in perfectly innocent sports. The capital of the Kurus, full as the ocean, was a second *Amaravati*[1], teeming with hundreds of palaces and mansions, and possessing gates and arches dark as clouds. And men in great cheerfulness sported constantly on rivers, lakes and in tanks, and in fine groves and charming woods. ... there were no misers and no widowed women...

Adi Parva section 109 The Kuru kingdom when ruled by Bhishma *Prosperity here is the direct result of virtue and the virtuous behaviour of the king.*

[1] The fabulous city of the god Indra.

For Yudhishthira ... worked for the good of all without making any distinctions. Indeed shaking off both anger and arrogance, Yudhishthira always said, Give unto each what is due to each, and the only sounds that he could hear were, -*Blessed be Dharma! Blessed be Dharma!*[1] ... The king cherished every one as belonging to his family[2], and Bhima ruled over all justly. Arjuna, used to employ both his hands with equal skill, protected the people from (external) enemies. And the wise Sahadeva administered justice impartially. ...Owing to all this, the kingdom became free from disputes and fear of every kind. And the people became attentive to their respective occupa-

Sabha Parva Section 13 A kingdom ruled justly & as one family
[1] Note Yudhishthira was the son of the god Dharma (justice)
[2] See also Cicero, Offices 3, 7 (page 45) & Ficino, Letters 1, 78 (page 49).

tions[3]. The rain became so abundant as to leave no room for desiring more; and the kingdom grew in prosperity. And in consequence of the virtues of the king, money lenders, the articles required for sacrifices, cattle-rearing, tillage, and traders, all and everything in prosperity. Indeed, during the reign of Yudhishthira who was ever devoted to truth, there was no extortion, no stringent realisation of arrears of rent, no fear of disease, of fire, or of death by poisoning and incantations, in the kingdom. It was never heard at that time that thieves or cheats or royal favourites ever behaved wrongfully ... the traders of the different classes came to pay him the taxes[4] leviable on their respective occupations. And accordingly ...the prosperity of the kingdom was increased not by these alone but even by persons wedded to voluptuousness and indulging in all luxuries to their fill[5].

[3] People were attentive to their own occupation.

[4] Note, the tax payers came to the king.

[5] So that every person in society contributes (so long as the behaviour does not involve theft).

And by reason of equitable taxation and the virtuous rule of the monarch, clouds in his kingdom poured as much rain as the people desired, and cities and towns became highly prosperous ...

Sabha Parva Section 32 Equitable Taxation & Virtue cause Prosperity.

... I never act solicitous of the fruits of my actions. I give away, because it is my duty to give; I sacrifice because it is my duty to sacrifice! I accomplish to the best of my power whatever a person living in domesticity should do, regardless of the fact whether those acts have fruits or not... Knowing for certain that God is the giver of fruits in respect of virtue, they practice virtue in this world. This, O Drupadi, is the eternal (source of) prosperity.

Vana Parva Section 31 Virtue is the source of prosperity. *See Confucius, Great Learning 10 (page 48), Plato, Apology 30b (page 127), MhB, Santi 123 (page 97) and Bible, Job 8, 3-6 (page 22).*

There may not be even one in a thousand who truly knoweth the utility of acts or work. One must act for protecting as also increasing his wealth[1]; for if without seeking to earn, one continueth to only spend, his wealth, even if it were a hoard huge as Himavat, would soon be exhausted[2]...
This body is only the instrument in the hands of God, for doing the acts that are done. Itself, inert, it doth as God urgeth it to do. O son of Kunti, it is the Supreme Lord of all who maketh all creatures do what they do. The creatures themselves are inert...Man, having first settled some purpose in his mind, accomplisheth it, himself working with the aid of his intelligence. We, therefore say that man is himself the cause (of what

Vana Parva Section 32 Wealth is a product of man's intelligence
[1] See also Sukra 4, 2, 64-71 (page 177) & MhB, Santi 133 (page 99)
[2] Encouragement to exert one's self.

he doeth). O bull among men, it is impossible to number the acts of men, for mansions and towns are the results of men's acts[3]. Intelligent men know, by help of intellect, that oil may be had from sesame, curds from milk, and that food cooked by means of igniting fuel. They know the means for accomplishing all these.

[3] See also Cicero, Offices 2, 4 (page 43).

If any person accidentally acquireth any wealth, it is said he deriveth it from chance, for no-one's effort hath brought about that result. And, O son of Pritha, whatever of good fortune a person obtaineth in consequence of religious rites, that is called providential. The fruit, however that a person obtaineth by acting himself, and which is the direct result of those acts of his, is regarded as proof of personal ability...

Vana Parva Section 32 Sources of Wealth. *This is the nearest description to 'the fruit of labour belonging to the worker'. See L of M 10, 115 (page 73) for modes of acquiring wealth.*

And, O child, that Yuga is called Krita when the one eternal religion was extant... And then virtue knew no deterioration; nor did people decrease... And there was no buying and selling... And there was no manual labour. And then the necessaries of life were obtained only by being thought of.

Vana Parva Section 148 No trade in the Golden Age *See MhB, Adi 68 above & Hesiod, Works & Days 225 (page 60).*

From religious observances proceedeth merit; and in merit are established the Vedas; and from the Vedas sacrifices come into existence; and by sacrifices are established the gods. The gods are maintained by the (celebration of) sacrifices prescribed by the Vedas and the religious ordinances; while men maintain themselves by (following) the ordinances of Vrihaspati[1] and Usanas and also by these avocations, by which the world is maintained, serving for wages, (receiving) taxes, merchandise, agriculture and tending kine and sheep.

The world subsisteth by profession[2]. The (study of the) three Vedas and agriculture and trade and government constitutes, it is ordained by the wise, the professions of the twice born ones; and each order maintaineth itself by following the profession prescribed for it. And when these callings are properly pursued, the world is maintained with ease. If, however, people do not righteously lead their lives, the world becometh lawless, in consequence of the want of Vedic merit and government. And if people do not resort to (their) prescribed vocations, they perish, but by regularly following the three professions, they bring about religion.

Vana Parva Section 150 Pursuit of the proper profession is applauded. *[1]Vrihaspati an author of whom only fragments remain (some included herein. Usanas, Author of the Sukra Niti (see page 167 For extracts)..* *[2]Expanded in Srimad 7, 11 (page 162). See also Confucius, Analects 16, 1 (page 47), Vana 162 & 206 below Santi 295 (page 103) & refer Rama, Uttara Kanda 76, on importance of people staying within the proper bounds of society.*

Thereat the Rakshasas said, 'O foremost of men, this spot is dear unto *Kuvera*, and it is his sporting region. Men subject to death cannot sport here. First taking permission of the chief of the Yakshas, drink of this lake and sport herein' ... Bhimasena said ... And, further this lotus-lake hath sprung from the cascades of the mountain; it hath' not been excavated in the mansion of *Kuvera*. Therefore it belongeth equally to all creatures with Vaisravana. In regard to a thing of such a nature, who goeth to beseech another?"

Vana Parva Section 154 Nature (unaltered) belongs to no man. *See also Cicero, Offices 1, 7 (page 41) & L of M 9, 44 (page 72). Note:- Rakshasas & Yakshas are servants of Kuvera (the god of wealth), Vaisravana - another name for Kuvera.*

"The lord of treasures said, 'O Yudhishthira, patience, ability, appropriate time and place and prowess-these five lead to success in human affairs. O Bharata, in the Krita Yuga, men were patient and able in their respective occupations[1] and they knew how to display prowess. And, O foremost of the *Kshatriyas,* a *Kshatriya* that is endued with patience and understandeth the propriety regarding place and time and is versed in all mortal regulations, can alone govern the world for a long time,- nay, in all transactions. He that behaveth thus, acquireth, O hero, fame in this world and excellent state in the next.

Vana Parva Section 162 Time and place is important for the acquisition of wealth. *[1] See Section 150 above.*

O king, no one can enjoy landed possessions unless he giveth away land, and no one can go on cars and vehicles unless he giveth away these[1]. Indeed a person on rebirth obtaineth the fruition of whatever objects he hath in view at the time of making a gift to a *Brahmana*. Gold hath sprung from Fire; the Earth from Vishnu; and the cows from the Sun. He, therefore, that giveth away gold, land, and kine attaineth all the regions of *Agni*, Vishnu, and the Sun. There is nothing so eternal as a gift[2]. Where, therefore, in the three worlds is anything that is more auspicious? It is for this, O king, that they who have great intelligence say that there is nothing higher and greater in the three worlds than gift !' "

Vana Parva Section 199. Gift is required for enjoyment *[1] See L of M 4, 227 (page 67), Santi 191 (page 102), Anusasana 62 (page 106), Vana 257 below, Luke 3, 11 (page 31) & Sukra 1, 418 (page 169) on gifts. [2] Note gift is the principle duty of this age.*

"...And, O great king, that son with whom the father and the mother are gratified, achieveth eternal fame and eternal virtue both here and thereafter. As regards women again, neither sacrifice nor sraddhas[1], nor fasts are of any efficacy. By serving their husbands only they can win heaven. O king, O Yudhishthira,..."

Vana Parva Section 204 Women *See MhB, Vana 231 (page 80), Anusasana 46 (page 105). [1] sraddhas - faith, belief*

In this world there are three principle professions, Viz.,

Vana Parva Section 206

agriculture, rearing of cattle, and trade. As regards the other world, the three Vedas, knowledge, and the science of morals are efficacious. Service (of the other three orders) hath been ordained duty of the *Sudra*. Agriculture hath been ordained for the Vaisyas, and fighting for the *Kshatriyas*, while the practice of the Brahmacharya vow, asceticism, recitation of mantras, and truthfulness have been ordained for the *Brahmanas*. Over subjects adhering to their proper duties, the king should rule virtuously; while he should set those thereto that have fallen away from the duties of their order. Kings should ever be feared, because they are the lords of their subjects. They restrain those subjects of theirs that fall away from their duties as they restrain the motions of the deer by means of their shafts...

There are three principle professions

See Vana 150 above

Note, the implication read here is that the three professions are 'self employed' or employers.

And the slender waisted Satyabhama, the favourite wife of Krishna and the daughter of Satrajit, then asked Draupadi in private, saying, 'By what behaviour is it, O daughter of Drupada, that thou art able to rule the sons of Pandu -... Beautiful lady, how is it that they are so obedient to thee and are never angry with thee? Without doubt the sons of Pandu, O thou of lovely features, are ever submissive to thee and watchful to do thy bidding!.. Tell me now, O princess of Panchala, of that blessed and auspicious thing by which, O Krishna, Krishna may ever be obedient to me." "When the celebrated Satyabhama, having said this, ceased, the chaste and blessed daughter of Drupada answered her, saying, 'Thou askest me, O Satyabhama, of the practices of women that are wicked. How can I answer thee, O lady, about the cause that is pursued by wicked females? It doth not become thee, lady, to pursue the questions, or doubt me, after this, for thou art endued with intelligence and art the favourite wife of Krishna. When the husband learns that his wife is addicted to incantations and drugs from that hour he beginneth to dread her like a serpent ensconced in his sleeping chamber. And can a man that is troubled with fear have peace, and how can one that hath no peace have happiness? A husband can never be made obedient by his wife's incantations. We hear of painful disease being transmitted by enemies. Indeed, they that desire to slay others, send poison in the shape of customary gifts, so that the man that taketh the powders so sent, by tongue or skin, is, without doubt, speedily deprived of life. Women have sometimes caused

Vana Parva Section 231

Women (Drupadi as the epitome of womanly virtue).

Drupadi to Satyabhama - the wife of the Lord Krishna. Drupadi was concurrently married to Yudhishthira & his 4 brothers N.B. The name Krishna in this text is also one of the names applied to Drupadi.

Note the similarity to Proverbs 31, 10-31:-

Who can find a virtuous woman? for her price is far above rubies. The heart of her husband doth safely trust in her, so that he shall have no need of spoil. She will do him good and not evil all the days of her life.

She seeketh wool, and flax, and worketh willingly with her hands. She is like the merchants' ships; she bringeth her food from afar. She riseth also while it is yet night, and giveth meat to her household, and a portion

dropsy and leprosy, decrepitude and impotence and idiocy and blindness and deafness in men. These wicked women, ever treading in the path of sin, do sometimes (by these means) injure their husbands. But the wife should never do the least injury to her lord. Hear now, O illustrious lady, of the behaviour I adopt towards the high-souled sons of Pandu. Keeping aside vanity, and controlling desire and wrath, I always serve with devotion the sons of Pandu with their wives. Restraining jealousy, with deep devotion of heart, without a sense of degradation at the services I perform, I wait upon my husbands. Ever fearing to utter what is evil or false, or to look or sit or walk with impropriety, or cast glances indicative of the feelings of the heart, do I serve the sons of Pritha-those mighty warriors blazing like the sun or fire, and handsome as the moon, those endued with fierce energy and prowess, and capable of slaying their foes by a glance of the eye. Celestial, or man, or Gandharva, young or decked with Ornaments, wealthy or comely of person, none else my heart liketh. I never bathe or eat or sleep till he that is my husband hath bathed or eaten or slept,-till, in fact, our attendants have bathed, eaten, or slept. Whether returning from the field, the forest, or the town, hastily rising up I always salute my husband with water and a seat. I always keep the house and all household articles and the food that is to be taken well-ordered and clean. Carefully do I keep the rice, and serve the food at the proper time. I never indulge in angry and fretful speech, and never imitate women that are wicked. Keeping idleness at distance I always do what is agreeable. I never laugh except at a jest, and never stay for any length of time at the house-gate. I never stay long in places for answering calls of nature, nor in pleasure-gardens attached to the house. I always refrain from laughing-loudly and-indulging in high passion, and from everything that may give offence. Indeed, O Satyabhama, I always am engaged in waiting upon my lords. A separation from my lords is never agreeable to me. When my husband leaveth home for the sake of any relative, then renouncing flowers and fragrant paste of every kind, I begin to undergo penances. Whatever my husband drinketh not, whatever my husband leaveth not, whatever my husband enjoyeth not, I ever renounce. O beautiful lady, decked in ornaments and ever controlled by the instruction imparted to me, I always devotedly seek the good of my lord. Those duties that my mother-in-law had told me of in respect of relatives, as

to her maidens. She considereth a field, and buyeth it: with the fruit of her hands she planteth a vineyard. She girdeth her loins with strength, and strengtheneth her arms. She perceiveth that her merchandise is good: her candle goeth not out by night. She layeth her hands to the spindle, and her hands hold the distaff. She stretcheth out her hand to the poor; yea, she reacheth forth her hands to the needy. She is not afraid of the snow for her household: for all her household are clothed with scarlet. She maketh herself coverings of tapestry; her clothing is silk and purple. Her husband is known in the gates, when he sitteth among the elders of the land. She maketh fine linen, and selleth it; and delivereth girdles unto the merchant. Strength and honour are her clothing; and she shall rejoice in time to come. She openeth her mouth with wisdom; and in her tongue is the law of kindness. She looketh well to the ways of her household, and eateth not the bread of idleness. Her children arise up, and call her blessed; her husband also, and he praiseth her. Many daughters have done virtuously, but thou excellest them all. Favour is deceitful, and beauty is vain: but a woman that feareth the LORD, she shall be praised. Give her

also the duties of alms-giving, of offering worship to the gods, of oblations to the diseased, of boiling food in pots on auspicious days for offer to ancestors and guests of reverence and service to those that deserve our regards, and all else that is known to me, I always discharge day and night, without idleness of any kind. Having with my whole heart recourse to humility and approved rules I serve my meek and truthful lords ever observant of virtue, regarding them as poisonous snakes capable of being excited at a trifle. I think that to be eternal virtue for women which is based upon a regard for the husband. The husband is the wife's god, and he is her refuge. Indeed, there is no other refuge for her. How can, then, the wife do the least injury to her lord? I never, in sleeping or eating or adorning my person, act against the wishes of my lord, and always guided by my husbands, I never speak ill of my mother-in-law. O blessed lady, my husbands have become obedient to me in consequence of my diligence, my alacrity, and the humility with which I serve superiors. Personally do I wait every day with food and drink and clothes upon the revered and truthful Kunti-that mother of heroes. Never do I show any preference for myself over her in matters of food and attire, and never do I reprove in words that princess equal unto the Earth herself in forgiveness. Formerly, eight thousand *Brahmanas* were daily fed in the palace of Yudhishthira from off plates of gold. And eighty thousand *Brahmanas* also of the Snataka sect leading domestic lives were entertained by Yudhishthira with thirty serving-maids assigned to each. Besides these, ten thousand yatis with the vital seed drawn up, had their pure food carried unto them in plates of gold. All these *Brahmanas* that were the utterers of the Veda, I used to worship duly with food, drink, and raiment taken from stores only after a portion thereof had been dedicated to the Viswadeva. The illustrious son of Kunti had a hundred thousand well-dressed serving-maids with bracelets on arms and golden ornaments on necks, and decked with costly garlands and wreaths and gold in profusion, and sprinkled with sandal paste. And adorned with Jewels and gold they were all skilled in singing and dancing O lady, I knew the names and features of all those girls, as also what they are and what they were, and what they did not. Kunti's son of great intelligence had also a hundred thousand maid servants who daily used to feed guests, with plates of gold in their hands. And while Yudhishthira lived in Indraprastha a hundred

of the fruit of her hands; and let her own works praise her in the gates.

In a passage in the Srimad Krishna advises the ladies that service to their husbands is the same as service to, and the proximity of Krishna.

thousand horses and a hundred thousand elephants used to follow in his train. These were the possessions of Yudhishthira while he ruled the earth. It was I however, O lady, who regulated their number and framed the rules to be observed in respect of them; and it was I who had to listen to all complaints about them. Indeed, I knew everything about what the maid-servants of the palace and other classes of attendants, even the cow-herds and the shepherds of the royal establishment, did or did not. O blessed and illustrious lady, it was I alone amongst the Pandavas who knew the income and expenditure of the king and what their whole wealth was. And those bulls among the Bharatas, throwing upon me the burden of looking after all those that were to be fed by them, would, O thou of handsome face, pay their court to me. And this load, so heavy and incapable of being borne by persons of evil heart, I used to bear day and night, sacrificing my ease, and all the while affectionately devoted to them. And while my husbands were engaged in the pursuit of virtue, I only supervised their treasury inexhaustible like an ever-filled receptacle of Varuna. Day and night bearing hunger and thirst, I used to serve the Kuru princes, so that my nights and days were equal to me. I used to wake up first and go to bed last. This O Satyabhama, hath ever been my charm for making my husbands obedient to me ! This great art hath ever been known to me for making my husbands obedient to me."

Vaisampayana said, "Once on a time[1], as Yudhishthira lay down at night in the Dwaita woods, some deer, with accents choked in tears, presented themselves before him in his dreams. To them standing with joined hands, their bodies trembling all over that foremost of monarchs said, 'Tell me what ye wish to say. Who are ye? And what do ye desire?' Thus accosted by Kunti's son-the illustrious Pandava, those deer, the remnant of those that had been slaughtered, replied unto him, saying, 'We are, O Bharata, those deer that are still alive after them that had been slaughtered. We shall be exterminated totally. Therefore, do thou change thy residence. O mighty king, all thy brothers are heroes, conversant with weapons; they have thinned the ranks of the rangers of the forest. We few-the remnants,- O mighty minded one, remain like seed[2]. By thy favour, O king of kings, let us increase.' Seeing these deer, which remained like seed after the rest had been destroyed

Vana Parva Section 256
Care of the earth and all creatures

[1] *After Yudhishthira & his very large entourage had occupied the same place in the forest for a considerable period of time.*

[2] *Note the injunction is not to prevent killing deer, only to ensure the ability to restore the*

trembling and afflicted with fear, Yudhishthira the just was greatly affected with grief. And the king, intent on the welfare of all creatures, said unto them, 'So be it. I shall act as ye have said.'

stock.

"Vyasa said, 'There is nothing, O child, in this world harder to practise than charity. Men greatly thirst after wealth, and wealth also is gotten with difficulty. Nay, renouncing even dear life itself, heroic men, O magnanimous one, enter into the depths of the sea and the forest for the sake of wealth. For wealth, some betake themselves to agriculture and the tending of kine, and some enter into servitude. Therefore, it is extremely difficult to part with wealth that is obtained with much trouble. Since nothing is harder to practise than charity, therefore, in my opinion, even the bestowal of boons is superior to everything. Specially is this to be borne in mind that well-earned gains should, in proper time and place, be given away to pious men.

Vana Parva Section 257
Wealth, acquisition is easier than Charity *See also Vana 199 above.*
Note:- This then needs to be maintained - See Sukra 4, 2, 64 (page 179).

Behold, the soil is moistened and divested of weeds by human exertion. Without rain, however, O son of Kunti, it never yieldeth crops. Indeed in the absence of rain some speak of artificial irrigation, as a means of success due to human exertion, but even then it may be seen that the water artificially let in is dried up in consequence of providential drought. Beholding all this, the wise men of old have said that human affairs are set agoing in consequence of the cooperation of both providential and human expedients.

Udyoga Parva Section 79
Human and divine co-operation is important for the acquisition of wealth.

'Because it is created by *Agni*[1], in the bowels of the earth and augmented by Vayu, and because also the earth itself is said to be Hiranmaya, therefore, is wealth called Hiranya. And because wealth supports the world and sustains life, therefore, is it called Dhana[2]. It is for serving these ends that Dhana (wealth) exists from the beginning in the three worlds. On that Friday, when either of the two constellations-the Purvabhadra or the Uttarabhadra-is ascendant, *Agni*, creating wealth by a fiat of his will, bestoweth it on mankind for the increase of *Kuvera*'s stock. The wealth that is embowelled in the Earth is guarded by the deities called the Ajaikapats[3] and the Ahivradnas[4], and also by *Kuvera*. Exceedingly difficult of attainment, that wealth therefore, ...is rarely attained.

Udyoga Parva Section 114
Wealth Supports and sustains life. [1] *Agni - Fire, Vayu - Wind, or Air, Hiranmaya - Golden, Hiranya - Gold*
[2] *Dhana - literally - 'the prize of a contest' also wealth, property, money, treasure. Can also be translated as gift. Kuvera - god of wealth*
[3] *Ajaikapats - not known,* [4] *Ahivradnas - possibly red snakes.*

A virtuous person, upon acquiring a kingdom, should in this world make all persons his own, attaching some by gift, some by force, and some by sweet words[1]. A *Brahmana* should adopt mendicancy; a *Kshatriya* should protect (subjects); a *Vaisya* should earn wealth; and a *Sudra* should serve the other three. Mendicancy, therefore, is forbidden to thee. Nor is agriculture suited to thee. Thou art a *Kshatriya* and therefore, the protector of all in distress.

Udyoga Parva Section 133
Kings should protect all in distress. *See also MhB, Santi 58 (page 88). Note, it is Vaisyas (merchants & farmers that produce wealth).*
[1] *See also Sukra 2, 836 (page 176).*

The next Yuga, called Kali... *Brahmanas* then perform the acts that are reserved for the *Sudras*, and the *Sudras* betake themselves to the acquisition of wealth ... and numerous Mleccha[1] kings then rule over the earth! And those sinful monarchs, addicted to false speech, govern their subjects on principles that are false. And people leading domestic lives, afraid of the burden of taxes, become deceivers,... And, O sinless one, the earth then becometh full of sin and immorality. And, O lord of the earth, he that becometh virtuous at such periods doth not live long. Indeed, the earth cometh reft of virtue in every shape. And, O tiger among men, the merchants and traders then full of guile, sell large quantities of articles with false weights and measures[2]. And they that are virtuous do not prosper; while they that are sinful prosper exceedingly. And virtue then loseth her strength while sin becometh all powerful. And men that are devoted to virtue become poor and short-lived; while they that are sinful become long-lived and win prosperity. And in such times, people behave sinfully even in places of public amusements in cities and towns. And men always seek the accomplishment of their ends by means that are sinful. And having earned fortunes that are really small they become intoxicated with the pride of wealth. And O monarch, many men at such periods strive to rob the wealth that hath from trust been deposited with them in secrecy[3]. And wedded to sinful practices, they shamelessly declare-there is nothing in deposit.

Udyoga Parva Section 187
Kali or Iron Age *see Srimad 12, 2 (page 164) & 12, 3 (page 164) & Hesiod (page 59).*
[1] *Mleccha - Barbarian, non Sanskrit speaking, and by implication, ignorant.*

[2] *see Plato, Laws 918 (page 141), Cicero, Offices 3, 16 (page 46), note regarding Caanan in Bible, Leviticus 18 (page 12).*

[3] *See Plato, Republic 554 b (page 133).*

Sanjaya said,-'... Creatures in this world are of two kinds, mobile and immobile. Mobile creatures are of three kinds according to their birth, viz., oviparous, viviparous, and those engendered by heat and damp. Of mobile creatures, O king, the foremost are certainly those called viviparous. Of viviparous creatures the foremost are men and animals. Animals, O king, of diverse forms, are of fourteen species. Seven have their

Bishma Parva Section 4
The Earth is the refuge of all creatures.

abodes in the woods, and seven of these are domestic. Lions tigers, boars, buffaloes, and elephants as also bears and apes, are, O king, regarded as wild. Kine, goats, sheep, men, horses, mules, and asses, - these seven amongst animals are reckoned as domestic by the learned. These fourteen, O king, complete the tale of domestic and wild animals, mentioned, O lord of earth, in the Vedas, and on which the sacrifices rest. Of creatures that are domestic, men are foremost, while lions are the foremost of those that have their abode in the woods. All creatures support their life by living upon one another[1]. Vegetables are said to be immobile, and they are of four species viz., trees, shrubs, creepers, creeping plants existing for only a year, and all stemless plants of the grass species. Of mobile and immobile creatures, there are thus one less twenty; -and as regards their universal constituents[2], there are five. Twenty-- four in all, these described as Gayatri [3](Brahma) as is well-- known to all. He who knows these truly to be the sacred Gayatri possessed of every virtue, is not liable, O best of the Bharatas, to destruction in this world. Everything springeth from the earth[4] and everything, when destroyed, mergeth into the Earth. The Earth is the stay and refuge of all creatures[5], and the Earth is eternal. He that hath the Earth, hath the entire universe with its mobile and immobile population. It is for this that longing for (the possession of the) Earth, kings slay one another[6].'

[1] *All creates live on one an-other.*

[2] *Ether, Air, Fire, Water, Earth*

[3] *Gayatri - in this context, a sacred hymn consisting of 24 syllables.*

[4] *See MhB, Santi 190 (page 101), Bible, Genesis 1, 24 (page 5) & 2, 19 (page 6).*

[5] *See Bishma 9 below & Atharveda 12, 1, 6 (page 1).*

[6] *See Sukra 1, 357-358 (page 168) & Bishma 9 below.*

Earth, if its resources are properly developed according to its qualities and prowess, is like an ever-yielding cow, from which the three-fold fruits of virtue, profit and pleasure, may be milked. Brave kings conversant with virtue and profit have become covetous of Earth. Endued with activity, they would even cast away their lives in battle, from hunger of wealth. Earth is certainly the refuge of creatures endued with celestial bodies as also of creatures endured with human bodies. Desirous of enjoying Earth, the kings, O chief of the Bharatas, have become like dogs that snatch meat from one another. Their ambition is unbounded, knowing no gratification. It is for this that the Kurus and the Pandavas are striving for posses-sion of Earth, by negotiation, disunion, gift, and battle, O Bharata. If Earth be well looked after, it becometh the father, mother, children, firmament and heaven, of all creatures[1], O bull among men.'

Bishma Parva Section 9
Abundance of the Earth. *See Bishma 4 above. This state-ment is the central conflict of the drama of the Mahabharata.*

[1] *See also Atharveda 12, 1, 6 (page 1).*

The *Vedas* are concerned with three qualities, (viz., religion, profit and pleasure). Be thou, O Arjuna free from them, Unaffected by the pairs of contraries (such as pleasure and pain, heat and cold, etc), without anxiety for new acquisitions or protection of those already acquired, and self-possessed, ... Thy concern is with work only, but not with the fruit (of work). Let not the fruit be thy motive for work; nor let thy inclination be for inaction. Staying in devotion, apply thyself to work, casting off attachment (to it).

Bishma Parva Section 26
Geeta Chapter 2, Verse 47

This is the eternal duty sanctioned for the *Kshatriya, viz.,* that they should fight, protect subjects, and perform sacrifices, all without malice.

Bishma Parva Section 109
Duty of king. *See Sukra 1, 375 (page 169) & Cicero, Offices 1, 25 (page 43).*

Making no provision for the morrow is a practice that suits Rishis... That however, which has been called the religion of royalty depends entirely on wealth. One who robs another of wealth, robs him of his religion as well. Who amongst us, therefore, O king, would forgive an act of spoilation that is practised on us? It is seen that a poor man, even when he stands near is accused falsely. Poverty is a state of sinfulness[1]. It behoveth thee not to applaud poverty, therefore... He that has wealth has friends. He that has wealth has kinsmen. He that has wealth is regarded as a true man of the world. He that has wealth is regarded as a learned man. If a person with no wealth desires to achieve a particular purpose, he meets with failure. Wealth brings about accessions of wealth[2], like elephants capturing wild elephants[3]. Religious acts, pleasures, joy, courage, wrath, learning and sense of dignity, all these proceed from wealth, O king! From wealth one acquires family honour. From wealth, one's religious merit increases... The man that hath no wealth succeeds not in performing religious acts, for these latter spring from wealth, like rivers from a mountain... If the appropriation of wealth of others be not regarded as righteous, how O monarch, will kings practice virtue on this earth? Learned men have, in the Vedas, laid down this conclusion. The learned have laid it down that kings should live, reciting every day the three Vedas, seeking to acquire wealth, and carefully performing sacrifices with the wealth thus acquired... The eternal precepts of the Vedas also sanction it. To learn, teach, sacrifice, and assist at other's sacrifices, - these

Santi Parva Section 8
Wealth, *eulogised. See also Santi 167 below.*

[1] *Poverty is sinful (because wealth is required for virtue)- see Santi 123 (page 97), Refer Apocrypha - Ecclesiasticus Chapter 13.*

[2] *See also Bible, Matthew 25, 29 (page 30).*
[3] *See also Bible, Mark 4, 25 (page 31) Note there is a that like attracts like.*

are our principle duties. The wealth that kings take from others becomes the means of their prosperity. We never see wealth that has been earned without doing some injury to others[4]. It is even thus that kings conquer the world.

[4] *Acquisition of wealth must involve some injury - see also Sukra 2, 527-531 (page 171). But limits apply, see MhB, Santi 38 below.*

The Supreme Ordainer created wealth for sacrifice, and He created man also for taking care of that wealth and for performing sacrifice. For this reason the whole of one's wealth should be applied to sacrifice. Pleasure would follow from it as a natural consequence. Possessed of abundant energy, *Indra*[1], by the performance of diverse sacrifices with profuse gifts of valuables, surpassed all the gods. Having got their chiefship by that means, he shineth in heaven. Therefore, everything should be applied to sacrifices.

Santi Parva Section 20 Wealth is for sacrifice. *See Santi 123 (page 97). Note:- this is a statement from the bronze age when it was said sacrifice was the principle duty.*
[1] *Indra took over from Varuna as king of the Gods.*

That king bent upon the practice of virtue who strives judiciously for acquiring Heaven and Earth and who takes of earthly goods just what is ordained (as the king's share) in the scriptures, wins a reputation that spread all over the worlds and among all creatures, mobile and immobile.

Santi Parva Section 38 Correct behaviour of King. *See Confucius, Great Learning 10, 5-7 (page 48) & Mencius 3, A (page 111).*

In the first place, O foremost one of Kuru's race, the king should, from desire of pleasing (his subjects), wait with humility upon the gods and the *Brahmanas*, always bearing himself agreeably to the ordinance. By worshipping the deities and the *Brahmanas*, O perpetuator of Kuru's race, the king pays off his debt to duty and morality, and receives the respect of his subjects.

Santi Parva Section 56 Kings are to serve gods & priests.

He is the best of kings in whose dominions men live fearlessly like sons in the house of their sire[1]. He is the best of kings whose subjects do not have to hide their wealth and are conversant with what is good and bad for them. He, indeed, is a king whose subjects are engaged in their respective duties and do not fear to cast off their bodies when duty calls for it[2]; whose people, protected duly, are all of peaceful behaviour, obedient, docile, tractable, unwilling to be engaged in disputes, and inclined to liberality. That king earns eternal merit in whose dominions there is no wickedness and dissimulation and deception and envy. That king truly deserves to rule who honours knowledge, who is devoted to the scriptures and the

Santi Parva Section 58 The protection afforded by a king upholds the world. [1] *See also Sabha 13 (page 76), Bishma 109 (page 87), Udyoga 133 (page 85), L of M 7, 2-3 (page 67), Cicero, Offices 2, 21 (page 44) & Ficino, Letters 2, 53 (page 50).*
[2] *See Sukra 2, 523 (page 171)*

good of his people, who treads in the path of the righteous and who is liberal. That king deserves to rule, whose spies and counsels and acts, accomplished and unaccomplished, remain unknown to his enemies. The following verse was sung in days of old by Usanas[3] of Bhrigu's race, in the narrative called Ramacharita, on the subject, O Bharata, of kingly duties: 'One should first select a king (in whose dominions to live). Then should he select a wife, and then earn wealth[4]. If there be no king, what would become of his wife and acquisition?' Regarding those that are desirous of kingdom, there is no other eternal duty more obligatory than the protection (of subjects). The protection the king grants to his subjects upholds the world.

[3] Author of Sukra Niti, see Notes on Texts.

[4] see Confucius, Analects 13 (page 47).

A Vaisya should make gifts, study the Vedas, perform sacrifices, and acquire wealth by fair means. With proper attention he should also protect and rear all (domestic) animals as a sire protecting his sons. Anything else that he will do will be regarded as improper for him. By protecting the (domestic) animals, he would obtain great happiness[1]. The Creator, having created the (domestic) animals, bestowed their care upon the Vaisya. Upon the *Brahmana* and the *Kshatriya* he conferred (the care of) all creatures. I shall tell thee what the Vaisya's profession is and how he may take the milk of one cow as remuneration; and if he keeps (for others) a hundred kine, he may take a single pair as such fee. If he trades with other's wealth, he may take a seventh part (as his share). A seventh also is his share in the profit arising from the trade in horns, but he should take a sixteenth if the trade be in hoofs. If he engages in cultivation with seeds supplied by others, he may take a seventh part of the yield[2]. This should be his annual remuneration. A Vaisya should never desire that he should not tend cattle. If a Vaisya desires to tend cattle, no one else should be employed in that task. I should tell thee, O Bharata, what are the duties of a *Sudra* are. The Creator intended the *Sudra* to become the servant of the other three orders. For this, the service of the three other classes is the duty of *Sudra*. By such service of the other three, a *Sudra* may obtain great happiness. He should wait upon the three other classes according to order of seniority. A *Sudra* should never amass wealth, lest, by his wealth, he makes the members of the three superior classes obedient to him. By this he would incur sin. With the king's permission, however, a *Sudra*, for performing religious acts,

Santi Parva Section 60.
Income for Vaisyas & Sudras

[1] Note (here and below for Sudra) happiness is obtained by attending to the duty arising from each man's nature. Note also it is the Vaisya's that are taxed.

[2] See L of M 9,53 (page 72)

may earn wealth. I shall now tell thee the profession he should follow and the means by which he may earn his livelihood. It is said that *Sudras* should certainly be maintained by the (three) other orders[3]. Worn-out umbrellas, turbans, beds and seats, shoes, and fans, should be given to the *Sudra* servants. Torn clothes which are no longer fit for wear, should be given away by the regenerate classes unto the *Sudras*. These are lawful acquisitions. Men conversant with morality say that if the *Sudra* approaches any one belonging to the three regenerate orders from desire of doing menial service, the latter should assign him proper work. Unto the sonless *Sudra* his master should offer the funeral cake. The weak and the old amongst them should be maintained[4]. The *Sudra* should never abandon his master, whatever the nature or degree of distress into which the latter may fall. If the master loses his wealth, he should be supported by the *Sudra* servant. A *Sudra* cannot have any wealth that is his own. Whatever he possesses belongs lawfully to his master.

[3] See also Sukra 2, 788 (page 174) & L of M 10, 123 with following verses (page 73).

[4] See also L of M 8, 215 (page 71).

The king, possessed of compassion for all creatures, should regard these to be the foremost of his duties, *viz,* reclaiming the land for cultivation and fertilizing it, performance of great sacrifices for cleansing himself, a disregard for begging, and protection of subjects.

Santi Parva Section 65. The King to make land available. *See also notes on L of M 7, 80 & Shu King. The effect being to ensure rents remain modest.*

Yudhishthira said, ...'Tell me now, O grandsire, what are the principal duties of a kingdom.' Bhishma said, 'The (election and) coronation of a king is the first duty of a kingdom. A kingdom in which anarchy prevails becomes weak and is soon afflicted by robbers. In kingdoms torn by anarchy, righteousness cannot dwell. The inhabitants devour one another[1]. An anarchy is the worst possible of states. The *Srutis* declare that in crowning a king, it is *Indra* that is crowned (in the person of the king). A person who is desirous of prosperity should worship the king as he should worship *Indra* himself.

Santi Parva Section 67. The duty of a kingdom.

[1] See Plato on Tyranny, Republic 562c (page 136).
Srutis - Scriptures
Indra - King of the Gods.

Vrihaspati said, 'The duties of all men, O thou of great wisdom, may be seen to have their root in the king. It is through fear of the king only that men do not devour one another. It is the king that brings peace on earth, through due observance of duties, by checking all disregard for wholesome restraints and all kinds of lust. Achieving this he shines in glory. As, O king,

Santi Parva Section 68. Duties have their root in the king. *See L of M 7, 13-27 (page 67) & Lao Tszu, Tao Te Ching 57 (page 63).*

all creatures become unable to see one another and sink into utter darkness if the sun and the moon do not rise, as fishes in shallow water and birds in a spot safe from danger dart and rove as they please (for a time) and repeatedly attack and grind one another with force and then meet with certain destruction, even so men sink in utter darkness and meet with destruction if they have no king to protect them, like a herd of cattle without the herdsman to look after them. If the king did not exercise the duty of protection, the strong would forcibly appropriate the possessions of the weak[1], and if the latter refused to surrender them with ease, their very lives would be taken. Nobody then, with reference to any article in his possession would be able to say 'This is mine.' Wives, sons, food, and other kinds of property, would not then exist[2]. Ruin would overtake everything, if the king did not exercise the duty of protection...

[1] See Plato on Tyranny, Republic 562c (page 136).

[2] Property requires law and protection. See Cicero, Offices 2, 21 (page 44). Property therefore doesn't exist in either the Golden or the Iron age.

The world depends upon agriculture and trade and is protected by the Vedas. All these again are duly protected by the king exercising his principle duty[1]. Since the king, taking a heavy load on himself, protects his subjects with the aid of a mighty force, it is for this that the people are able to live in happiness. ... No one should disregard the king by taking him for a man, for he is really a high divinity in human form. The king assumes five different forms according to the five different occasions. He becomes *Agni*, Aditya, *Mrityu*, Vaisravana and Yama[2]. When the king, deceived by falsehood, burns with his fierce energy the sinful before him, he is then said to assume the form of *Agni*. When he observes through his spies the acts of all persons and does what is for the general good, he is then said to assume the form of Aditya. When he destroys in wrath hundreds of wicked men with their sons, grandsons and relatives, he is then said to assume the form of the destroyer. When he restrains the wicked by inflicting upon them severe punishments and favours the righteous by bestowing rewards upon them, he is then said to assume the form of Yama. When he gratifies with profuse gifts of wealth those that have rendered him valuable services, and snatches away the wealth and precious stones of those that have offended him, indeed, when he bestows prosperity upon some and takes it away from others, he is then, O king, said to assume the form of *Kuvera* on earth...

Santi Parva Section 68.
A king is a god incarnate.
[1] See Santi 68 above

[2] See Brihad 1, 4, 11 (page 35), L of M 7, 4 (page 67), Sukra 1, 141 (page 167). Vaisravana - another name for Kubera, the god of wealth, Mrityu - another name for Yama, death.

Vrihaspati has said that a king possessed of intelligence should always avoid war for the acquisition of territory. The acquisition of dominion should be made by the three well-known means (of conciliation, gift, and disunion). The king that is possessed of wisdom should be gratified with those acquisitions that are made by means of conciliation, gift and disunion. The king, O delighter of the Kurus, should take a sixth[1] of the incomes of his subjects as tribute for meeting the expenses of protecting them. He should forcibly take away wealth, much or little (as the case may require), from the ten kinds of offenders mentioned in the scriptures, for the protection of his subjects. A king should, without doubt, look upon his subjects as his own children[2]. In determining their disputes, however, he should not show compassion... The king should always appoint persons possessed of wisdom and a knowledge of the affairs of the world, for the state really rests upon a proper administration of justice[3]. The king should set honest and trustworthy men over his mines, salt, grain, ferries and elephant corps[4]. The king who always wields with propriety the rod of chastisement earns great merit. The proper regulation of chastisement is the high duty of kings and deserves great applause[5].

Santi Parva Section 69. On acqisition of territory. *Vrihaspati - A sage of great antiquity.*

[1] *The same rate is frequently used, but may be intended as a guide, See L of M 7, 130 (page 69) & associated notes.*

[2] *See Ficino, Letters 2, 53 (page 50).*

[3] *Such as described in Rama 1, 7 (page 145).*
[4] *Note the sources of wealth & see note with L of M 7, 80 (page 69).*
[5] *See L of M 7, 13 (page 67).*

Whether it is the king that makes the age, or, it is the age that makes the king, is a question about which thou shouldst not entertain any doubt. The truth is that the king makes the age. When the king rules with a complete and strict reliance on the science of chastisement[1], the foremost of ages called Krita is then said to set in.

Santi Parva Section 69. The king makes the age. *See Santi 141 (page 101) & Sukra 1, 145-152 (page 167).*
[1] *See L of M 7, 13 (page 67).*

... With a sixth part upon a fair calculation, of the yield of the soil as his tribute, with fines and forfeitures levied upon offenders, with imposts, according to the scriptures, upon merchants and traders in return for the protection granted to them, a king should fill his treasury. Realising this just tribute and governing the kingdom properly the king should, with heedfulness, act in such a way that his subjects may not feel the pressure of want. Men become deeply devoted to that king who discharges the duty of protection properly, who is endued with liberality, who is steady in observance of righteousness, who is vigilant, and who is free from lust and hate. Never desire to fill thy treasury by acting unrighteously or from covetousness... That avaricious king who through folly oppresses his subjects

Santi Parva Section 72. Taxation. *Note, taxation is calculated on the productivity of the land. Fair calculation is presumably based on the net profit.*

by levying taxes not sanctioned by the scriptures, is said to wrong his own self[1]. As a person desirous of milk never obtains any by cutting off the udders of a cow, similarly a kingdom afflicted by improper means, never yields any profit to the king.

[1] See Sukra 2, 345 (page 171), L of M 7, 129 (page 69) & MhB, Santi 120 (page 97).

Persons conversant with duties regard that to be the highest merit of the king when, engaged in protecting all creatures, the king displays compassion towards them. The sin a king incurs by neglecting for a single day to protect his subjects from fear is such that he does not attain to the end of his sufferings (for it) in hell till after a thousand years. The merit a king earns by protecting his subjects righteously for a single day is such that he enjoys its rewards in heaven for ten thousand years...

Santi Parva Section 72.
King to protect all creatures.
See L of M 7, 2-3 (page 67), Santi 88 (page 96) & 139 (page 100).

All orders should protect the wealth of a *Brahmana* even as they should the *Brahmana*'s boy or life ... Everything is protected by protecting the *Brahmana*'s wealth. Through the grace of the *Brahmana*, which may be thus secured, the king becomes crowned with success...

Santi Parva Section 75.
Priests to be protected.

I shall tell thee how a kingdom may be consolidated, and how it may be protected. A headman should be selected for each village. Over ten villages (or ten headmen) there should be one superintendent. Over two such superintendents there should be one officer (having control, therefore, of twenty villages). Above the latter should be appointed persons under each of whom should be a century of villages; and above the last kind of officers, should be appointed men each of whom should have a thousand villages under his control. The headman should ascertain the characteristics of every person in the village and all the faults that need correction. He should report everything to the officer (who is above him..)... The village headman should have control over all the produce and the possessions of the village[1]. Every headman should contribute his share for maintaining the lord of ten villages, and the latter should do the same for supporting the lord of twenty villages. The lord of a hundred villages should receive every honour from the king and should have for his support a large village, O chief of the Bharatas, populous and teeming with wealth. Such a village, so assigned to a lord of a hundred villages, should be, however, within the control of the lord of a thousand villages. That high officer, again, viz., the lord of a thousand villages, should have

Santi Parva Section 87.
Administration of the Kingdom.
See Shu King Notes (page 160). For another system & Refer L of M 7, 113 & MhB, Santi 88.

[1] See Sukra 2, 242 (page 171).

a minor town for his support. He should enjoy the grain and gold and other possessions derivable from it... Taking note of the sales and the purchases, the state of the roads, the food and dress, and the stocks and the profits of those that are engaged in trade[2], the king should levy taxes on them. Ascertaining on all occasions the extent of the manufactures, the receipts and expenses of those that are engaged in them, the state of the arts, the king should levy taxes upon the artisans in respect of the arts they follow[3]. The king, O Yudhishthira, may take high taxes, but he should never levy such taxes as would emasculate his people[4]. No tax should be levied without ascertaining the outrun and the amount of labour that has been necessary to produce it. Nobody would work or seek for outturns without sufficient cause[5]. The king should, after reflection, levy taxes in such a way that he and the person who labours to produce the article taxed may both share the value. The king should not, by thirst, destroy his own foundations as also those of others. ...The subjects hate that king who earns a notoriety for voraciousness of appetite (in the matter of taxes and imposts)[6]. ...A king who is possessed of sound intelligence should milk his kingdom after the analogy of (men acting in the matter of) calves. If the calf be permitted to suck, it grows strong, O Bharata, and bears heavy burdens. If on the other hand, O Yudhishthira, the cow be milked to much, the calf becomes lean and fails to do much service to the owner. Similarly, if the kingdom be drained much, the subjects fail to achieve any act that is great. That king who protects his kingdom himself and shows favour on his subjects (in the matter of taxes and imposts) and supports himself upon what is easily obtained, succeeds in earning many good results. Does not the king then obtain wealth sufficient for enabling him to cope with his wants?[7].. A king conversant with the considerations relating to time should, with such agreeable, sweet and complimentary words, send his agents and collect imposts from his people. Pointing out to them the necessity of repairing his fortifications and of defraying the expenses of his establishment and other heads, inspiring them with the fear of foreign invasion, and impressing them with the necessity that exists for protecting them and enabling them to ensure the means of living in peace, the king should levy imposts upon the Vaisyas of his realm[8]. If the king disregards the Vaisyas, they become lost to him, and abandoning his dominions remove themselves to the woods[9].

[2] See L of M 7, 127 (page 69), & Sukra 2, 207 - 214 (page 170).

[3] Presumably upon the owner of the business the individuals are required to work. See L of M 7, 137 (page 69) & Sukra 4, 2, 241 (page 180).

[4] See Plato, Laws 744 (page 140) & Sukra 2 345 (page 171).

[5] Tf:- The sense seems to be that if a sufficient margin of profit, capable of maintaining one at ease, be not left, one would refrain absolutely from work. The king, therefore, in taxing the outturns of work, should leave such a margin of profit to the producers. See also L of M 7, 127 (page 69).

[6] See Sukra 2, 547 (page 171).

[7] Tf:- The sense is that the subjects then, on occasions of their sovereign's want, hasten to place their resources at his disposal. See also Confucius, Analects 12 (page 47).

[8] Note taxation is on merchants & farmers (businesses).

[9] Or perhaps in contemporary

The king should, therefore, behave with leniency towards them. The king, O son of Pritha, should always conciliate and protect the Vaisyas, adopt measures for inspiring them with a sense of security and for ensuring them in the enjoyment of what they possess[10], and always do what is agreeable to them. The king, O Bharata, should always act in such a way towards the Vaisyas that their productive powers may be enhanced[11]. The Vaisyas increase the strength of a kingdom, improve its agriculture, and develop its trade. A wise king should always gratify them. Acting with heedfulness and leniency, he should levy mild imposts upon them. It is always easy to behave with goodness towards the Vaisyas. There is nothing productive of greater good to a kingdom. O Yudhishthira, than the adoption of such behaviour towards the Vaisyas of the realm.

Yudhishthira said, 'Tell me, O grandsire, how should the king behave if, notwithstanding his great wealth, he desires for more.'

... A king ... should devote himself to the good of his subjects and protect them according to the considerations of place and time and to the best of his intelligence and power. He should, in his dominions, adopt all such measures as would in his estimation secure their good as also his own. A king should milk his kingdom like a bee gathering honey from plants. He should act like the keeper of a cow who draws milk from her without boring her udders and without starving the calf. The king should (in the matter of taxes) act like the leech drawing blood mildly. He should conduct himself towards his subjects like a tigress in the matter of carrying her cubs, touching them with her teeth but never piercing them therewith. He should behave like a mouse which though possessed of sharp and pointed teeth still cuts the feet of sleeping animals in such a manner that they do not at all become conscious of it. A little by little should be taken from a growing subject and by this means should he be shorn. The demand should be increased gradually till what is taken assumes a fair proportion[1]. The king should enhance the burdens of his subjects gradually like a person gradually increasing the burden of a young bullock. Acting with care and mildness, he should at last put the reigns on them. If the reins are thus put, they would not become intractable[2]. Indeed adequate means should be employed for making them obedient. Mere entreaties to reduce them to

terms 'move off-shore'. See also Srimad 12, 2 (page 164).

[10] Security is required for encouragement. In contemporary terms we may say 'create a climate of confidence'.

[11] Presumably this includes provision of infra-structure, see notes on L of M 7, 80 (page 69).

Santi Parva Section 88
On Taxation

[1] Note that tax is increased until the proportion is fair.

[2] See Sukra 2, 547 (page 171). 'New taxes are vexatious'.

subjection would not do. It is impossible to behave equally towards all men[3]. Conciliating those that are foremost, the common people should be reduced to obedience ... The king should never impose taxes unseasonably[4] and on persons unable to bear them. He should impose them gradually and with conciliation[5], in the proper season and according to due forms. These contrivances that I declare unto thee are legitimate means of king-craft. They are not reckoned as methods fraught with deceit. One who seeks to govern steeds by improper methods only makes them furious. Drinking-shops, public women, pimps, actors, gamblers and keepers of gaming houses, and other persons of this kind, who are sources of disorder to the state, should all be checked. Residing within the realm, these afflict and injure the better classes of subjects. Nobody should ask anything of anyone when there is no distress. Manu himself in days of old has laid down this injunction in respect to all men. If all men were to live by asking or begging and abstain from work, the world would doubtless come to an end...

Let there be no beggars in thy kingdom[6], nor robbers. It is the robbers (and not the virtuous men) that give unto beggars. Such givers are not real benefactors of men.

Let such men reside in the kingdom that advance the interests of others and do them good, but not exterminate others.

Agriculture, rearing of cattle, trade and other acts of a similar nature, should be carried on by many persons on the principle of division of labour...

[3] *Reading as 'even tax rates are not equal'.*

[4] *Taxes not be imposed unseasonably, see Santi 120 below.*

[5] *see also Santi 120 below.*

[6] *Note beggars are not permitted.*

... The king should always honour subjects that are rich and should say unto them 'Do ye, with me, advance the interest of the people.'. In every kingdom, they that are wealthy constitute an estate in the realm. Without doubt, a wealthy person is the foremost of men. He that is wise, or courageous, or wealthy or influential, or righteous, or engaged in penances, or truthful in speech, or gifted with intelligence, assists in protecting (his fellow subjects).

Santi Parva Section 88.
The wealthy to be honoured.
see Ficino, Letters 1, 73 (page 49), and Mencius, 4, A (page 117).

Let not such trees as yield edible fruits be cut down in thy dominions. Fruits and roots constitute the property of the *Brahmanas*. The sages have declared this to be an ordinance of religion. The surplus, after supporting the *Brahmanas*, should go to the support of other people.

Santi Parva Section 89.
Support of Priests and the poor.
Refer also Bible, Deut 20, 20 & See Bible, Leviticus 19, 9 (page 12).

It is true, kings desirous of victory afflict many creatures, but after victory they advance and aggrandise all. By the power of gifts, sacrifices, and penances, they destroy their sins, and their merit increases in order that they may be able to do good to all creatures. The reclaimer of a field, for reclaiming it, takes up both paddy-blades and weeds. His action, however, instead of destroying the blades of paddy, makes them grow more vigorously. They that wield weapons, destroy many that deserve destruction. Such extensive destruction, however, causes the growth and advancement of those that remain.

Santi Parva Section 97.
Destruction causes growth.

He should always act heedfully (in the matter of levying his taxes) after examining the incomes and expenses of his subjects like men repairing to a full-grown palmyra for drawing its juice.

Santi Parva Section 120.
Tax based on the ability to pay.

The king should take wealth from his subjects at the proper time. He should never proclaim what he does. Like an intelligent man milking his cow every day, the king should milk his kingdom every day. As a bee collects honey from flowers gradually, the king should draw wealth gradually from his kingdom and store it. Having kept apart a sufficient portion, that which remains should be spent upon acquisition of religious merit and the gratification of the desire for pleasure. The king who is acquainted with duties and who is possessed of intelligence would never waste what has been stored. The king should never disregard any wealth for its littleness; ... Steadiness, cleverness, self-restraint, intelligence, health, patience, bravery, and attention to the requirements of time and place, - these eight qualities lead to the increase of wealth, be it small or be it much.

Santi Parva Section 120.
Tax to be taken gradually. *See L of M 7, 129 (page 69), MhB, Santi 72 (page 92, 93) & 88 (page 92, 93) & Sukra 2, 345 (page 171). Note that this conforms to Adam Smith's principles of Taxation.*

Yudhishthira said, 'I wish to hear the settled conclusions on the subject of Virtue, Wealth, and Pleasure. Depending on which does the course of life proceed? What are the respective roots of Virtue, Wealth, and Pleasure? What again are the results of those three?...'
Bhishma said, 'When men in this world endeavour with good hearts to achieve Wealth with the aid of Virtue, then those three, viz., Virtue, Wealth, and Pleasure, may be seen to co-exist in a state of union in respect of time, cause, and action.[1] Wealth has its root in Virtue, and Pleasure is said to be the fruit

Santi Parva Section 123
Virtue, wealth & pleasure. *See also Cicero, Offices 1, 2 (page 42). In the Platonic tradition a 4th is added, 'glory', by implication in Republic 8, an articulated by Gemistos Plethon (Refer Plethon's Laws).*
[1] *Tf:- The commentator illustrates this by the action of a*

of Wealth. All these three have their root in Will. Will is concerned with objects. All objects, again, in their entirety, exist for gratifying the desire of enjoyment. Upon these then does the aggregate of three depend. Entire abstraction from all objects is Emancipation. It is said that Virtue is sought for the protection of the body, and Wealth is for the acquisition of Virtue. Pleasure is only the gratification of the senses. All three have, therefore, the quality of Passion. Virtue, Wealth, and Pleasure, when sought for the sake of heaven or other such rewards, are said to be remote because the rewards themselves are remote. When sought, however, for the sake of knowledge of self, they are said to be proximate. One should seek them when they are of such a character. One should not cast them off even mentally. If Virtue, Wealth, and Pleasure are to be abandoned, one should abandon them when one has freed one's self by ascetic penances. The aim of the triple aggregate is towards emancipation[2]. Would that man could attain it! One's acts, undertaken and completed with even the aid of intelligence may or may not lead to the expected results. Virtue is not always the root of Wealth, for other things than Virtue lead to Wealth (such as service, agriculture &c)... As regard this topic, therefore, a dullard whose understanding has been debased by ignorance, never succeeds in acquiring the highest aim of Virtue and Wealth, viz., Emancipation. Virtue's dross consists in the desire of reward; the dross of Wealth consists in hoarding it[3]; when purged of these impurities, they are productive of great results.

virtuous husband seeking congress with his wedded wife in the proper season. There is religious merit in the performance of the rites known by the name of Garbhadhana; there is pleasure in the act itself; and lastly, wealth or profit in the form of a son is also acquired. Refer also to L of M 2, 224.

[2] *Refer Geeta 14.*

[3] *See notes with Santi 140 below & see Varna 199 (page 79) for right use.*

Through the decrease of the treasury, the king's forces are decreased. The king should, therefore, fill his treasury (by any means) like to one creating water in a wilderness which is without water. Agreeable to this code of quasi-morality practised by the ancients, the king should, when the time for it comes, show compassion to his people. This is eternal duty ... In seasons of distress, however, one's duties are of a different kind[1]. Without wealth a king may (by penances and the like) acquire religious merit. Life, however, is much more important than religious merit[2]. (And as life cannot be supported without wealth, no such merit should be sought which stands in the way of the acquisition of wealth)...
The profession ordained for a *Kshatriya* is the acquisition of wealth by battle and victory. ... The person who supports

Santi Parva Section 130. Times of distress. *See also Sukra 4, 2, 19 (page 179)*

[1] *See also Plato, Statesman 294b (page 127)*
[2] *Life is the first priority, then wealth, then religious merit.*

himself at ordinary times by following the practises primarily laid down for him, may in seasons of distress ...live by even unjust and improper means ...a *Kshatriya* may (by force) take what he can from persons that are rich. Know that the *Kshatriya* is the protector and the destroyer of the people. Therefore, a *Kshatriya* in distress should take (by force) what he can, with a view to (ultimately) protecting the people[3]. No person in this world, O King, can support life without injuring other creatures[4]... The king and the kingdom should always mutually protect each other[4]. This is the eternal duty. As the king protects, by spending all his possessions, the kingdom when it sinks into distress, even so should the kingdom protect the king when he sinks into distress[5]. The king even at the extremity of distress, should never give up his treasury, his machinery for chastising the wicked, his army, his friends and allies and other necessary institutions and the chiefs existing in his kingdom[6]. Men conversant with duty say that one must keep one's seeds, deducting them from one's very food. This is the truth cited from the treatise of Samvara...

[3] *See also L of M 10, 118 (page 73).*

[4] *See MhB, Santi 8 (page 87).*

[5] *See MhB, Santi 67 (page 90). The principle here, when related to economics, could be seen exactly the same as Keynes theory.*

[6] *As listed in L of M 9, 294 (page 73).*

The king should, by drawing wealth from his own kingdom as also from the kingdoms of his foes, fill his treasury. From the treasury springs religious merit[1], O son of Kunti, and it is by consequence of the treasury that the roots of his kingdom extend. For these reasons the treasury must be filled; and when filled[2]; it should be carefully protected (by putting a stop to all useless expenditure)[3], and even sought to be increased. This is the eternal practise. The treasury cannot be filled by (acting with) purity and righteousness, nor by (acting with) heartless cruelty. It should be filled by adopting the middle course.

Santi Parva Section 133.
The treasury must be filled.
[1] *In the form of both sacrifice & execution of temporal duties.*

[2] *explained in Sukra 4, 2 25-29 (page 177)*

[3] *see Sukra 4, 2, 64-72 (page 177).*

In this connection, viz., the method by which a king should fill his treasury, persons acquainted with the scriptures of olden days cite the following verses sung by Brahman himself. The wealth of persons who are given to the performance of sacrifices, as also the wealth dedicated to the deities should never be taken. A *Kshatriya* should take the wealth of such persons as never perform religious rites and sacrifices as are on that account regarded to be equal to robbers. All the creatures that inhabit the earth and all the enjoyments that appertain to sovereignty, O Bharata, belong to the *Kshatriyas*. All the wealth of the earth belongs to the *Kshatriya* and not to any

Santi Parva Section 136.
All wealth belongs to the king.

[1] *But see L of M 1, 100 (page 65), MhB, Anusasana 62 (page 106) & Santi 321 (page 104).*

person else[1]. That wealth the *Kshatriya* should use for keeping up his army[2] and for the performance of sacrifice. Tearing up such creepers and plants as are not of any use, men burn them for cooking such vegetables as serve for food[3]. Men conversant with duty have said that his wealth is useless who does not, with libations of clarified butter, feed the gods, the Pitris[4], and men. A virtuous ruler, O king should take away such wealth. By that wealth a large number of good people can be gratified. He should not however, hoard that wealth in his treasury. He who makes himself an instrument of acquisition and taking away wealth from the wicked gives them to those that are good is said to be conversant with the whole science of morality...

Both friends and foe arise from considerations of interest and gain. ... Self interest is very powerful. This whole world of creatures is moved by the desire of gain (in some form or other)... I do not know any kind of affection between any persons that does not rest upon some motive of self interest.

Knowledge, courage, cleverness, strength, and patience are said to be one's natural friends. They that are possessed with wisdom pass their lives in this world with the aid of these five. Houses, precious metals, land, wife, and friends, - these are said by the learned to be secondary sources of good. A man may obtain them everywhere.

If the king happens to be sinful, his subjects, in consequence of his oppressions, meet with destruction[1]. The king is the root of one's triple aggregate (i.e. Virtue, Wealth, and Pleasure). He should protect his subjects with heedfulness. Taking from his subjects a sixth share[2] of their wealth, he should protect them all. That king who does not protect his subjects is truly a thief.

The triple aggregate has three disadvantages with three inseparable adjuncts. Carefully considering those adjuncts, the disadvantages should be avoided. The unpaid balance of a debt, the unquenched remnant of a fire, and the unslain remnant of foes, repeatedly grow and increase. Therefore all should be completely extinguished and exterminated. Debt, which always grows, is certain to remain unless wholly extinguished.

Footnotes:

[2] *See Sukra 4, 2, 25 (page 177).*
[3] *Tf:- The king should similarly, by punishing the wicked, cherish the good.*
[4] *Spirits of deceased ancestors.*

Santi Parva Section 138.
Desire of gain motivates all.
See L of M 2, 1 (page 66) and note therewith & Santi 167 below. See also Santi 190 below on the desire is for happiness.

Santi Parva Section 139.
Primary sources of good.

Santi Parva Section 139.
The king protects his subjects.
[1] *See Santi 141 below.*
[2] *Same rate often used in Vedic texts, but not always, see Sukra 4, 2, 222-230 (page 180).*

Santi Parva Section 140[1].
Unpaid debts grow
See Cicero, Offices 2, 24 (page 43) In the Bible & Hammurabi legal limitations are imposed to protect the debtor.

O mighty armed one, the peace and prosperity of subjects, sufficiency and seasonableness of rain, disease, death, and other fears, are all dependent on the king[1]. I have no doubt also in this. O bull of Bharatas race, that Krita, Treta, Dwapara, and Kali, as regards their setting in, are all dependent on the king's conduct.

Santi Parva Section 141. Everything Depends on the King *See Santi 139 above.*
[1] *The king makes the age, see Santi 69 above & Sukra 1, 145-152 (page 167).*

The goat, the horse and the *Kshatriya* were created for a similar purpose (viz., for being useful to everybody). A *Kshatriya*, therefore, should incessantly seek the happiness of all creatures.

Santi Parva Section 142. Service

Arjuna said, 'This world, O king is the field of action. Action, therefore, is applauded here. Agriculture, trade, keeping of cattle, and diverse kinds of arts, constitute what is called Profit. Profit, again, is the end of all such acts. Without Profit or Wealth, both virtue and the objects of Desire cannot be won. This is the declaration of the Sruti. Even persons of uncleansed souls, if possessed of diverse kinds of Wealth are able to perform the highest acts of virtue and gratify desires that are apparently difficult of being gratified. Virtue and desire are the limbs of wealth as the Sruti declares. With the acquisition of Wealth both Virtue and the objects of desire may be won.

Santi Parva Section 167. Profit is required for both virtue & objects of desire. *See also Santi 8 above.*

Bhimasena said, 'One without Desire never wishes for Wealth. One without Desire never wishes for Virtue. One who is destitute of Desire can never feel any wish... Traders, agriculturalists, keepers of cattle, artists and artisans, and those who are employed in rites of propition, all act from Desire.'

Santi Parva Section 167 Desire motivates all. *See MhB, Santi 138 (page 100), L of M 2, 1 (page 66) & Cicero, Offices 1, 8 (page 41).*

... Wisdom is not competent to bring an accession of wealth; nor is wealth competent to bring an accession of happiness. Intelligence is not the cause of wealth, nor stupidity the cause of penury.

Santi Parva Section 174 Wisdom does not produce wealth.

Both in this and the other world, the visible and the fruits (of action) are specified (in the Vedas) for the sake of happiness. There is nothing more important than happiness and among the fruits or consequences of the triple aggregate. Happiness is desirable. It is an attribute of the Soul[1]. Both Virtue and Profit are sought for its sake. Virtue is its root. This, indeed, is its origin. All acts have for their end the attainment of happiness.

Santi Parva Section 190. Pursuit of happiness motivates all.
[1] *The essential nature of man is said to be 'Sat-chit-ananda', being, knowledge, consciousness and happiness, unlimited.*

The Earth is the progenitrix of all creatures. Females partake of her nature. The male animal is like Prajapati[1] himself. The vital seed, it should be known, is the creative energy. In this way did Brahman ordain in days of old that the creation should go on. Each, affected by his own acts, obtains happiness or misery.

Santi Parva Section 190.
The Earth is the mother of all creatures. *See also Bishma 4 (page 85), Atharveda 12, I, 17 (page 1) & Bible, Genesis 1, 24 (page 5) & 2, 19 (page 6). [1]*
Prajapati = The Creator.

By pouring libations on the sacred fire, sin is burnt. By study of the Vedas one obtains blessed tranquillity. By penances, one acquires blessed heaven. Gift is said to be of two kinds: gifts for the other world, and those for this. Whatever is given to the good attends the giver in the other world. Whatever is given to those that are not good produces consequences enjoyable here. The consequences of gifts are commensurate with the gifts themselves.

Santi Parva Section 191
The consequence of gifts
See L of M 4, 227 (page 67), Brihaspati (page 39), Yaj (page 187) & MhB, Vana 199 (page 79).

A thing that is acquired by a person is that which is already arrived and intended for his acquisition ... It is time that gives everything and again that takes away everything. It is time that ordains all things.

Santi Parva Section 224
Time dictates all things. *The following text expands on this. See also Bible, Ecclesiastes 3, 1 (page 23).*

... The duties set down for the Krita Yuga are of one kind. Those for the Treta are otherwise. Those for the Dwapara are different. And those for the Kali are otherwise. This is in accordance with the decline that marks every succeeding Yuga. In the Krita, Penance occupies the foremost place. In the Treta, Knowledge is foremost. In the Dwapara, Sacrifice has been said to be foremost. In the Kali Yuga, only Gift[1] is the one thing that has been laid down. ...
The slaughter of animals is the sacrifice laid down for the Kshatriyas[2]. The growing of corn is the sacrifice laid down for the Vaisyas[3]. Serving the three other orders is the sacrifice laid down for the *Sudras*. In the Krita age the performance of sacrifice was not necessary. Such performance became necessary in the Treta age. In the Dwapara, sacrifices have begun to fall off. In the Kali, the same is the case with them.

Santi Parva Section 232
Foremost duties of different ages *See Srimad 11 & 12 on the succession of the ages (page 163).*
[1] See Brihaspati (page 39) & Yaj (page 187) For legitimate gifts.
[2] See Santi 248 & 263 below.
[3] Because corn that could be enjoyed is forgone for the sake of a potential new crop. Merchants would make similar sacrifices.

Wise men apply themselves to agriculture and tillage, and the acquisition of crops (by those means) and of vehicles (for locomotion) and seats and carpets and houses. They attend also

Santi Parva Section 237
Wise men apply themselves for wealth.

to the laying of pleasure-gardens, the construction of commodious mansions, and the preparation of medicines, for diseases of every kind. It is wisdom (which consists in the application of means) that leads to the fruition of purpose.

The libations poured on the sacrificial fire rise up to the sun. From the sun springs rain. From rain springs food. From food are born living creatures. In former days, men righteously devoted to Sacrifices used to obtain therefrom the fruitions of all there wishes. The earth yielded crops without tillage. The blessing uttered by the *Rishi* produced herbs and plants. The men of former times never performed Sacrifices from desire of fruits and never regarded themselves as called upon to enjoy those fruits.

Santi Parva Section 248 Everything arises from Sacrifice *Refer Geeta 3, 9. Sacrifices, in which injury is done to animal & vegetable life are for Kshatriyas. The only sacrifice for Brahmanas is Yoga. See Santi 232 above, 263 & 343 below, & Anusasana 46 below.*

There are men that live by trafficking in living creatures! When they earn a living by such a sinful course, what scruples need they feel in selling dead carcases? The goat is *Agni*. The sheep is Varuna. The horse is Surya. Earth is the deity Virat. The cow and the calf are Soma. The man who sells these can never obtain success. But what fault can attach to the sale of oil, or Ghirita, or honey, or drugs, O regenerate one?

Santi Parva Section 262 All living Creatures are embodied gods. *Agni - fire, Varuna - ocean, Surya - sun, Virat - supreme God, Soma - Nectar.*

From Sacrifices spring progeny like clear water from the firmament. The libations poured on the sacrificial fire rise up to the Sun. From the sun springs rain. From rain springs food. From food are born living creatures. In former days, men righteously devoted to Sacrifices used to obtain therefrom the fruition of all their wishes. The earth yielded crops without tillage. The blessings uttered by the *Rishis* produced herbs and plants. The men of former times never performed Sacrifices from desire of fruits and never regarded themselves as called upon to enjoy those fruits.

Santi Parva Section 263 Sacrifice produces all mens needs. *See Santi 232 & 248 above. Refer also Geeta chapter 3 verse 9 and following.*

The lowest order, it is proper, should derive their sustenance from the three other orders. Such service, rendered with affection and reverence, makes them righteous. ... Truly, he should apply himself to service as his occupation... Dhatri created a son who was engaged in upholding all the worlds (the god of the clouds). Worshipping that deity, the Vaisya employs himself, for means of support, in agriculture and rearing cattle. The *Kshatriyas* should employ themselves in the task of

Santi Parva Section 295 The Correct Occupations of the different Orders of Society *see Vana 150 (page 78), Adi 49 (page 75), Srimad 4, 21 (page 161), Confucius, Analects 16, 1 (page 47).* [1] *The process of diminution &*

humbly protecting all the other classes. The *Brahmanas* should enjoy only... If each order acts in this way, righteousness will not suffer any diminution[1]. If righteousness is preserved in its entirety, all creatures inhabiting the earth would be happy. Beholding this happiness of all creatures on earth, the deities in heaven become filled with gladness. ... The *brahmana* shines by self restraint; the *Kshatriya* by victory; the Vaisya by wealth[2]; while the *Sudra* always shines in glory through cleverness in serving (the other three orders).

its consequences are illustrated in Plato, Republic 8 (page 131).

See also Confucius, Analects 16, 1 (47).

[2] Note that it is the Vaisya (merchants and farmers) that produce wealth.

...All orders of men are *Brahmanas*. All are sprung from Brahma. All men utter Brahma... Indeed this whole universe is Brahma. From the mouth of Brahma sprung the *Brahmanas*; from his arms, sprung the *Kshatriyas*; from the navel, the Vaisya; and from his feet, the *Sudras*. All orders in this way should not be regarded as pilfering from one another[1].

Santi Parva Section 319 All men are really the same, & the highest. *See Brihad 1, 4, 11 (page 35)*
[1] See also Ficino, Letters 1, 78 (page 49).

That man who has to rule the whole world must, indeed, be a single king without a second. He is obliged to live in only a single palace. In that palace he has again only one sleeping chamber. In that chamber he has only one bed on which at night he is to lie down. Half that bed again he is obliged to give to his Queen-consort. This may serve as an example of how little the king's share is of all he is said to own. This is the case with the food he eats, and with the robes he wears. ... The king is always dependent on others. He enjoys a very small share of all he is supposed to own... In matters also of peace and war, the king cannot be said to be independent. In the matter of women, of sports and other kinds of enjoyment, the king's inclinations are extremely circumscribed. In the matter of taking counsel and in the assembly of his councillors what independence can the king be said to have? When, indeed, he sets his orders on other men, he is said to be thoroughly independent. But then the moment after, in the several matters of his orders, his independence is barred by the very men who he has ordered... *the passage continues ...*

Santi Parva Section 321 Private property is an impression only, and the King, really has very little freedom. *See Shantanand 'The man who wanted to meet God' (page 153). See also Cicero, Offices 1, 7 (page 41).*

Thou regardest this kingdom and this palace to be thine. Thou thinkest also this army, this treasury, and these counsellors to belong to thee. Whose, however, in reality are they, and whose are they not? Allies, ministers, capital, provinces, punishment, treasury, exist, depending upon one another, like three sticks

Santi Parva Section 321 The servants of the King are not his. *See Ficino, Letters 1, 78 (page 49). [1] Tf:- The three others are Vriddhi, Kshaya, and*

standing with one another's support. The merits of each are set off by the merits of the others[1]. Which of them can be said to be superior to the rest? At those times those particular ones are regarded as distinguished above the rest when some important end is served through their agency. Superiority, for the time being, is said to attach to that one whose efficacy is thus seen. The seven limbs already mentioned[2], O best of kings, and the three others, forming an aggregate of ten, supporting one another, are said to enjoy the kingdom like the king himself.

Sthana, all of which arise from policy. Some of the seven limbs are inanimate, such as the treasury. But it is said that the treasury supports the ministers, and the ministers support the treasury.
[2] See L of M 9, 294 (page 73).

In this world it is seen that the friends and followers only of those that are rich behave towards the rich with devotion. The friends and followers of those, however that are poor fall away fall away during even the life-time of the poor.

Santi Parva Section 322
People are devoted to the wealthy. *And the wise apply themselves to wealth Santi 237 (page 102).*

The sacrifices (which the *Brahmanas* perform) strengthen the deities. Strengthened in this way, the deities fructify the Earth (and thereby support all living creatures).

Santi Parva Section 343
Sacrifice Supports all *See Santi 248 (page 103).*

Persons are very rare, O king, that are devoted to Narayana[1] with whole souls. If, O son of Kuru's race the world had been full of such persons, that are full of universal compassion, that are endured with knowledge of the soul, and that are always employed in doing good to others, then the Krita age would have set in.

Santi Parva Section 349
Universal Compassion leads to a Golden Age
[1] Narayana=the Supreme God

Women have no sacrifices ordained for them. There are no Sraddhas which they are called upon to perform. They are not required to observe any facts. To serve their husbands with reverence and willing obedience is their only duty. Through the discharge of that duty they succeed in conquering heaven. In childhood, the sire protects her. The husband protects her in youth. When she becomes old, her sons, protect her. At no period in life does she deserve to be free. The deities of prosperity are women[1]. The person that desires affluence and prosperity should honour them. By cherishing women, O Bharata, one cherishes the goddess of prosperity herself, and by afflicting her, one is said to afflict the goddess of prosperity.

Anusasana Parva Section 46
The only duty of women is to serve their husbands *See also Vana 204 (page 79) and on sacrifice see MhB, Santi 232 & 248 above.*

[1] Specifically the Goddess Lakshmi.

Yudhistira said, 'I desire, O chief of the Bharatas, to hear from thee what rewards are attached... to the planting of trees and

Anusasana Parva Section 48 Tanks and irrigation are

digging of tanks[1].'

... A tank full of water is agreeable and beneficial as the house of a friend. It is gratifying to Surya[2] himself. It also contributes to growth to the deities. The wise have said that the excavation of a tank contributes to the aggregate of three, Righteousness, Wealth and Pleasure. A tank is said to be subservient to all the four purposes of living creatures... The deities and human beings and Gandharvas and Pitris and Uragas and Rakshasas[3] and even immobile beings -- all resort to a tank full of water as their refuge... Water, especially in the other world, is difficult to obtain, O son. A gift of a drink produces eternal happiness[4]. By planting trees one acquires fame in the world of men and auspicious rewards in the world hereafter... Trees gratify the deities by their flowers; the Pitris by their fruits; and all guests and strangers by the shadow they give. Kinnaras and Uragas and Rakshasas and deities and Gandharvas and human beings, as also Rishis, all have recourse to trees as their refuge. Trees that bear flowers and fruits gratify all men... Therefore, the man that is desirous of achieving his own good, should plant trees by the side of tanks and cherish them like his own children[5].

Yudhistira said, '... What, however, O grandsire, is the best or foremost of all gifts.'

'Bhishma said, 'Of all kinds of gifts, the gift of the earth has been said to be the first (in point of merit). Earth is immovable and indestructible. It is capable of yielding unto him who owns it all the best things upon which his heart may be set. It yields robes and vestments, jewels and gems, animals, paddy and barley. Amongst all creatures, the giver of earth grows in prosperity for ever and ever... Earth is prosperity's self. She is a mighty goddess. ...The measure of one's enjoyment in this life is commensurate with the measure of one's gifts in a previous life[1]... Like one's mother, earth, when given away, cleanses the giver and the taker. ... Hence a king as soon as he gets earth, should make gifts of earth unto *Brahmanas*. None but a lord of earth, is competent to make gifts of earth. ...After the coronation ceremony has been performed of a king, this Vedic declaration should be recited to him, so that he may make gifts of earth and may never take away earth from a righteous person. Without doubt, the entire wealth owned by the king belongs to the *Brahmanas*[2]. A king well-conversant

supported.

[1] *Trees & tanks are also useful for Boundaries, L of M 8, 246 - 248 (page 71).*

[2] *Surya = Sun.*

[3] *Gandharvas = cestial singers, Pitris =spirits of ancestors, Uragas= snakes, Rakshasas= Demons.*

[4] *But note, this affects the tax rate, see Sukra 4, 2, 242 (page 180 & $, 2, 227 (page 180)), & other uses L of M 8, 248 (page 73).*

[5] *Note, there is a tradition among Mediterranean peoples that olive trees are planted for the grand children, and the planter never sees the tree fully productive.*

Anusasana Parva Section 62

Land to be given away *See also notes on L of M 7,80 (page 69) & Brihaspati (page 39).*

[1] *ie wealth in this life arises from virtue in a previous life See also Vana 199 (page 79).*

[2] *The wealth of the kings be-*

with the science of duty and morality is the first requisite of the kingdom's prosperity...

Vrihaspati ... said 'That king... who desires to have prosperity and who wishes to win happiness for himself, should always make gifts of earth, with due rites, unto deserving persons... The merit that a person acquires by making a gift of earth is incapable of being acquired by the performance of even such great sacrifices as the Agnishtoma[3] and others with plentiful gifts in the shape of Dakshina[4]... The merit that attaches to a gift of earth increases every time the earth given bears crops for the benefit of the owner.

longs to the Brahmanas*, see L of M 1, 100 (page 65).

[3] *Fire sacrifice.*
[4] *A donation to a priest usually for officiating at a ceremony. In the most ancient times, consisting of a cow.*

Then Yudhishthira gave away unto the *Brahmanas* a thousand cores of golden *nishkas*, and then unto Vyasa he gave away the whole earth. Satyavati's son Vyasa, having accepted the Earth, addressed that foremost one of Bharata's race, *viz.,* king Yudhishthira the just and said, O best of kings, the Earth which thou has given me I return unto thee. Do thou give me the purchasing value[1], for *Brahmanas* are desirous of wealth (and have no use with the Earth).'...

Aswamedha Parva Section 89
The earth is not wealth

[1] *Note that the earth had purchasing value, so that some form of land enclosure must have operated.*

There are thousands of occasions for joy and hundreds of occasions for fear. These affect only him that is ignorant but never him that is wise. With uplifted arms I am crying aloud but nobody hears me. From Righteousness is Wealth as also pleasure. Why should not righteousness, therefore be courted? For the sake neither of pleasure, nor fear, nor cupidity should anyone cast off Righteousness.

Swargarohanika Parva Section 5
Wealth and pleasure are from Virtue.

Supplementary Notes:-

1. Mahabharata Santi Parva 140. The following footnote appears in the translation:- The triple aggregate consists of Virtue, Wealth & Pleasure. The dis-advantages all arise from injudicious pursuit of each. Virtue stands as an impediment in the way of Wealth; Wealth stands in the way of Virtue; & Pleasure stands in the way of both. The inseparable adjuncts of these three, in the case of the vulgar, are that Virtue is practised as a means of Wealth; Wealth is sought as a means of Pleasure; & Pleasure is sought for the gratifying the senses. In the case of the truly wise, those adjuncts are purity of the soul as the end of Virtue; performance of sacrifices as the end of Wealth; and upholding the body as the end of Pleasure.

Mencius

5. '...A territory of a hundred li[1] square,' answered Mencius, 'is sufficient to enable its ruler to become a true King. If Your Majesty practises benevolent government towards the people, reduces punishment and taxation, gets the people to plough deeply and weed promptly, and if the able-bodied men learn, in their spare time, to be good sons and good younger brothers, loyal to their prince and true to their word, so that they will, in the family, serve their fathers and elder brothers, and outside the family, serve their elders and superiors[2], then they can be made to inflict defeat on the strong armour and sharp weapons of Ch'in and Chu, armed with nothing but staves.

'These other princes take the people away from their work during the busy seasons[3], making it impossible for them to till the land and so minister to the needs of their parents. Thus parents suffer cold and hunger while brothers, wives and children are separated and scattered. These princes push their people into pits and into water[4]. If you should go and punish such princes, who is there to oppose you? Hence it is said, "The benevolent man has no match." I beg of you not to have any doubts.'

2. King Hsüan of Ch'i asked, 'Is it true that the park of King Wen[1] was seventy *li* square[2]?'

'It is so recorded,' answered Mencius.

'Was it really as large as that?'

'Even so people found it small.'

'My park is only forty *li* square, and yet the people consider it too big. Why is this?'

'True, King Wen's park was seventy *li* square, but it was open to woodcutters as well as catchers of pheasants and hares. As he shared it with the people, is it any wonder that they found it small?

'When I first arrived at the borders of your state, I enquired about major prohibitions before I dared enter. I was told that within the outskirts of the capital there was a park forty *li* square in which the killing of deer was as serious an offence as the killing of a man. This turns the park into a trap forty *li* square in the midst of the state. Is it any wonder that the people

Book I Part A

Light taxation is best *See also MhB, Adi 63 (page 75).*

[1] *NB 1 english mile = 3.5 li.*

[2] *Expansion of these relationships is contained in a book called 'The Hsiâo King' (The Book of Filial Piety).*

[3] *See Srimad 12, 2 (7-9) in the context of the different ages (page 164), & MhB, Santi 88 & 93 (page 96).*

[4] *Perhaps a reference to the behaviour of a particularly cruel Chinese ruler - Shâu, king of Shang - described in the Shu King (refer Shu King, Books of Kau, Book 1).*

Book I Part B. 2

Private land versus Common land

[1] *The Father of King Wu, the founder of the Chan Dynasty C11th B.C.*

[2] *One English mile is approximately 3½ Li.*

109

consider it too big?'

5. ...'May I hear about Kingly government? '

'Formerly, when King Wen ruled over Ch'i, tillers of land were taxed one part in nine[1]; descendants of officials received hereditary emoluments[2]; there was inspection but no levy at border stations and market places; fish-traps were open for all to use; punishment did not extend to the wife and children of an offender. Old men without wives, old women without husbands, old people without children, young children without fathers- these four types of people are the most destitute and have no one to turn to for help. Whenever King Wen put benevolent measures into effect, he always gave them first consideration. The *Book of Odes* says,

Happy are the rich[3];

But have pity on the helpless[4].

'Well spoken,' commented the King.

'If you consider my words well spoken, then why do you not put them into practice?'

'I have a weakness. I am fond of money.'

'In antiquity Kung Liu was fond of money too. *The Book of Odes* says,

He stocked and stored;

He placed provisions

In bags and sacks[5].

He brought harmony and so glory to his state.

On full display were bows and arrows,

Spears, halberds and axes.

Only then did the march begin.

It was only when those who stayed at home had full granaries and those who went forth to war had full sacks that the march could begin[6]. You may be fond of money, but so long as you share this fondness with the people, how can it interfere with your becoming a true King?'

'I have a weakness,' said the King. 'I am fond of women.'

'In antiquity, T'ai Wang was fond of women, and loved his concubines. The *Book of Odes* says,

Ku Kung Tan Fu

Early in the morning galloped on his horse

Along the banks of the river in the West

Till he came to the foot of Mount Ch'i.

He brought with him the Lady Chiang,

Book I Part B 5 Good Government

[1] *A reference to the 'ching' method of taxation, see note 1 below (page 119).*

[2] *Dobson translates this as '.. And officials enjoyed hereditory tenure'.*

[3] *Dobson translates this as 'Lucky are the rich'.*

[4] *Shi King II, iv Ode 8 verse 13. See MhB, Santi 8 (page 87).*

[5] *Dobson translates as 'not only those who accompanied, but those who remained behind had ample provision'. See also Sukra 4, 2, 25-27 (page 177).*

[6] *See Sukra 4, 2 verse 5, 25 & 41 (page 177).*

[7] *Dobson translates as '..Coming to the foot of Mount Ch'i He met the Lady Chiang. Together they chose the site'. This king here, established a city for the benefit of his people. The next verse says '...And there he proceeded to build'*

Looking for a suitable abode[7].

At that time, there were neither girls pining for a husband nor men without a wife. You may be fond of women, but so long as you share this fondness with the people, how can it interfere with your becoming a true King?'

(Legge translation of the Shih King). The import of this quotation being that despite the kings propensity he remained devoted to his people.

5. Mencius said, 'If you honour the good and wise and employ the able so that outstanding men are in high position, then Gentlemen throughout the Empire will be only to pleased to serve at your court[1]. In the market-place, if goods are exempted when premises are taxed, and premises are exempted when the ground is taxed[2], then traders throughout the Empire will only be too pleased to store their goods in your market-place. If there is inspection but no duty at the border stations, then travellers throughout the Empire will only be too pleased to go by way of your roads[3]. If tillers help in the public fields but pay no tax on the land[4], then farmers throughout the Empire will be only too pleased to till the land in your realm. If you abolish the levy in lieu of corvée[5] and the levy in lieu of the planting of the mulberry, then all the people of the Empire will be only too pleased to come and settle in your state. If you can truly execute these five measures, the people of your neighbouring states will look up to you as to their father and mother; and since man came into this world no one has succeeded in inciting children against their parents. In this way, you will have no match in the Empire. He who has no match in the Empire is a heaven-appointed officer, and it has never happened that such a man failed to become a true king.'

Book 2 Part A Land Tax is preferable *See Alternate Translation in note 2 below (page 119).*

[1] *See MhB, Adi 109 (page 76), Santi 58 (page 88) & Confucius Analects 13 (page 47).*

[2] *Note, only the land is taxed. See also Sukra 4, 2, 257 (page 180).*

[3] *Free trade is encouraged.*

[4] *See note 1 regarding 'Ching' below (page 119).*

[5] *corvée - a feudal tradition of providing taxation in the form of labour.*

3. Duke Wen of T'eng asked about government.

'The business of the people,' said Mencius, 'must be attended to without delay. The *Book of Odes* says,

In the day time they go for grass;
At night they make it into ropes.
They hasten to repair the roof;
Then they begin sowing the crops[1].

This is the way of the common people. Those with constant means of support will have constant hearts, while those without constant means will not have constant hearts[2]. Lacking constant hearts, they will go astray and get into excesses, stopping at nothing[3]. To punish them after they have fallen foul of the law is to set a trap for the people. How can a benevolent

Book 3 part A 3 Forms of Taxation

[1] *see also Plato, Republic 2, 370 (page 129) & Ecclesiastes 3, 1 (page 23).*

[2] *See also Sukra 2, 807 (page 174) & Shantanand 1982 on the family (page 153).*

[3] *See Plato, Republic 562c onwards (page 136)*

man in authority allow himself to set a trap for the people[4]? Hence a good ruler is always respectful and thrifty, courteous and humble, and takes from the people no more than is prescribed[5]. Yang Hu said, "If one's aim is wealth one cannot be benevolent; if one's aim is benevolence one cannot be wealthy."

'In the Hsia Dynasty, each family was given fifty mu of land, and the "kung" method of taxation was used; in the Yin, each family was given seventy mu and the *"chu"* method was used; in the Chou, each family was given a hundred mu and the *"ch'e"* method was used. In fact, all three amounted to a taxation of one in ten. *"ch'e"* means "commonly practised"; *"chu"* means "to lend help". Lung Tzu said, "In administering land, there is no better method than *chu* and no worse than *kung.*" With the kung method, the payment due is calculated on the average yield over a number of years[6]. In good years when rice is so plentiful that it goes to waste, the people are no more heavily taxed, though this would mean no hardship; while in bad years, when there is not enough to spare for fertilizing the fields, the full quota is insisted upon. If he who is father and mother to the people makes it necessary for them to borrow because they do not get enough to minister to the needs of their parents in spite of having toiled incessantly all the year round, and causes the old and young to be abandoned in the gutter, wherein is he father and mother to the people[7]?

'Hereditary emolument as a matter of fact is already practised in T'eng.

'The *book of Odes* says,

The rain falls on our public land,
And so also on our private land[8].

There is "public land" only when *chu is* practised. From this we see that even the Chou practised chu...

The Duke sent Pi Chan to ask about the well-field system[9].

'Your prince,' said Mencius, 'is going to practise benevolent government and has chosen you for this mission. You must do your best. Benevolent government must begin with land demarcation. When boundaries[10] are not properly drawn, the division of land according to the well-field system and the yield of grain used for paying officials cannot be equitable. For this reason, despotic rulers and corrupt officials always neglect the boundaries. Once the boundaries are correctly fixed, there will be no difficulty in settling the distribution of land and the

[4] *Note, Sudras cannot be punished. See L of M 7, 14 (page 67) & by way of example Mencius 1, B, 2 above.*

[5] *See also MhB, Santi 38 (page 88).*

Short comings of different tax methods.

[6] *A variation of this form used currently in Australia for calculating taxation for farmers but the surplus is retained.*

[7] *See Nehemiah 5, 1-8 (page 22).*

[8] *The consideration for the people is for the whole before themselves. See note below on this form of land tenure (page 119). The verse quoted continues 'ears (of grain) untouched for the benefit of widows', like Bible, Deut 24, 19-22 (page 17).*

[9] *well-field, ching - see note below (page 119).*

[10] *See Plato, Laws 843 (page 141), Bible, Deut 19, 14 (page 16), L of M 8, 245 (page 71) & Cicero, Offices 2, 21. (page 44). Any producer must have*

determination of emolument.

This state is limited in territory. Nevertheless, there will be men in authority and there will be the common people. Without the former, there would be none to rule over the latter; without the latter, there would be none to support the former[11]. I suggest that in the country the tax should be one in nine, using the method of *chu,* but in the capital it should be one in ten, to be levied in kind[12]. From Ministers downwards, every official should have fifty *mu* of land for sacrificial purposes. In ordinary households every extra man is to be given another twenty-five *mu.* Neither in burying the dead, nor in changing his abode, does a man go beyond the confines of his village. If those who own land within each *ching* befriend one another both at home and abroad, help each other to keep watch, and succour each other in illness, they will live in love and harmony. A *ching*[13] is a piece of land measuring one *li* square, and each *ching* consists of 900 *mu.* Of these, the central plot of 100 *mu* belongs to the state, while the other eight plots of 100 *mu* each are held by eight families who share the duty of caring for the plot owned by the state. Only when they have done this duty dare they turn to their own affairs. This is what sets the common people apart.

'This is a rough outline. As for embellishments, I leave them to your prince and yourself.'

4. There was a man by the name of Hsü Hsing who preached the teachings of Shen Nung[1]. He came to T'eng from Ch'u, went up to the gate and told Duke Wen, 'I, a man from distant parts, have heard that you, my lord, practise benevolent government. I wish to be given a place to live and become one of your subjects.'

The Duke gave him a place.

His followers, numbering several score, all wore unwoven hemp and lived by making sandals and mats.

Ch'en Hsiang and his brother Hsin, both followers of Ch'en Liang, came to T'eng from Sung carrying ploughs on their backs. 'We have heard ' said they, 'that you, my lord, practice the government of the sages. In that case you must yourself be a sage. We wish to be the subjects of a sage.'

Ch'en Hsiang met Hsü Hsing and was delighted with his teachings, so he abjured what he had learned before and became follower of Hsü Hsing.

certainty of tenure before he is prepared to expend money or effort.

[11] *See MhB, Santi 67 (page 90) & 68 (page 90).*

[12] *Note, tax is not collected in cash for rural production.*

[13] *ching- see note 1 on page 119 below.*

Book 3 part A, 4
On Trade and Specialisation *See also Plato, Republic 2, 370 (page 129), Cicero, Offices 2, 4 (page 43) & refer Plato, Republic 2, 374.*

[1] *Shen Nung- was the legendary Emperor credited with the invention of Agriculture.*

Ch'en Hsiang saw Mencius and cited the words of Hsü Hsing 'The prince of T'eng is a truly good and wise ruler. However he has never been taught the Way. To earn his keep a good and wise ruler shares the work of tilling the land with his people. He rules while cooking his own meals. Now T'eng has granaries and treasuries. This is for the prince to inflict hardship on the people in order to keep himself. How can he be a good and wise prince?'

'Does Hsü Tzu only eat grain he has grown himself?' asked Mencius.

'Does Hsü Tzu only wear cloth he has woven himself?'

'No. He wears unwoven hemp.'

'Does Hsü Tzu wear a cap?'

'Yes.'

'What kind of cap does he wear?'

'Plain raw silk.'

'Does he weave it himself?'

'No. He trades grain, for it.'

'Why does Hsü Tzu not weave it himself?'

'Because it interferes with his work in the fields.'

'Does Hsü Tzu use an iron pot and an earthenware steamer for cooking rice and iron implements for ploughing the fields?'

'Yes'

'Does he make them himself?'

'No. He trades grain for them.'

'To trade grain for implements is not to inflict hardship on the potter and the blacksmith. The potter and the blacksmith, for their part, also trade their wares for grain. In doing this, surely they are not inflicting hardship on the farmer either. Why does Hsü Tzu not be a potter and a blacksmith as well so that he can get everything he needs from his own house? Why does he indulge in such multifarious trading with men who practise the hundred crafts? Why does Hsü Tzu put up with so much bother?'

'It is naturally impossible to combine the work of tilling the land with that of a hundred different crafts[2]'

'Now, is ruling the Empire such an exception that it can be combined with the work of tilling the land? There are affairs of great men, and there are affairs of small men. Moreover, it is necessary for each man to use the products of all the hundred crafts. If everyone must make everything he uses, the Empire will be led along the path of incessant toil. Hence it is said,

[2] *Note that trade is essential then for practical society. The alternative is incessant toil.*

"There are those who use their minds and there are those who use their muscles. The former rule; the latter are ruled[3]. Those who rule are supported by those who are ruled." This is a principle accepted by the whole Empire.

[3] See opening lines of MhB, Santi 88 (page 96).

'In the time of Yao[1] the Empire was not yet settled. The Flood still raged unchecked, inundating the Empire; plants grew thickly; birds and beasts multiplied; the five grains did not ripen, birds and beasts encroached upon men, and their trail criss-crossed even the Central Kingdoms. The lot fell on Yao to worry about this situation. He raised Shun to a position of authority to deal with it. Shun put Yi in charge of fire. Yi set the mountains and valleys alight and burnt them, and the birds and beasts went into hiding. Yu[2] dredged the Nine Rivers, cleared the courses of the Chi and the T'a to channel the water into the Sea, deepened the beds of the Ju and the Han, and raised the dykes of the Huai and Ssu to empty them into the River. Only then were the people able to find food for themselves. During this time Yu spent eight years abroad and passed the door of his own house three times without entering. Even if he had wished to plough the fields, could he have done it?

'Hou Chi taught the people how to cultivate land and plough the fields. kinds of grain. When these ripened, the people multiplied. This is the way of the common people: once they have a full belly and warm clothes on their back they degenerate to the level of animals if they are allowed to lead idle lives, without education and discipline[3]. This gave the sage King further cause for concern, and so he appointed Hsieh as the Minister of Education whose duty was to teach the people human relationships: love between father and son, duty between ruler and subject, distinction between husband and wife, precedence of the old over the young, and faith between friends[4]. Fang Hsün said,

Encourage them in their toil,
Put them on the right path,
Aid them and help them,
Make them happy in their station,
And by bountiful acts further relieve them of hardship. The Sage worried to this extent about the affairs of the people. How could he have leisure to plough the fields. Yao's only worry was that he should fail to find someone like Shun, and Shun's only worry was that he should fail to find someone like Yu and Kao

Book 3 part A, Continued
On The establishment of the Kingdom & Public Works.
[1] *The legendary first king of China*

[2] *See Shû King 3, 1 (page 155)*

[3] *See Srimad 4, 21 (page 161)*

[4] *See Mencius 1, A above & associated notes.*

Yao. He who worries about his plot of a hundred mu not being well cultivated is a mere farmer.

'To share one's wealth with others is generosity; to teach others to be good is conscientiousness, to find the right man for the Empire is benevolence. Hence it is easier to give the Empire away than to find the right man for it...

'It is not true that Yao and Shun did not have to use their minds to rule the Empire. Only they did not use their minds to plough the fields.

'If we follow the way of Hsü Tzu there will only be one price in the market, and dishonesty will disappear from the capital[5]. Even if you send a mere boy to the market, no one will take advantage of him. For equal lengths of cloth or silk for equal weights of hemp, flax or raw silk, and for equal measures of the five grains, the price will be the same, for shoes of the same size, the price will also be the same.

[5] *Prices are naturally different. See Sukra 2, 718 (page 173).*

'That things are unequal is part of their nature. Some are Worth twice or five times, ten or a hundred times, even a thousand and ten thousand times, more than others. If you reduce them to the same level, it will only bring confusion to the Empire. If a roughly finished shoe sells at the same price as a finely finished one, who would make the latter? If we follow the way of Hsü Tzu, we will be showing one another the way to being dishonest. How can one govern a state in this way?'

4. ... 'But it is not right for a Gentleman not to earn his keep.' 'If people cannot trade the surplus of the fruits of their labours to satisfy one another's needs, then the farmer will be left with surplus grain and the women with surplus cloth. If things are exchanged, you can feed the carpenter and the carriage-maker. Here is a man. He is obedient to his parents at home and respectful to his elders abroad and acts as custodian of the way of the Former Kings for the benefit of future students. In spite of that, you say he ought not to be fed. Why do you place more value on the carpenter and the carriage maker than on a man who practises morality?'

Book III part B, 4
People are paid for their results
See Book 3, part A, 4 above

'It is the intention of the carpenter and the carriage maker to make a living. When a Gentleman pursues the Way, is it also his intention to make a living? '

'What has intention got to do with it? If he does good work for you then you ought to feed him whenever possible. Moreover, do you feed people on account of their intentions or on account of their work?'

'Their intentions.'

'Here is a man who makes wild movements with his bowel, ruining the tiles. Would you feed him because his intention is to make a living?'

'No.'

'Then you feed people on account of their work, not on account of their intentions[1].'

[1] The consequence being that the desirability of the product is what is important.

5. Mencius said, 'There is a common expression, "The Empire, the state, the family". The Empire has its basis in the state, the state in the family, and the family in one's own self.'

Book IV Part A 5
Hierarchy of Society

6. Mencius said, 'It is not difficult to govern. All one has to do is not to offend the noble families. Whatever commands the admiration of the noble families will command the admiration of the whole state; whatever commands the admiration of a state will command the admiration of the Empire. Thus moral influence irresistibly fills to overflowing the whole Empire within the Four seas.'

Book IV Part A 6
Importance of Nobility
See MhB, Santi 88 (page 96).

10. Po Kuei said, 'I should like to fix the rate of taxation at one in twenty. What do you think of it?'

'Your way,' said Mencius. 'Is that of the Northern Barbarians. In a city of ten thousand households, would it be enough to have a single potter?'

'No. There will be a shortage of earthenware.'

"In the land of the Northern barbarians, the five grains do not grow. Millet is the only crop that grows. They are without city walls, houses, ancestral temples or sacrificial rites. They do not have diplomacy with its attendant gifts and banquets, nor do they have the numerous offices and officials. This is why they can manage on a tax of one in twenty. Now in the Central Kingdoms, how can human relationships and men in authority be abolished? The affairs of a city cannot be conducted when there is a shortage even of potters. How much more so if the shortage is of men in authority? Those who wish to reduce taxation to below the level laid down by Yao and Shun are all, to a greater or less degree, barbarians; while those who wish to increase it are all, to a greater or less degree, Chiehs[1].'

Book VI Part B 10
Amounts of taxation

[1] Note that more sophisticated societies require more tax.

14. Mencius said, Benevolent words do not have as profound an

Book VII Part B 14

effect on the people as benevolent music. Good government does not win the people as does good education. He who practises good government is feared by the people; he who gives the people good education is loved by them. Good government wins the wealth of the people; good education wins their hearts.'

Education

22. Mencius said... 'If the mulberry tree is planted at the foot of the walls in every homestead of five *mu* of land and the women of the house keeps silkworms, then the aged can wear silk. If there are five hens and two sows, and these do not miss their breeding season, then the aged will not be deprived of meat. If a man tills a hundred *mu* of land, there will be enough for his family of eight mouths not to grow hungry.
'When Hsi Po was said to"take good care of the aged", what was meant is this. He laid down the pattern for the distribution[1] of land, taught the men the way to plant trees and keep animals, and showed their womenfolk the way to care for the aged. A man needs silk for warmth at fifty and meat for sustenance at seventy. To have neither warm clothes nor a full belly is to be cold and hungry. The people under King Wen had no old folk who were cold and hungry.'

Book VII Part A 22
Care of the aged

[1] *Note:- Care of the aged does not require direct support from the coffers of government.*

23. Mencius said, Put in order the fields of the people, lighten their taxes, and the people can be made affluent. If one's consumption of food is confined to what is in season and one's use of other commodities is in accordance with the rites, then one's resources will be more than sufficient. The common people cannot live without water and fire, yet one never meets with refusal when knocking on another's door in the evening to beg for water and fire. This is because these are in such abundance. In governing the Empire, the sages tried to make food as plentiful as water and fire. When this happens, how can there be any amongst his people who are not benevolent?'

Book VII Part A 23
Prosperity

Supplementary Notes

1. Ching (or Chu) system of taxation. So named because the land is divided into 9 parts which looks like '#', similar to the character 'ching' - translated as 'a well'. This method involved eight families cultivating their own land and sharing the cultivation of the public land, the product of which was for the state. The centre block (government block) also contained the houses of the farmers. Ode 6 (decade 6) of the book of Odes describes each block being 100 mau and the central block including 2½ mau for each family on which they erected their huts.

Other references speak of a system of land tenure not unlike the patchwork spread of fields around English villages before the enclosure movement involving numerous strips scattered over a wide area. An observer writes' On across such and such a stream; up to the side of the willow tree... a plot on the T'ung road... a plot on the Chou road'

2. **Alternate Translation** of Book 2 part A: Mencius said: Respect the worthy and employ the capable; put talented people in key positions, then all the shih of the realm will be pleased and will want to be members of your court.
In the market-places, charge land-rent, but don't tax the goods; or make concise regulations and don't even charge rent. Do this, and all the merchants in the realm will be pleased, and will want to set up shop in your markets.
At the borders, make inspections but don't charge tariffs, then all the travellers in the realm will be pleased and will want to traverse your highways.
If the farmers merely have to help each other with the government fields, and do not have to pay an additional tax, then all the farmers in the realm will be pleased, and will want to till your fields.
If you do not charge fines to the unemployed in your marketplaces, then all the people in the realm will be pleased, and will want to become your subjects.
If you are really able to put these five points into practice, then the people from the neighbouring states will look up to you as a parent. Now, there has never been a case of someone being able to consistently succeed in making children attack their own parents. This being the case, you will have no enemies in the realm. The one who has no enemies in the realm is the vicegerent of Heaven. There is no case of one who attained to this level, and who did not attain to true kingship. (Translator unknown).

Narada Smriti

1. Where a man wishes to resume what he has given, because it has been unduly given by him, it is called Resumption of Gift, a title of law.

3. ... Again, what may not be given is eightfold; what may be given is of one kind only; of valid gifts there are seven species; and sixteen sorts of invalid gifts.

4. An Anvâhita deposit, a Yâkita, a pledge, joint property, a deposit, a son, a wife, the whole property of one who has offspring,

5. And what has been promised to another man; these have been declared by the spiritual guides to be inalienable by one in the worst plight even.

6. What is left (of the property) after the expense of maintaining the family has been defrayed, may be given. But by giving away anything besides, a householder will incur censure.

7. He who has, for three years, property sufficient to provide for those whom he is bound to maintain, or who has even more than that, shall drink the Soma juice.

8. The price paid for merchandise. wages, (a present offered) for an amusement, (a gift made) from affection, or from gratitude, or for sexual intercourse with a woman, and a respectful gift, are the seven kinds of valid gifts.

9. Invalid gifts are the following (sixteen): what has been given by a man under the influence of fear, anger, hatred, sorrow or pain; as a bribe; in jest; fraudulently, under false pretences;

10. Or by a child; or by a fool; or by a person not his own master; or by one distressed; or by one intoxicated; or by one insane; or in consideration of a reward, thinking 'This man will show me some service;'

11. And so is invalid what was given from ignorance to an unworthy man thought to be worthy, or for a purpose (thought to be) virtuous.

12. Both the donee who covets invalid gifts and accepts them from avarice, and the donor of what ought not to be given who yet gives it away, deserve punishment.

Book IV Resumption of Gift
See also Brihaspati (page 39)

1. Tf 'unduly' means unlawful, ie against what is here stated.

4. Anvahita deposit = a deposit made to be delivered ultimately to the rightful owner.

Philo

40. You see therefore, that all good things spring up and shoot out from labour as from one general root, and this you must never allow yourself to neglect; for if you do, you will without being aware of it, be also letting slip the collected heap of goods which it brings with it; for the Ruler of the universe, of heaven, and of the world, both himself possesses and bestows on whomsoever he pleases, his good things, with all ease and abundance. Since formerly he created this world, vast as you see it is, without any labour, and how too he never ceases holding it together, so that it may last for ever. And absence from all labour and fatigue is the most appropriate attribute of God; but nature has not given the acquisition of good things to any mortal without labour...

41. ... For as those persons who are desirous to live must not neglect food, so too they who are anxious to attain to good things must pay due attention to labour, for what food is to life that labour is to virtue.

The Sacrifices of Abel & Cain IX,
All wealth is produced by labour.

41. Note that Philo sees a nexus between virtue & labour.

92. But there are men who are so sordid in their minds, being wholly devoted to the acquisition of money and labouring to death for every description of gain, without paying any attention to the source from which it is derived, that they glean their vineyards again after they have gathered the fruit, and beat their olive branches a second time, and reap the whole of the land which bears barley and the whole of the land which bears wheat, convicting themselves of an illiberal and slavish littleness of soul, and displaying their impiety;

93. For they themselves have contributed but a small part of what was necessary for the cultivation of their lands, but a greater number and the most important of the means to render the land fertile and productive have been supplied by nature, such as the seasonable rains, a proper temperature of the atmosphere, those nurses of the seeds sown and springing up -- heavy and continual dews, vivifying breezes, the beneficial bestowal of the seasons of the year, so that summer shall not scorch the crops nor the frost chill them, nor the revolutions of spring and autumn deteriorate or diminish what is produced.

94. And though these men know and actually see that nature is continually perfecting her work by these means, and enriching

On the Virtues, XVII
The majority of the product is the result of nature.
What should be taken? Only that which is required.
92. See Bible, Leviticus 19, 9 (page 12).

93. Men contribute little. Nature contributes the bulk.

them with her abundant bounties, nevertheless they endeavour to appropriate the whole of her liberality to themselves, and, as if they themselves were the causes of everything, they give no share of any of their wealth to any one, showing at one and the same time their inhumanity and their impiety...

95. The laws command that the people should offer to the priests first fruits of corn, and wine, and oil, and of their domestic flocks, and of wools. But that of the crops which are produced in the fields, and of the fruits of the trees, they should bring in full baskets in proportion to the extent of theirs lands; with hymns made in praise of God ... And moreover, they were not to reckon the first-born of the oxen, and sheep, and goats in their herds and flocks as if they were their own, but were to look upon these also as first fruits, in order that being thus trained partly to honour God, and partly also not to seek for every possible gain, thy might be adorned with those chief virtues, piety and humanity.

95. See Bible, Deuteronomy 18, 4 (page 16).

46. But the unerring law is right reason; not an ordinance made by this or that mortal, a corruptible and perishable law, a lifeless law written on lifeless parchment or engraved on lifeless columns; but one imperishable, and stamped by immortal nature on the immortal mind.

Every Good man is Free

76. But the temple has for its revenues not only portions of land, but also other possessions of much greater extent and importance, which will never be destroyed or diminished; for as long as the race of mankind shall last, the revenues likewise of the temple will always be preserved being coeval in their duration with the universal world. (77) For it is commanded that all men shall bring their first fruits to the temple, from twenty years old and upwards; and this contribution is called their ransom[1]. On which account they bring in the first fruits with exceeding cheerfulness, being joyful and delighted...

The Special Laws, 1
The first fruits are due to the priests. *Commentary on Bible, Deuteronomy 18, 4 (page 16).*

[1]Ranson - the Hebrew can also be interpreted as 'redemption'.

131. The law did not allot any share of the land to the priests, in order that they like others might derive revenues from the land, and so possess a sufficiency of necessary things...
137. Moreover the law, going beyond all these enactments in their favour, commands the people to bring them first fruits, not only of all their possessions of every description...
143. And they are accordingly given to them in a manner quite contrary to that in which cities usually furnish them to their

Special Laws, 1
Advantages of the Hebrew Tax System
See Bible, Leviticus 19, 9 (page 12).

rulers; for cities usually furnish them under compulsion, and with great unwillingness and lamentation, looking upon the collectors of taxes as common enemies and destroyers, and making all kinds of different excuses at different times, neglecting all laws and ordinances, and with all this jumbling and evasion do they contribute the taxes and payments which are levied on them.

60. Not that the law is the advisor of idleness, for it is always accustoming its followers to submit to hardships, and training them to labour, and it hates those who desire to be indolent and idle; at all events, it expressly commands us to labour diligently for six days[1], but in order to give some remission from uninterrupted and incessant toil, it refreshes the body with seasons of moderate relaxation exactly measured out, so as to renew it again for fresh works.

Special Laws II XV
Encouragement against idleness

[1] *Bible, Exodus 20, 9 (see page 10).*

71. ... on every seventh year he ordains a remission of debts, assisting the poor, and inviting the rich to humanity...
73. For while it does not permit them to lend on usury to their fellow countrymen, it has allowed them to receive interest from foreigners; calling the former, with great felicity of expression, their brothers, in order to prevent any one's grudging to give of his possessions to those who are as if by nature joint inheritors with themselves; but those who are not their fellow countrymen are called strangers, as is very natural. For being a stranger shows a person has no right to a participation in any thing, unless, indeed, any one out of excess of virtue should treat even those in conditions of strangers as kindred and related, from having been bred up under a virtuous state of things, and under virtuous laws which look upon what is virtuous alone as good.
74. But the action of lending on usury is blameable; for a man who lends on usury has not abundant means of living, but is clearly in some want; and he does so as being compelled to add the interest to his principle in order to subsist, and so he at last becomes of necessity very poor; and while he thinks he is deriving advantage he is in reality injured, just as foolish animals are when they are deceived by a present bait. (75)

Special Laws II XVII
Care of Poor

On Usury
See also Bible, Exodus 24, 25 (page 11) and Deuteronomy 23, 19 (page 17).

86. ... Moses commands the people to leave the land fallow and untilled evert seventh year, for many reasons; first of all that they may honour the number seven, or each period of days months, and years; for every seventh day is sacred, which is

Special Laws XVII
On the Purpose of the Sabbath
See Bible Leviticus 25: 1-7 (page 13).

called by the Hebrews the sabbath; and the seventh month in every year has the greatest of the festivals allotted to it, so that very naturally the seventh year also has a share of veneration paid to this number, and receives special honour.

87. And the second reason is this, 'Be not,' says the lawgiver, 'wholly devoted to gain, but even willingly submit to some loss,' that you may bear with the more indifference involuntary calamity if it should ever fall upon you ... (88) But the followers of Moses, all who are true disciples, being practised in good laws, are accustomed, from the earliest age, to bear want with patience, by the custom of leaving their fertile land fallow; and being also taught magnanimity, and one may almost say, to let slip out of their hands, from deliberate intention, revenues of admitted certainty.

89. The third reason appears to me to be, ... to show that it does not become any one whatever to weigh down and oppress men with burdens; for if one is to allow a period of rest to the portions of the earth which cannot by nature have any share in the feelings of pleasure or of pain, how much the more must men be entitled to a similar relaxation...

92. Moreover let the governors of cities cease to oppress them with continual excessive taxes and tributes, filling their own stores with money, and in preserving as a treasure the illiberal vices which defile their whole lives; (93) for they do, on purpose, select as collectors of their revenues the most pitiless of men, persons full of all kinds of inhumanity, giving them abundant opportunity for the exercise of their covetousness; ... (94) therefore they throw everything into disorder and confusion, levying their exactions, not only on the possessions of the citizens, but also on their persons, with insults and violence, and the invention of new and unprecedented torture.

96. ... The earth ..(97).. although it seems to be inanimate, is nevertheless fully prepared to make requital and to recompense favours, hastening to pay back any gift which it has received; for as it receives an exemption every seventh year, and is set wholly free for the circle of the year, in subsequent year produces double, or sometimes, many times, larger crops than usual from its great productiveness.

100. And I have learnt all this from all-wise nature, which, knowing the industrious and labourious condition of our race, has distributed them into day and night, giving to us the one for wakefulness, and the other for sleep; (101) for she felt a natural anxiety, like a careful mother, that her offspring should not be

worn out with toil...

105. For he commands his people every seventh year to forbear to enclose any piece of land, but to let all the olive gardens and vineyards remain open, and all other possessions, whether they be seed-land or trees, that so the poor may be able to enjoy the spontaneously growing crops without fear, in a greater, or in all events not in a less degree than the owners themselves.

107. Is it not then fit to love these laws which are full of such abundant humanity? By which the rich men are taught to share the blessings which they have with and to communicate them to others: and the poor are comforted, not being for ever compelled to frequent the houses of the indigent to supply the deficiencies by which they themselves are oppressed...

109. And all those who breed flocks and herds lend their own cattle with fearlessness and impunity to graze on the land of others, choosing the most fertile plains, and the lands most suitable for the feeding of their cattle.

110. Having laid down these principles as a kind of foundation of gentleness and humanity, he puts together seven sevens of years, and so makes the fiftieth year an entirely sacred year enacting with reference to it some ordinances of especial honour beyond those which relate to the ordinary years of communication of property.

Special Laws 2 XXII
The Jubilee Year
Commentary on Bible, Leviticus 25:8-17 (page 13).

111. In the first place he gives this commandment. He thinks it fitting that all property alienated should now be restored to its original masters in order that inheritances originally apportioned to the different tribes may be preserved, and that no one who originally received an allotment may be wholly deprived of his possessions.

113. For the law says Do not give price as if for an everlasting possession, but only for a definite number of years, which must be less than fifty; for the sale effected ought not be a sale of the lands owned, but a sale of the crops, for two most weighty reasons; one, that the whole country is called the possession of God, and it is impious for any one else to be recorded as the masters of the possessions of God; and secondly because a separate allotment has been assigned to each land-owner, of which the law does not choose the man who originally received the allotment to be deprived.

Plato

For know that this is the command of God; and I believe that no greater good has ever happened in the state than my service to the God. For I do nothing but go about persuading you all, old and young alike, not to take thought for your persons or your properties, but first and chiefly to care about the greatest improvement of the soul. I tell you that virtue is not given by money, but that from virtue comes money and every other good of man, public as well as private.

Apology - 30 b
Money arises from virtue.
see also Confucius, Great Learning 10 (page 48). In MhB, Santi 123 this is explained at length (page 97), see also Plato, Laws 743 (page 140).

Law can never issue an injunction binding on all which really embodies what is best for each: it cannot prescribe with perfect accuracy what is good and right for each member of the community at any one time. The differences of human personality, the variety of men's activities and the inevitable unsettlement attending all human experience make it impossible for any art whatsoever to issue unqualified rules holding good on all questions at all times. I suppose that so far we are agreed. Yes most emphatically.

But we find practically always that the law tends to issue just this invariable kind of rule. It is like a self-willed, ignorant man who lets no one do anything but what he has ordered and forbids all subsequent questioning of his orders even if the situation has shown some marked improvement on the one for which he originally legislated.

Yes, that is just how the law treats us all.

It is impossible then, for something invariable and unqualified to deal satisfactorily with what is never uniform and constant.

Statesman 294b
The limitations of human law.
See Cicero, Offices 1, 10 (page 42). The L of M proposes different arrangements in times of distress. See also Shantanand 1978 regarding Natural Law (page 150) & Plato, Laws 743 (page 140) On the objects of Law.

For I must remark, Thrasymachus, if you will recall what was previously said, that although you began by defining the true physician in an exact sense, you did not observe a like exactness when speaking of the shepherd; you thought that the shepherd as a shepherd tends the sheep not with a view to their own good, but like a mere diner or banqueter with a view to the pleasures of the table; or, again, as a trader, for sale in the market, and not as a shepherd. Yet surely the art of the shepherd is concerned only with the good of his subjects; he has only to provide the best for them, since the perfection of the

Republic 345c
Earnings are not related to ability in a mans work.
The argument here is that the power of earning is unrelated to a man's skill in the art or craft he undertakes (or his output). As shown in Sukra 2, 788 (page 174) for example wages are paid based on effort

127

art itself is already ensured whenever the shepherd's work is perfectly performed... (345e)

Let me ask you a question: Are not the several arts different, by reason of their each having a separate function? And, my dear illustrious friend, do say what you think, that we may make a little progress.

Yes, that is the difference, he replied.

And each art gives us a particular good and not merely a general one - medicine, for example, gives us health; navigation, safety at sea; and so on?

Yes, he said. (346b)

And the art of earning has the special function of giving pay: but we do not confuse this with other arts, any more than the art of the pilot is to be confused with the art of medicine, because the health of the pilot may be improved by a sea voyage. You would not be inclined to say, would you, that navigation is the art of medicine, at least if we are to adopt your exact use of language?

Certainly not.

Or because a man is in good health when he receives pay, you would not say that the art of earning is medicine?

I should not.

Nor would you say that medicine is the art of receiving pay, because a man takes fees when he is engaged in healing? (346c)

No.

And we have admitted, I said, that the good of each art is specially confined to the art?

Let us take it for granted.

Then, if there be any good which all craftsmen have in common, that is to be attributed to something of which they all make common use?

True, he replied.

Moreover, we say that if the craftsman is benefited by receiving pay, that comes from his use of the art of earning in addition to his own?

He gave a reluctant assent to this. (346d)

Then the benefit, or receipt of pay, is not derived by the several craftsmen from their respective crafts. But it is more accurate to say that while the art of medicine gives health, and the art of the builder builds a house, another art attends them which is the art of earning. The various arts may be doing their own

expended for a period of time or from a measure of effort. If they are based on time the production of the worker is completely unrelated to the amount paid.

business and benefiting that over which they preside, but would the craftsman receive any benefit from his art unless he were paid as well?

I suppose not. (346e)

But does he therefore confer no benefit when he works for nothing?

Certainly, he confers a benefit.

Then now, Thrasymachus, there is no longer any doubt that neither arts nor governments provide for their own interest; but, as we were before saying, they rule and provide for the interests of their subjects who are the weaker and not the stronger-to their good they attend and not to the good of the superior[1].

[1] Note, the beneficiary of any art, trade or indeed any job is not the 'doer' of the job, but the subject of his attention.

A State, I said, arises, as I conceive, out of the needs of mankind; no one is self-sufficing, but all of us have many wants. Can any other origin of a State be imagined?

There can be no other.

Then, as we have many wants, and many persons are needed to supply them, one takes a helper for one purpose and another for another; and when these partners and helpers are gathered together in one habitation the body of inhabitants is termed a State[1].

True, he said.

And it is in the belief that it is for his own good, that one man gives to another or receives from him in exchange[2].

Very true.

Republic 369a A State arises from the needs of mankind The first need being to establish government, and for that government to protect the people, See MhB, Santi 67 (page 90) & MhB, Santi 72 (page 92, 93).
[1] See Mencius 3, A, 4 (page 113).
[2] men will only trade for advantage, since this is universal, all parties must gain. See Shantanand 74/88 (page 149).

And how will they proceed? Will each bring the result of his labours into a common stock? --the individual husbandman, for example, producing for four, and labouring four times as long and as much as he need in the provision of food with which he supplies others as well as himself; or will he have nothing to do with others and not be at the trouble of producing for them, but provide for himself alone a fourth of the food in a fourth of the time, and in the remaining three fourths of his time be employed in making a house or a coat or a pair of shoes, not bothering to form a partnership with others, but supplying himself all his own wants?

Adeimantus thought that he should-aim at producing food only and not at producing everything.

Probably, I replied, that would be the better way; and when I

Republic Book II 370 On the Division of Labour (Using an example of a community of 4 people). Refer also to 374 for continuance of this argument. See also Mencius 3, A, 4 (page 113) & Cicero, Offices 2, 4 (page 43). As Shakespeare puts it (Henry V):-
'Therefore doth Heaven divide the state of man into divers functions, Setting endeavour in continual

hear you say this, I am myself reminded that we are not all alike; there are diversities of natures among us which are adapted to different occupations[1].

Very true.

And will you have a work better done when every workman tries his hand at many occupations, or when each has only one.

When he has only one.

Further, there can be no doubt that a work is spoilt when not done at the right time?[2]

No doubt.

For business is not disposed to wait until the doer of the business is at leisure; but the doer must follow up his opportunity, and make the business his first object.

He must.

motion;...' But note how much more humane this approach is than Adam Smith's illustration of the manufacture of pins.- Wealth of Nations Bk 1 Ch 1.

[1] See also Sukra 2, 9-12 (page 170).

[2] See Bible, Ecclesiastes 3, 1 (page 23) & Mencius 3, A, 3 (page 111).

Hence, I said, it can be seen what will be the best limit for our rulers to fix when they are considering the size of the State and the amount of territory which they are to include, and beyond which they will not go.

What would you propose?

I would allow the State to increase so far as is consistent unity; that, I think, is the proper limit.

Republic Book IV 423c
Best size for a State

...The intention was that, in the case of the citizens generally, each individual should be put to the use for which nature intended him, one to one work, and then every man would do his own business, and become one and not many; and so the whole city would be one and not many.

Republic Book IV 423d
Specialisation is Natural *See Ficino, Letters 1, 78 (page 49), Cicero, Offices 3, 6 (page 45) & L of M 9, 296 (page 73) & Mencius 3, A, 4 (page 113).*

Shall we try to find a common basis by asking of ourselves what ought to be the chief aim of the legislator in making laws- - what is the greatest good, and what is the greatest evil, in the organization of a State; ...

By all means.

Can we name anything more harmful for a State than a force, whatever it may be, which causes distraction and plurality where unity ought to reign? or any greater good than the bond of unity[1]?

We cannot.

And there is unity where there is community of pleasures and pains--where all the citizens are glad or grieved in the same

Republic Book V 462 b
Objective of Laws

[1] See Plato, Laws 739 (page 139) & Republic 4, 423d above.

130

degree on the same occasions of joy and sorrow[2]?
No doubt.
But where there is no common but only private feeling a State is disorganized--when you have one half triumphing and the other plunged in grief at the same events happening to the city or the citizens?[3]
Certainly.
Such differences commonly originate in a disagreement about the use of the terms 'mine' and 'not mine', 'his' and 'not his'.
Exactly so.

And so Glaucon, we have arrived at the conclusion that in the perfect State wives and children are to be in common[1], and that all education and the pursuits of war and peace are also to be common, and, those who have proved to be both the best philosophers[2] and the bravest warriors[3] are to be their kings. [543 a]
Governors ... will take their soldiers and place them in houses ... which are common to all, and contain nothing private or individual... (not having) any of the ordinary possessions of mankind ... receiving from the other citizens, as their annual stipend, only the maintenance necessary for their duties[4], ... they were to be responsible for themselves and the whole State ... In the succeeding generation rulers will be appointed who have lost the guardian power and hence there will arise dissimilarity and inequality and irregularity (Which are always and in all places causes of hatred and war). Two races arise. The iron and brass pulling towards the acquisition of money and land and houses and gold and silver, and the gold and silver races having true riches in their own nature, inclined towards virtue and the ancient order of things[5]. [546 e]
They compromise, agreeing to distribute the land and houses among individual owners; ... their friends and maintainers who they formerly protected in the condition of free men, were to be enslaved and held as subjects and servants[6]; they themselves were to keep watch against them, besides attending to warfare. [547]

An intermediate state between oligarchy and aristocracy. [547 c] Like the Aristocracy "in the honour given to rulers, in the abstinence of the warrior class from agriculture, handicrafts and trade in general, in the institution of common meals, and

[2] *See MhB, Sabha 13 (page 76) For example.*

[3] *See Ficino, Letters 1, 78 (page 49)*

Republic Book 8 *(abridged)*
Aristocracy 543a *The passage reflects the principles illustrated in the Vedic texts for the 4 ages & the 4 orders of society. See Srimad 12, 18 (page 164). Note how the desires & the nature of goods required change. Aspects of this are laid out in Gibbon's 'Decline & Fall ... Roman Empire'.*
[1] *Whether sharing is actual or in terms of responsibility is not clear see Laws 739 below.*
[2] *That is to say, the wisest.*
[3] *See MhB, Bishma 109 (page 87).*
[4] *See Sukra 4, 2, 3-8 (page 177). Note the self discipline required for this - see note on Pythagoras beside Ficino, Letters 1, 73 (page 49).*
[5] *See MhB - the King makes the age Santi 69 (page 92).*
[6] *See Cicero, Offices 1, 7 (page 41).*

Timocracy 547c
Note, Plato regards this as a transitional stage.

the attention paid to gymnastics and military training". Unique in the fear of philosophers as rulers (preferring passionate less complex characters more fitted for war than peace), and in the value placed on military stratagems and contrivances, and in the waging of everlasting wars. Like the Oligarchy in the covetousness of money ("they will have a fierce secret longing after gold and silver, which they will hoard in dark places, having magazines and treasuries of their own for the deposit and concealment of them". [547 d])

They will spend large sums of money on women, and others who please them; "they are miserly because they have no means of openly acquiring the money which they prize; they will spend that which is another man's on the gratification of their desires, stealing their pleasures and running away like children from the law, their father[1]". They honour gymnastic more than music. [548 a]

[1] Bracton is quoted as saying with reference to English law - 'The King is under no man, but is under the Law and God, for the Law creates the King'.

"He should have more of self-assertion and be less cultivated, though still a friend of culture; and a good listener, but no speaker". Apt to be rough with slaves, courteous to freemen, and remarkably obedient to authority. He is a lover of power and honour, and a lover of gymnastic exercises and the chase. [548 e]

The Timocratic Man.
Which sounds like a common view of medieval nobility (perhaps romanticised).

"A government resting on the valuation of property, in which the rich have power and the poor man is deprived of it." [550 c]

Oligarchy 550c

The accumulation of gold in the treasury of private individuals is the ruin of timocracy; for first, they invent for themselves new modes of expenditure and wrest the laws to allow of these; for what do they or their wives care about the law? Seeking to rival rich men, the great mass of citizens become lovers of money. The more they think of money the less they honour virtue[1]. At last instead of loving contention and glory, men became lovers of money and money-making; they honour and look up to the rich man, & promote him to high office, and dishonour the poor man[2]. A law is passed which fixes a sum of money as qualification of citizenship[3].

Its Origin See Plato, Laws 729 (page 138) & measures to prevent this, Laws 744 (page 140). See Also Srimad 12, 2 (page 164).
[1] See MhB, Santi 123 (page 97).
[2] See MhB, Santi 322 (page 105).
[3] Such as the in the Venetian Republic. [550d]

Consider the nature of the qualification. What would happen if sea captains were chosen according to their wealth (You mean

Its Attributes
See Republic 370 (page 129)

that the voyage would be very unpleasant?). How much more so then a city? There is a further defect, its division. The State is not one but two States, the one of the poor, the other of rich men, living on the same spot and always conspiring against one another[1]. [551 c]

Another discreditable feature is that they are incapable of carrying on any war (because they must arm the multitude, of whom they are afraid). At the same time their fondness of money makes them unwilling to pay taxes. And, perhaps the greatest evil of all, a man may sell all that he has and live without participating in anyway (the drone); thus poverty arises, and with that arise thieves and cut purses. [551 d]

The son of a representative of timocracy who begins by emulating his father, but sees him foundering against the State and losing all that he has. The son, knocks "ambition and passion head foremost from his bosom's throne; humbled by poverty he takes to money-making and by mean and miserly savings and hard work gets a fortune together" seating the concupiscent and covetous element on the vacant throne[1]. [553 a]

"When he has made reason and spirit sit down on the ground obediently on either side of their sovereign, and made them his slaves, he compels the one to think only of how lesser sums may be turned into larger ones, and will not allow the other to worship and admire anything but riches and rich men." Also "the individual only satisfies his necessary appetites, and confines his expenditure to them; his other desires he subdues, under the idea that they are unprofitable[2]." [553 d]

He is not a man of cultivation, and possesses suppressed desires which are drone like, and which will manifest whenever he is granted sufficient liberty to act dishonestly (such as in the guardianship of an orphan)[3]; "in his ordinary dealings which give him a reputation for honesty he coerces his bad passions by an enforced virtue... because he fears for his possessions." His drone like nature will come to the surface most frequently when he has to spend what is not his own. [554 b]

For these reasons such a one will be more respectable than many people; yet the true virtue of a unanimous and harmonious soul will flee far away and never come near him. [554 e]

The miserly individual will be an ignoble competitor in a State for any prize of victory, or other object of honourable ambition;

Cicero, Offices 2, 4 (page 43) and Mencius 3, A, 4 (page 113) on specialisation.
[1] *See also Plato, Laws 744 below.*

Oligarchical Man

[1] *See end of MhB, Santi 123 (page 97).*

[2] *Perhaps illustrated by the large numbers of post WW2 emigrants who left Europe for the new worlds and became prosperous businessmen in their adopted countries.*
[3] *See also end of extract from MhB, Udyoga 187 (page 85).*

he will not spend his money in the contest for glory; so afraid [555 a]
is he of awakening his expensive appetites and inviting them to
help and join in the struggle; in true oligarchical fashion he
fights with a small part only of his resources, and the result
commonly is that he loses the prize and saves his money."

This then seems likely to be the fairest of States, being like an
embroidered robe which is spangled with every sort of flower.
And just as women and children think a variety of colours to be
of all things most charming, so there are many men to whom
this State, which is spangled with manners and characters of
mankind, will appear to be the fairest of States[1]. [557 c]
Because owing to the liberty which reigns there, it offers a
complete assortment of constitutions; and he who has a mind
to establish a State, as we have been doing, must go to a
democratic city as he would to a bazaar at which they sell
constitutions, and pick out the one that suits him[2]; then, when
he has made his choice, he may found his State. [557]

Democracy 556

[1] See Srimad 12, 3, 35 (page 164).

[2] Not only of forms of democracy, but all forms from Aristocracy to Tyranny.

The rulers (of the Oligarchy), being aware that their power
rests upon their wealth, refuse to curtail by law the liberty of
undisciplined young men to spend and waste their money;
wishing to buy up their estates or lend money on them, and
thus increase their own wealth and importance.[555c]
Unchecked self indulgence, even among men of good family
often reduces them to beggary, hating and conspiring against
those who have got their property (and against everybody else).
They are eager for revolution. On the other hand, the men of
business stoop as they walk, and pretend not even to see those
whom they have already ruined, insert their sting - that is their
money - into some one else who is not on his guard against
them. The young men of the governing class are prone to lead
a life of luxury and idleness both of body and of mind (unable
to resist either pleasure or pain). The poor will be despised by
the rich, and in the course of time the poor will draw the
conclusion that rich men are only rich because no one has had
the courage to despoil them. [555 d]
And then democracy comes into being after the poor have
conquered their opponents, slaughtering some and banishing
some, while to the remainder they give an equal share of
freedom and power; and in this form of government the
magistrates are commonly elected by lot[1].[557]

Its Origin

[1] Such as some of the Italian cities in later medieval times.

The people are free, the city is full of freedom and frankness, and a man may say and do what he likes. An individual is able to order his life as he pleases. [557 b]

Its Attributes

There is no necessity to govern if you have the capacity, or to be governed unless you wish to be. No necessity to go to war, or to be at peace when others are at peace. There is humanity towards the condemned, a forgiving spirit, and a 'don't care' about trifles. All fine principles are ignored (except in the case of some rarely gifted nature) and no regard is taken for the pursuits from which a man has come into political life, and the promoting to honour of anyone who professes to be the peoples friend. [557 e]

These and other kindred characteristics are proper to democracy, which will be so it seems, a charming form of government, full of variety and disorder, and dispensing a sort of equality to equals and unequals alike.

[558c]

He comes into being as the son of a miserly and oligarchical father who has trained him in his own habits, and like his father, he keeps under by force the pleasures which are of the spending and not of the getting sort (eg necessary pleasures such as eating simple food are permitted, but that which goes beyond this, is not)[1]. [558 d]

Democratic Man

When a young man who has been brought up in a vulgar and miserly way has tasted the drones honey, and has come to associate with fierce and crafty natures who are able to provide him with all sorts of refinements and varieties of pleasures[2] - then, as you may imagine, the change will begin of the oligarchical principle within him into the democratical" (the change being effected by an alliance from without assisting the desires within him). [559 d]

[1] Some of the principles behind this may be gained from MhB, Santi 123 (page 97) and the Translators footnote follows MhB, Santi 140 (page 101).
[2] See 564a below.

"If there be any ally which aids the oligarchical principle within him, whether the influence of a father or of kindred advising him or rebuking him, then there arises in his soul a faction and an opposite faction, and so he comes to be at war with himself." [560 a]

Sometimes the oligarchical principles dominate and some of his desires die and others are banished; a spirit of reverence enters into the young mans soul and order is restored. And then again fresh desires spring up, and because their father does not know how to educate them, wax fierce and numerous. At length they seize upon the citadel of the young man's soul, which they perceive to be devoid of noble studies, pursuits and principles and false and boastful conceits and phrases mount upwards and take possession of the stronghold. Honour they call silliness, temperance is called unmanliness and moderation and orderly expenditure are called vulgarity and meanness. Insolence is termed breeding, anarchy called liberty, waste called magnificence and impudence courage. [560 a]

After this the young man lives on, spending time, labour and [561 b] money on unnecessary pleasures as much as on necessary ones, and, if he is fortunate and is not to much disordered in his wits, when the years have elapsed and the heyday of passion is over, he balances his pleasures and lives a sort of equilibrium, putting the government of himself into the hands of the one who comes first and wins the turn, and when he has had enough of that into the hands of another, despising none but encouraging them all equally.

He rejects advice that the satisfaction of some desires is good and noble and the satisfaction of others is evil saying that they are all alike, indulging the appetite of the hour, sometimes lapped in drink, then trying to get thin; sometimes idle and neglecting everything, sometimes living the life of a philosopher; sometimes busy with politics, saying and doing whatever comes into his head; sometimes emulous of a warrior, sometimes of men of business. "His life has neither law nor order, and this distracted existence, which he terms joy and bliss and freedom, continues throughout his life." [562 c]

Democracy is brought to dissolution by an insatiable desire for **Tyranny 562c** freedom. The insatiable desire for this good, and the neglect of other things, introduces change in this constitution also, and occasions the demand for tyranny. [562 c]

When Democracy which has begun to thirst for freedom has evil cup-bearers presiding over the feast, and has drunk too deeply of the strong wine of freedom, then, unless her rulers are very amenable and give a plentiful draught, she calls them to account and punishes them, and says that they are cursed oligarches." Men who obey their rulers they call slaves. Democracy would have subjects who are like the rulers and rulers who are like their subjects. These men she praises and honours. [562 d]

By degrees anarchy must find its way into private houses. Fathers grow accustomed to descending to the level of their sons, who show no respect for either parent; the master fears and flatters his scholars, who despise their masters and tutors; the young man is on a level with the old, and competes with him; old men condescend to the young and are full of pleasantry and gaiety; they are both loth to be thought to be morose and authoritative. [562 e]

Slaves bought with money are just as free as the purchaser, and liberty and equality exist between the two sexes in relation to each other. Animals who are under the dominion of man also have greater liberty in a democracy. Citizens chafe impatiently at any sign of authority and cease to care for the laws [1]. [563 b]

[1] See also 559 d above (When a young man...)

The excessive increase of anything often causes a reaction in the opposite direction. The harshest form of tyranny arising out of the most extreme form of liberty. [564 a]

In a democracy there are three classes, the drones (rather more numerous of monstrous winged drone), and they are almost the entire ruling power (hence in democracies also everything is managed by the drones).

Then there is another class which is always being served from the mass, who are most orderly by nature, which in a nation of traders is sure to be the richest. They are the most squeezable persons and yield the largest amount of honey to the drones. And this is called the wealthy class. [565]

The people are the third class, consisting of those who work with their own hands; they are not politicians, and have not much to live upon. This, when assembled, is the largest and most powerful class in a democracy. [565b]

"And when other lusts, amid clouds of incense and perfumes and garlands and wines, and all the dissolute pleasures of such company, come buzzing around him, and when they implant in his drone-like nature the sting of desire, while they fatten and nourish him, then at last this lord of the soul, having Madness for the captain of his guard, breaks out into a frenzy; and if he finds in the man such opinions or appetites as are deemed to be good, or still have the sense of shame about them, he kills them and casts them forth until he has purged away all temperance and brought in madness to the full. [573 b]

"At the next step in his progress there will be feasts and carousals and revellings and courtesans." His revenues, if he has any are soon spent, and he must plunder if he is to escape the horrid pains and pangs, and spend the property of his parents (by cheating, deceiving or force as necessary)[1]. He

How He Lives

[1] See also Hesiod, Works &

fancies some harlot under whose influence he falls. After his parents property is exhausted he breaks into other houses and subsequently the temple, the old opinions about good and justice finally being overthrown by those others which were lately emancipated and are now the bodyguard of love and share his empire. Now he will not abstain from the foulest murder, or from forbidden food, or from any other horrid act. "Love is his tyrant and lives in him in complete anarchy and lawlessness, and being himself sole king leads him on as a tyrant leads a State to the performance of any reckless deed by which he can maintain himself and the rabble of his associates." [573 d]

If there are only a few of them in the State, and the rest of the people are well disposed, they will go away and become the bodyguard of some other tyrant, or mercenary soldiers. If they stay at home they become a criminal class. If they come to power, they associate entirely with their own flatterers or ready tools, "if they want anything from anybody, they in turn are equally ready to bow down before them and perform any gesture of friendship for them; but when they have gained their point they know them no more." "The tyrannical nature never tastes of true freedom and friendship." The longer he lives the more of a tyrant he becomes. [575 b]

The same is true of the possession of money and goods: its value is measured by the same yardstick. Both, in excess, produce enmity and feuds in private and public life, while a deficiency almost invariably leads to slavery.

We should not forget that we are in the same fortunate position as the Heraclids when they founded their colony: we noticed how they avoided vicious and dangerous disputes about land and cancellations of debts and distribution of property. When an old-established state is forced to resort to legislation to deal with these problems, it finds that both leaving things as they are and reforming them are somehow equally impossible. The only policy left them is to mouth pious hopes and make a little cautious progress over a long period by advancing a step at a time. (This is the way it can be done. From time to time some of the reformers should be themselves great land-owners and have a large number of debtors; and they should be prepared, in a philanthropic spirit, to share their prosperity with those

Days 106-201 (page 59) - with whom Plato would have been familiar.

Laws - 729 Excess or deficiency to be avoided. *See Plato, Republic 550c (page 132) & Laws 744.*

Laws - 736 Re-distribution of land.
See Cicero, Offices 2, 21 (page 44).

[1] Solon (594 B.C.) When establishing the Athenian constitution, cancelled all debts that

debtors who are in distress, partly by remitting debts and partly by making land available for distribution[1]. Their policy will be a policy of moderation, dictated by the conviction that poverty is a matter of increased greed rather than diminished wealth. This belief is fundamental to the success of a state, and is the firm base on which you can later build whatever political structure is appropriate to such conditions as we have described. But when these first steps towards reform falter, subsequent constitutional action in any state will be hard going.)...

were secured against land, or persons (ie that would lead to slavery if they were not honoured), but in doing so incurred the wrath of the poor (who wanted a greater share of the wealth of the state), and the rich (who saw that they had lost greatly).

You'll find the ideal society and state, and the best code of laws, where the old saying 'friends property is genuinely shared' is put into practice[1] as widely as possible throughout the entire state. Now I don't know whether in fact this situation - a community of wives, children and all property - exists anywhere today, or will ever exist, but at any rate in such a state the notion of 'private property' will have been by hook or by crook completely eliminated from life. Everything possible will have been done to throw into a sort common pool even what is by nature 'my own', like eyes and ears and hands, in the sense that to judge by appearances they all see and hear and act in concert. Everybody feels pleasure and pain at the same things, so that they all praise and blame with complete unanimity. To sum up, the laws in force impose the greatest possible unity on the state - and you'll never produce a better or truer criterion of an absolutely perfect law than that.

Laws - 739 Common Property is best *See Republic 8, 543 (page 131); Ficino, Letters 1, 78 (page 49) & Cicero, Offices 1, 7 (page 41).*
[1] See also Plato, Republic 462b above.

First of all, the citizens must make a distribution of land and houses; they must not farm in common, which is a practice too demanding for those born and bred and educated as ours are[1]. But the distribution should be made with some such intention as this: each man who receives a portion of land should regard it as the common possession of the entire state. The land is his ancestral home and he must cherish it even more than children cherish their mother[2]; furthermore, Earth is a goddess, and mistress of mortal men. (And the gods and spirits already established in the locality must be treated with the same respect.)

Laws 740
Plato's proposal for ideal Laws of a new society in his time.
[1] See note re-Pythagoras beside Ficino, Letters 1, 73 (page 49).
See also Bible, Lev 25, 23 (page 14).
[2] See MhB, Adi 49 (page 75) & Artharveda 12, 1 (page 1).

All these considerations suggest a further law that runs like this: no private person shall be allowed to possess any gold or

Laws 741 Only sufficient money for normal trading

silver[1], but only coinage for day-to-day dealings which one can hardly avoid having with workmen and all other indispensable people of that kind (we have to pay wages to slaves and foreigners who work for money). For these purposes, we agree, they must possess coinage, legal tender among themselves, but valueless to the rest of mankind. The common Greek coinage is to be used for expeditions and visits to the outside world, such as when a man has to be sent abroad as an ambassador or to convey some official message; to meet these occasions the state must always have a supply of Greek coinage. If a private individual should ever need to go abroad, he should first obtain leave of the authorities, and if he returns home with some surplus foreign money in his pocket he must deposit it with the state and take local money to the same value in exchange[2].

should be kept.

[1] *A common situation in many countries in recent times. See also Republic 550d above. 'Money is Power', Shantanand 1974 (page 149).*

[2] *Note, this has become the practice in current times - Greek Coinage becoming for the most part US dollars - even to the extent that in many countries permission is required to convert money to foreign currency.*

The whole point of our legislation was to allow the citizens to live supremely happy lives in the greatest possible mutual friendship. However, they will never be friends if injuries and lawsuits arise among them on a grand scale, but only if they are trivial and rare. That is why we maintain that neither gold nor silver should exist in the state[1], and there should not be much money made out of menial trades and charging interest, nor from prostitutes; the citizens' wealth should be limited to the products of farming, and even here a man should not be able to make so much that he can't help forgetting the real reason why money was invented (I mean for the care of the soul and body, which without physical and cultural education respectively will never develop into anything worth mentioning). That's what has made us say more than once that the pursuit of money should come last in the scale of value. Every man directs his efforts to three things in all, and if his efforts are directed with a correct sense of priorities he will give money the third and lowest place, and his soul the highest, with his body coming somewhere between the two In particular, if this scale of values prevails in the society we're now describing, then it has been equipped with a good code of laws[2].

Laws 743
The Purpose of Laws

[1] *Note the impact of vast amounts of cash available on financial markets at present and the instability resulting from this.*

[2] *See Statesman 294b on the limitations of Law (page 127).*

In view of all this, the next law I'd pass would be along the following lines. (We maintain that if a state is to avoid the greatest plague of all - I mean civil war, though civil disintegration would be a better term - extreme poverty and wealth must not be allowed to arise in any section of the citizen-body,

Laws 744
Unequal Wealth to be Avoided
See also Laws 729 above, Plato, Republic on Oligarchy 550c above & Confucius,

because both lead to both these disasters. That is why the legislator must now announce the acceptable limits of wealth and poverty.) The lower limit of poverty must be the value of the holding (which is to be permanent: no official nor anyone else who has ambitions to be thought virtuous will ever overlook the diminution of any man's holding). The legislator will use the holding as his unit of measure and allow a man to possess twice, thrice, and up to four times its value. If anyone acquires more than this, by finding treasure-trove or by gift or by a good stroke of business or some other similar lucky chance which presents him with more than he's allowed, he should hand over the surplus to the state[2] and its patron deities thereby escaping punishment and getting a good name for himself.

Analects 12, 9, 4 (page 47).

[2] All unclaimed wealth belongs to the state - see Sukra 2, 656 (page 171), but this passage goes further to include any windfall profits, so that wealth can only be derived from work. This would be a form of taxation.

Let's first specify the 'agricultural' laws, as they're called. The first law - sanctioned by Zeus the Protector of Boundaries -shall run as follows:- No man shall disturb the boundary stones of his neighbour, whether fellow-citizen or foreigner (that is, when a proprietor's land is on the boundary of the state), in the conviction that this would be 'moving the immovable' in the crudest sense. Far better that a man should want to try to move the biggest stone that does not mark a boundary, than a small one separating friend's land from foe's, and established by an oath sworn to the gods. Zeus the God of Kin is witness in the one case, Zeus the Protector of Foreigners in the other. Rouse him in either capacity, and the most terrible wars break out. If a man obeys the law he will escape its penalties, but if he holds it in contempt he is to be liable to two punishments, the first at the hands of the gods, the second under the law. No man, if he can help it must move the boundary stones of his neighbour's land ...

Laws 843 Boundaries
See also Bible, Deut 19, 14 (page 17), & L of M 8, 254 (page 71).
Some gauge of the importance placed on this is to be had from Hammurabi (page 53) & Mencius 3, a, 3 (page 111).

...That is why everyone should do everything he can to avoid offending his neighbour; above all, he must always go out of his way to avoid all acts of encroachment.

Laws 843 c Neighbours not to be offended. *Text continues on aspects of the right to quiet enjoyment of land & supporting duties. See also Cicero, Offices 2, 21 (page 44).*

... come the practice of retail trade. First we should give a word of advice on the whole subject, then lay down legislation for it. The natural function in the state of retail trading in general is

Laws 918 Retail Trade
See Ficino, Letters 1, 78 (page 49), Cicero, Offices 3, 16

141

not to do harm, but quite the opposite. When goods of any kind are distributed disproportionately and unequally, anyone who makes the distribution equal and even cannot fail to do good. It needs to be stated that this redistribution, in which money too plays an effective role, is precisely the purpose the trader is meant to serve. Hired labourers, inn-keepers and other work-men of varying degrees of respectability all perform the function of satisfying the needs of the community by ensuring an even distribution of goods.

(page 46), Shantanand 1974 (page 149) & Srimad 7, 11, 15 (page 162).

My dear fellow, because they feared the line of argument I have mentioned, they passed the law allowing a man to dispose of his own property in his will exactly as pleases. But when people have come to death's door in your state, you and I will make a rather more appropriate response:
'Friends, you "creatures of a day" in more senses than one it's difficult for you in your present circumstances to know the truth about your own property and also "know your-selves", as the Delphic inscription puts it. Therefore, I as legislator, rule that neither you nor this property of yours belongs to yourselves, but to your whole clan, ancestors and descendants alike; and your clan and its property in turn belong, even more absolutely, to the state[1]. That being so, I should be reluctant to tolerate someone worming him into your good graces when you are smitten with illness or old age, and wheedling you into making a will that is not for the best. I shall legislate with a view to nothing except the interest of your clan and the entire state, relegating (as is only right) that of the individual to second place. So you go on your journey, which is the way of all flesh, show restraint and goodwill towards us: we will look after your affairs for the future and guard your interests with the utmost care, down to the smallest detail.'

Laws 923 Inheritance

[1] *See Cicero, Offices 1, 7 (page 41) on ownership of property, and see 1 Kings 21, 1-4 (page 21) for similar re-strictions on disposition of property.*

Ramayana

On the banks of the river Sarayu[1], there was a great and prosperous country named Koshala[2], inhabited by contented people. In it was the City of Ayodhya[3], famed in the three worlds, founded by the renowned Manu a lord among men. The city's thoroughfares extended for sixty miles; its beauty was enhanced by streets admirably planned, the extended highways being sprinkled with water and strewn with flowers.

King Dasaratha protected that city as Maghavan[4] protects Amaravati[5] and he dwelt there in splendour, as *Indra* in heaven that city had beautiful and massive gates and numerous markets; its fortifications were planned by skilful engineers and artificers. There were bards, ballad singers and public musicians in the city; the inhabitants were wealthy and had spacious houses with high arched porticos decorated with flags and banners. The capital was filled with extensive buildings and beautiful gardens and surrounded by mango groves, tall trees enhancing the outskirts, giving it the appearance of a lovely girl wearing a girdle of greenery. It was enclosed by strong fortifications and a deep moat, which no enemy, by any expedient whatsoever, could penetrate. Countless elephants, horses, cattle, camels and mules were to be seen in the city; innumerable ambassadors dwelt there and people from many lands traded peacefully within its walls.

Ayodhya, like *Indra*'s Amaravati[5], was resplendent with gilded palaces, the walls of which were set with precious stones the domes resembling mountain peaks. That marvellous city where gold abounded and beautiful women wandered about in groups, rich in jewels of every kind, was adorned with luxurious palaces and mansions. The dwellings of the artisans were so constructed that no space was left between them, and the ground on which they stood was perfectly levelled; all were abundantly stocked with rice and the juice of the sugar cane was employed instead of water.

On every side, the sound of trumpets, bugles, lutes and gongs was constantly heard; that city had no rival on earth but resembled the abode of the Gods attained through austerities. The gorgeous edifices contained therein were perfectly constructed and inhabited by the noblest of men, those who did not

Book 1 Chapter 5 Prosperity of the Silver Age *Refer to Bk 6 chap 39 for a similar description of prosperity in Lanka, & refer Plato's description of Atlantis (Critias 107).*

[1] *Sarayu = air, wind.*

[2] *Koshala = a store room, treasury, accumulated wealth.*

[3] *Ayodhya = irresistible in the sense of military might*

[4] *Maghavan - a name for Indra which carries the meaning of distributing gifts, bountiful, munificent etc*

[5] *Amaravati - the abode of the immortals, and the celestial city in which Indra is said to reside.*

slay a fleeing foe or one without defence, warriors who were skilled archers...

There dwelt in that city, King Dasaratha, a follower of the tradition of the illustrious Emperor Manu[1]. The king was learned in the interpretation of the Vedas[2], his chief wealth being pre-eminence in truth and virtue; he was one who never broke his word, who was ever prudent, sagacious and beloved of his subjects, a great charioteer, a worthy descendant of the dynasty of Ikshvaku, an observer of many sacrifices, he who ever delighted in the practice of righteousness, in authority over his people, equal to a great sage, a royal seer, renowned in the three worlds, triumphing over his enemies, a friend to all, having perfect control of his senses and appetites, in prosperity equal to *Indra*, in wealth equal to *Kuvera*[3]. That truth-loving monarch, striving to acquire perfection in virtue[4], worldly prosperity and happiness, ruled the city as the celestial king, *Indra*, rules Amaravati.

The people in that capital were happy, virtuous, learned, experienced, each satisfied with his state, practising his own calling, without avarice and of truthful speech. None was indigent or dwelt in a mean habitation, all lived happily with families, possessing wealth, grain, cattle and horses. In a city of Ayodhya, none was a miser or a swindler, none was mean-spirited, proud, rash, worthless or an atheist. Men and women were of righteous conduct, fully self-controlled and, in their pure and chaste behaviour, they equalled the Sages. None lacked earrings, coronets or necklaces; they bathed daily and rubbed their bodies with oil, using attar roses and sandal paste. None ate impure food, none allowed his neighbour to suffer hunger; all possessed ornaments and gold, and there was none who had not learnt to subdue his mind. No-one was mean, impious or failed to discharge his duties; there were no thieves and none were born of mixed castes.

The Brahmins were devoted to their respective duties[5], firm in self-control and authorized to accept gifts. None denied the existence of God; none uttered falsehood or were enamoured of worldly pleasure and none were guilty of slander. No Brahmin was unversed in the six systems of philosophy[6] nor did any neglect to fast at the full moon or on other appointed days; there were none who suffered from mental or physical infirmities and none were unhappy in that city.

Book 1 Chapter 6
Qualities of King in the Silver Age

[1] *The first man and author of the 'Laws of Manu'.*
[2] *Scriptural authority.*

[3] *Note the difference between Prosperity and Wealth.*
[4] *The prosperity described being due to this. For similar see MhB, Adi 109 (page 76).*

[5] *See L of M 1, 88 (page 65) For duties of Brahmins.*

[6] *Refer to for example 'The Spiritual Heritage of India'.*

Among the inhabitants of Ayodhya, there was no man or woman who was not endowed with beauty and wealth and none who were not devoted to the king and state[7]. Those who dwelt there, worshipped the Gods and the uninvited guest, they were both magnanimous and charitable. All attained to a ripe age as virtuous and truth-loving people, their homes were filled with children, grandchildren and virtuous women. The warriors were subject to the learned Brahmins and the merchants to the warrior caste; in accordance with their caste, the people served the Brahmins, the warriors and the merchants[8].

In the administration of the kingdom, the Emperor Dasaratha followed the example of the first ruler, Manu, who was supreme in wisdom and a God among men[9].

Ayodhya abounded in warriors undefeated in battle, fearless and skilled in the use of arms, resembling lions guarding their mountain caves.

The city was full of excellent horses, equal to *Indra*'s, the issue of Vanayu, born in the regions of Kambhoja and Bahlika or from the banks of the River Sindhu; and also mighty elephants of colossal strength as large as hills, whose temples ran with ichor, the denizens of the Vindhya and Himavat Mountains, and who were the issue of Airavata, Mahapadma, Anjana and Vamana. Ever filled with elephants, like unto mountains, intoxicated with Mada juice, of the Bhadra, Mandra and Mriga race or interbred of these, that city, the brilliance of which spread for four miles, was worthy of its name.

Ruled by the illustrious and mighty King Dasaratha ... that well-named city, the fortunate Ayodhya, with its gates and solid locks, adorned by edifices of every kind and peopled by thousands of men, had for its sovereign one who was equal to *Indra*.

The ministers of this magnanimous descendant of Ikshvaku were endowed with every virtue; wise counsellors and skilled physiognomists, they took pleasure in doing all that was agreeable and useful. That illustrious hero had eight ministers of impeccable conduct, ever devoted to the king's interests[1]... The renowned and excellent Rishis, Vasishtha and Vamadeva[2], also assisted the king with other counsellors..., associated in counsel with these Brahmarishis, were elderly priests of consummate prudence, venerable, experienced, masters of their senses, fortunate, magnanimous, skilled in the use of arms,

[7] *See also Ficino, Letters 1, 78 (page 49).*

[8] *That is all kept their proper place in society, see Confucius Analects, 16, 1 (page 47). But see L of M 1, 88 - 91 (page 65).*
[9] *Original king & author of the Laws of Manu.*

Book 1 Chapter 7
King Dasaratha's Court

[1] *See L of M 7, 54 (page 68) on ideal constitution of the cabinet.*
[2] *Two renown sages, the former being the author of 'Vasishtha's Yoga'. Note that the king*

steadfast, of great renown, loyal and obedient to the king's commands. Having acquired power and glory, they were friendly in intercourse and never uttered an unjust word either in anger, or from motives of expediency; conversant with all that concerned their friends and others, they knew what their enemies were doing or intended to do. Of sober conduct, proved friendship, they even passed judgment on their sons if they broke the law. Expert in the science of economics[3] and warfare, those counsellors never inflicted unmerited punishment on an enemy and were brave and unambitious. Conversant with every branch of political life, they protected all those who lived in the state and added to the royal treasury without burdening the learned[4] and the warriors; and they inflicted penalties on wrongdoers with regard to their capacity for bearing it.

These ministers were pure of heart and of chaste conduct. None consorted with his neighbour's wife, none were wicked and all lived together peaceably. Cultivating every quality and practising various arts[5], they were renowned for their courage, their fair name was published abroad and their lives were guided by reason. Skilled in the laws of the country and blessed with wealth, they issued wise edicts and exercised their minds in philosophical debate.

Acquainted with the moral code they conversed affectionately with each other, such were King Dasaratha's ministers, who, informed by their agents of the needs of the people, satisfied them and governed with prudence. In the administration of his kingdom, the king never allowed dissension to arise through unrighteousness and became known throughout the world as an ocean of truth... Honoured by his feudal lords surrounded by many friends, his neighbours favourably disposed to him, by his energy he had extracted the thorns from his kingdom and ruled the world as *Indra* rules the heavens. Encircled by skilled ministers adept in the law and what proper, who were devoted, intelligent and capable, that monarch acquired a glory equal to the sun's surrounded by its rays.

Then the virtuous Vishvamitra enquired of the king concerning the welfare of the empire, the prosperity of his subjects, relatives and friends and also as to the state of the royal treasury[1]. Thereafter, the Sage questioned the monarch further, saying, "Are thy vassals obedient to thee? Are thine enemies subdued? Are the Vedic sacrifices duly observed in thy domin-

had also spiritual guidance.

[3] *The only mention of the term in the Ramayana.*

[4] *Priests are exempt from taxation. See Bible, Genesis 47, 22 (page 9) & others shown at that point.*

[5] *The Arts are supported. See Sukra 1, 741 (page 170).*

Book 1 Chapter 18 Brahmana's interest in Temporal Affairs. *Refer to MhB, Sabha 5 for a similar but more complete greeting when the sage Narada meets King*

ion? Are strangers entertained with fitting hospitality?" Then, having enquired as to the well-being of Vasishtha and other Sages, Vishvamitra entered the palace.

Sitting at ease, Vasishtha, the chief of those who recite the Veda, and the son of Brahma, in his turn, interrogated King Visvamitra, saying:-- "O King, is it well with thee? Dost thou constitute the happiness of thy people and dost thou govern and protect them in accord with the spiritual law? Is thy revenue justly received and increased? Is it judiciously administered and distributed to those who are eligible and deserving? Are thy servants remunerated at the proper season[1]? Do thy subjects willingly obey thee? O Sovereign, hast thou subdued thine enemies? O Sinless King, is it well with thine army, thy treasury, thy friends, thy sons and grandsons?"
In reply to these questions, the illustrious King Vishvamitra answered the humble Sage, Vasishtha, that all was well with him...

Yudhishthira, encompassing all the responsibilities of the King.
[1] *See Sukra 4, 2, 25-29 (page 177).*

Book 1 Chapter 52
Brahmana's interest in Temporal Affairs

[1] *See Sukra 2, 799 (page 174).*

Shantanand Saraswati

Every man or creature in the universe essentially wants three things: he wants to know everything; he wants to be happy always; he would like to live forever and does not want to face death. These are the three basis desires, or the essential nature which reflects them as desires; and with this imprint he starts his journey. Somewhere, sometime, someone wants to secure these things without consideration for others, and the trouble starts; most people are then tempted to rush to secure their own truth consciousness & bliss so as to avoid their misery.
With this idea, people have taken to such ways and means that the proper pattern of the universe has been disrupted.

Conversations, 1965
The Source of Desires
And desire then motivates all action, see L of M 2, 1 (page 66).

You may give one hundred pounds to a man. If he is a businessman he will invest it, a student, he may buy books and study, a gambler would gamble, a criminal would buy a gun and so on. The money is a power[1], a Shakti[2], a value and it can be used in any way; but only in accordance with the Sanskara[3] of the Vyashti[4], the type of Vyashti you give the money".
"Take a shop keeper as an example. His job is to collect useful commodities from the main markets or producers, keep them in good order, place them before his customers when they need them and charge a reasonable living for his services[5]. If he keeps doing this he is serving society and the Lord. But nowadays prices are raised quickly due to short supply but do not seem to come down again even when the supply is enough. The shop keepers may think they make a better margin for themselves but do they[6]. The whole society is disrupted by this act and tensions and misery keep on building so that the shop keeper and everyone lose peace of mind and happiness of heart. The general spiritual level sinks and the results are obvious. Even the material level is now in danger of collapse.
There is a fundamental principle by which to know the righteousness of one's actions. When a work is for the satisfaction of the individual and also the society, if both gain from this production and use then it is righteous; and, if only the producer makes a gain at the loss of society or the nation, then it must be unrighteous. This principle applies to all times and all nations[7]. The more who can share in the goodness of a

Conversations, 1974
Money, and Retail Trade
[1] *See also Plato, Laws 741 (page 139).*
[2] *Shakti - Power strength, faculty, property, etc*
[3] *Sanskara - propensities accumulated from previous lives.*
[4] *Vyashti - limit, shape or form.*

[5] *See also Ficino, Letters 2, 53 (page 50), Plato, Laws 918 (page 141) & Cicero, Offices 3, 16 (page 46).*
[6] *See Ficino, Letters 1, 78 (page 49), 'It is the duty of a citizen to consider the state as one being'.*

Ethics

[7] *This mutual benefit is the basis of all trade. See also Plato, Republic 369c (page*

product the better for physical needs and also for mental or *129)*.
spiritual needs.

Every human being feels to be human being and thus always **Conversations, 10 Feb 1978**
behaves like one. If one is rich, one simply feels to be rich, and What it is to be Rich
every action would arise as if coming from a rich source. ...
Feeling rich doesn't demand carrying a load of money or gold
all the time and everywhere one goes, it only involves a feeling
of being rich and the capacity of being so.

The Natural Laws are the operational laws and there is much **Conversations, January 1978**
in common between the economic and spiritual laws. But today (a)
they seem to belong to a former age. The old Natural Laws do Natural Law is always the
not seem to be effective in this world of today as we have it[1]. same.
All that one needs to find out is the relationship of the same old *[1] See also Plato, Statesman 294*
laws to the modern conditions. One of the natural laws *b (page 127), Srimad on the*
prescribes truthfulness in everyday speech. Today it is much *Kali Yuga, 12, 2 (page 164) &*
more difficult to follow this. If you tell the truth about your *Cicero, Offices 1, 10 (page 42).*
wealth there will always be someone to organise a robbery and
your other works would remain uncompleted. If this is the
situation, then the question does arise whether the law to speak
the truth is useful or applicable. If it is a natural law it must be
quite useful and applicable for all time. But the present
conditions are so different that a new approach to these laws
has become necessary. Thus one must discover the relationship
by which the old natural laws may be made to tackle the new
situation. For example, a word may have different meanings
to suit different contexts and 'saindhawa ānaya'[2] is a good *[2] सैन्धव आनय*
example to consider. 'saindhawa ānaya' simply means 'bring
salt'. If so requested at a dinner party it would mean 'bring salt'
and in context of a journey it would mean the horse. Similarly,
the natural laws should be reinterpreted within the latitude or
meanings which they them-selves hold so that the good use and
application of the laws becomes a possibility. The direct
meaning of the law may not apply to the level of consciousness
today, so look at the different aspect of the law and make the
best use of it. There is a need to consider the lower level of
consciousness, weaker minds and hearts of the masses to
regulate them in the way they can be regulated. This calls for
(prudence), tact, intelligent weighing of the situation.

Those who were responsible to propound the natural laws also **Conversations, January** had the *Kaliyuga* within their vision. It was not out of their consideration. So the proclaimed natural laws must also be applicable to *Kaliyuga*, as they were the other three yugas. The natural laws are eternal and they cannot be changed because they are made for all situations. If, however, one tried to change the natural laws then he will have to face the consequences to keep on charging them to utter confusion and lawlessness. Call for the change of natural laws comes from men of weak mind and character. There can't be a law for the weak, for the weak law fails to prevail, so the law must remain as it was. Responsibility to hold on to the natural laws lies upon those who are responsible to execute the law. Unfortunately men of such places have become weak and they tremble to promulgate the law. One needs men of strong character who could execute the law with courage. One needs no new laws for the *Kaliyuga*. Nowadays, even in education the laws are being changed. In the old days there were no examinations because the education was not bookish. Now you have examinations and prescribed and promoted books. Books are being followed by "keys" which very much shorten the books. When even the keys fail to help, people demand lowering of the standard. If you do, one day they may ask for certificates without examinations. In the old set up the teacher was responsible to educate through his words and actions and only when he was sure of the understanding and practice he would declare him educated. Every day was an examination day. Answer to the problem needs no change in the law to suit the weaklings. One must hold on to the law as firmly as possible, but in view of this apathy one needs 'yukti'[2] (intelligent weighing of the circumstances and prescribing a workable interpretation of the law) to formulate the law in such way that it becomes palatable. Even the Shastras encourage to "speak the truth but in a pleasant way and discourage to speak pleasant untruth".

Suppose one has earned some money, one need not tell the truth to everyone. If an unsocial person does ask such a leading question one has to answer with great care and not spell out the amount which would land him in unforeseen trouble. Without speaking a lie one should by-pass. When a cow is being chased for slaughter one can't tell the truth about her whereabouts even if it is known. It is within the tradition even to speak a lie to save the life of a child, women, cows and brahmin and also one's own life and such similar circumstances, if it does not

1978 (b)
Principles of Government and Economics for this Age.
[1] The Kaliyuga (Iron Age) is the age in which we live. See Srimad 12, 3 for descriptions of the ages. Note the Kaliyuga has only just begun.

[2] युक्ति

hurt anyone. Every girl is not a Venus and yet she must be married, so without calling her ugly her appearance is described in a pleasant way or presented in a good form so that a happy marriage takes place, and a soul is saves from deprivation.

The weak does not like the law for he wants everything according to his own desire. Law can't be diluted for him, but he can be encouraged to accept the law in a sweet form. One has to educate to lift up the situation.

Every individual who comes into the world has his unmanifest nature with him, which will find its unfoldment in the course of time. ...Here in Indian tradition, when the child is six months old, in a ceremonial way he is presented with various types of things, such as play objects, tools, books and all household things in various colours. It is expected that he will pick up the things to his liking. This gives an indication as to what manner of nature will unfold when he grows up. This is based on the concept that every individual has something special of his own lying dormant and needing suitable conditions for its full development. If the parents do get to know this factor properly, the child would be helped to evolve according to his nature in the shortest time. Anything else is slow and cumbersome.

Conversations, 1980
Men's Talents

The owner of a business has overall responsibility for the organisation. He has to care for the future apart from the present. He alone carries the burden of finance, sales, supplies and image. He appoints a manager and delegates all the routine work. The talents of the manager are to be used in running the day to day production. He knows almost everything about the functioning aspects of the business. He wields most power and keeps the wheels moving. He is most busy but does not carry any burden or pressure which the proprietor carries. The manager has surrendered his talents to the service of the proprietor carries. There is no clash of wills and this is why the manager is more effective. The owner rather seems to be doing nothing. ...

Conversations, 1982
Management

World Wide recession follows when at some place production and labour is too cheap, and local recession follows when production and labour is too costly at home. Both are unreason-

Conversations, 1982
Causes of Recession

able, and both arise due to lack of love for one's Nation. Unemployment for too long and for too many can cause social unrest. Only love and reason can help.

Progress depends on wisdom and its practice. One who has acquired proper understanding and has seen the laws of nature can project his concepts of possible progress in a convincing manner. It is equally necessary that the findings must be put into practice within the new set of situations before they are exposed for public use. Economics is an aspect of Law and the goodness of ancient laws lies in their usefulness for contemporary situations as well as without damaging their basic form. The ultimate unit for economic considerations is the family which accounts for all individuals bound together with love, affection and sacrifice[1]. Happiness of a family depends upon the cultural, religious and philosophical traditions of the society. When cultural, religious and philosophical traditions become weak, the disintegration of family begins, individuals become greedy for security[2]. Once general greed takes over the economic structure begins to crack.

One of the laws of nature is the true expression of what lies within, for nothing in nature is concealed. This is known as the law of cause and effect. Conscious application of this law of nature is to speak the truth, but the major part of conscious energy is being spent in not disclosing the truth. The result is that everyone is trying to convince others of the truth of their inflated needs by minimising the natural needs of others. All this is being done by proposing new economic theories with total disregard to the laws of nature. One must understand the laws of nature first and then put them into practice on oneself before offering them to others.

We possess and we claim; this is all ignorance. The Absolute created the universe and we create boundaries--"This is my land, this is my country[1]." In fact the land belongs to no one. You can claim it for a time, but in the end you have to leave everything behind. The Creator creates men; we create the 'Indian' and the 'English.' The creation is consciousness, but we do not see this because of our ignorance[2].

Once a holy man was travelling. In the evening he asked to stay the night at a palace. He asked the doorkeeper, who enquired of the owner. The owner refused and said that this was not an

---

Conversations, 1982
The Ultimate Economic Unit is the Family.

[1] *Note the original of the word 'economics' is commonly accept as the Greek οἰκονομία. Traditionally translated as 'management of a household'*
[2] *See also Mencius, 3, A, 3 (page 111).*

The Man who wanted to meet God Story of the Holy man who tried to stay at a palace
[1] *See Cicero, Offices 1, 7 (page 41).*
[2] *See Ficino, Letters 1, 73 (page 49).*

inn where people could drop in.

The holy man asked the owner, "Who built this palace?"

"My father," came the answer.

"Now you own the palace?"

"Yes, I am the owner."

"Who will own it after you?"

"My sons" said the owner.

"Who after your sons?"

"My grandsons."

"Then this looks like an inn," said the holy man, "because people seem to come and stay for some time and go. Wouldn't you call it an inn? Had it belonged to your father, he certainly could have taken it with him." The owner realized his error[3].

[3] *A similar example is included in MhB, Santi 321 (page 104).*

There was a Sanyasin living on a plateau where there was a spring. He developed the place as a beautiful garden with flowers, plants and fruit trees. Once a king of that area and his minister came that way in search of water during their hunt. Seeing some birds around they went up to the hill top and saw this beautiful place and requested the Sanyasin for some water to quench their thirst. The Sanyasin plucked two pomegranates and squeezed them in two glasses which were then filled with juice. They quenched their thirst and paid their respects and they went on their way. The king was surprised with the quantity of juice the two fruits produced. He asked his minister if this land was in his domain and how much was the tax yield. The tax was nominal so the king thought that this was unjust as the land gives plentiful and the tax was so small compared to the yield and began to consider taking over the land or increasing the tax substantially. Per chance they had to come to the Sanyasin after two days and requested for drink to quench their thirst. The Sanyasin this time brought eight fruits but even these couldn't produce enough juice to fill the glasses. The king asked for an explanation. The Sanyasin said that the other day when you walked away satisfied you started talking about tax and confiscation of land. The trees heard it and since then have stopped producing juice. Your feelings have hurt them. The story ends there but it is simple to give the moral that it only needs a little initiation of some feelings of either love or hate or deceit or submission or devotion and you will find almost natural response to this.

Source Unknown

Taxation

This story aptly illustrates the principle that taxation discourages whatever is taxed.

The Shû King

1. Yü divided the land. Following the course of the hills, he cut down the trees. He determined the highest hills and largest rivers (in the several regions).

2. With respect to Ki Kau, he did his work at Hu-khau, and took effective measures at (the mountains) Liang and Khi. Having repaired the works on Thai-yuan, he proceeded on to the south of (mount) Yo. He was successful with his labours on Tan-hwai, and went on to the cross-flowing stream of Kang. The soil of this province was whitish and mellow. Its contribution of revenue was the highest of the highest class, with some proportion of the second. Its fields were the average of the middle class.

The (waters of the) Hang and Wei were brought to their proper channels, and Ta-lu was made capable of cultivation.

The wild people of the islands (brought) dresses of skins (I. e. fur dresses); keeping close on the right to the rocks of kieh they entered the Ho.

3. Between the Ki and the Ho was Yen Kau. The nine branches of the Ho were made to keep their proper channels. Lei-hsia was made a marsh, in which (the waters of) the Yung and the 3u were united. The mulberry grounds were made fit for silkworms, and then (the people) came down from the heights, and occupied the grounds (below).

The soil of this province was blackish and rich; the grass in it was luxuriant, and the trees grew high. Its fields were the lowest of the middle class. Its contribution of revenue was fixed at what would just be deemed the correct amount; but it was not required from it, as from the other provinces, till after it had been cultivated for thirteen years[1]. Its articles of tribute were varnish and silk, and, in baskets, woven ornamental fabrics. They floated along the Ki and Tha, and so reached the Ho.

4. The sea and (mount) Tai were the boundaries of khing Kau. (The territory of) Yu-l was defined; and the Wei and 3ze were made to keep their (old) channels.

Its soil was whitish and rich. Along the shore of the sea were wide tracts of salt land. Its fields were the lowest of the first class, and its contribution of revenue the highest of the second. Its articles of tribute were salt, fine cloth of dolichos fibre,

Part III Book 1. The Tribute of YÜ

Section 1. YÜ was the founder of the Hsia dynasty (B.C. 2205 - 1767). Place names are as given in the text and not the contemporary names for the same areas. Some further descriptions of YÜ are given in Mencius, 3 A (page 111).

1. i.e. Yu divided the country into 9 provinces each described in verses 2-10 below.

2. The productiveness of the soil at that time was classified by grade, Shan-high, Chung-middle, Hia-low, and within each first-rate, second rate, and third rate.

Yu dredged the channels of some rivers and drained the fields.

3. The land was drained so that the industry could be resumed.

In Egyptian mythology, similarly, Ptah ('The Developer') raised Egypt from under the waters of the Great Flood and made it habitable by extensive drainage and earthworks.

[1] The land was not taxed until it was capable of producing a 'normal' level of income. See Also Sukra 4, 2, 242 (page 180).

4. Dolichos was an especially strong silk, useful for stringed instruments.

productions of the sea of various kinds; with silk, hemp, lead, pine trees, and strange stones, from the valleys of Tai. The wild people of Lai were taught tillage and pasturage, and brought in their baskets the silk from the mountain mulberry tree.
They floated along the Wan, and so reached the Ki.

5. The sea, mount Tai, and the Hwai were (the boundaries of) Hsu k'au.

The Hwai and the I (rivers) were regulated. The (hills) Mang and Yu were made fit for cultivation (The waters of) Ta-yeh were confined (so as to form a marsh); and (the tract of) Tung-yuan was successfully brought under management.

The soil of this province was red, clayey, and rich. Its grass and trees grew more and more bushy. Its fields were the second of the highest class; its contribution of revenue was the average of the second. Its articles of tribute were--earth of five different colours, variegated pheasants from the valleys of mount Yui, the solitary dryandra from the south of mount Yi, and the sounding-stones that (seemed to) float on the (banks of the) Sze. The wild tribes about the Hwai brought oyster-pearls and fish, and their baskets full of deep azure and other silken fabrics, chequered and pure white.

They floated along the Hwai and the Sze, and so reached the Ho.

6. The Hwai and the sea formed (the boundaries of) Yang kau. The (lake of) Phang-li was confined to its proper limits, and the sun-birds (the wild geese) had places to settle on. The three Kiang were led to enter the sea, and it became possible to still the marsh of Kan. The bamboos, small and large, then spread about; the grass grew thin and long, and the trees rose high; the soil was miry.

The fields of this province were the lowest of the lowest class; its contribution of revenue was the highest of the lowest class, with a proportion of the class above. Its articles of tribute were gold, silver, and copper; yao and khwan stones; bamboos, small and large; (elephants') teeth, hides, feathers, hair, and timber. The wild people of the islands brought garments of grass, with silks woven in shell-patterns in their baskets. Their bundles contained small oranges and pummeloes,--rendered when specially required.

They followed the course of the Kiang and the sea, and so reached the Hwai and the Sze.

7. (Mount) King and the south of (mount) Hang formed (the

5-10 These verses are similar, but illustrate both the variety of produce available and the specialised nature of different regions.

General Observations

Apart from the fact taxes were not collectable until the land was fully productive, there are a couple of other thing to note here:-

~ The establishment of a tax revenue base was attended to simultaneously with making the land habitable, as was the establishment of tittle to land.

~ Tax rates were established based on the productiveness of the site (within general categories).

~ Taxes were gathered in the form of produce that was from the district. Hence taxes were easy to pay.

~ The tax rates were known well in advance.

boundaries of) King Kau.

The Kiang and the Han pursued their (common) course to the sea, as if they were hastening to court. The nine Kiang were brought into complete order. The Tho and Khien (streams) were conducted by their proper channels. The land (in the marsh of) Yun (became visible), and (the marsh of) Mang was capable of cultivation.

The soil of this province was miry. Its fields were the average of the middle class; and its contribution of revenue was the lowest of the highest class its articles of tribute were feathers, hair, (elephants') teeth, and hides; gold, silver, and copper; khun trees, wood for bows, cedars, and cypresses; grindstones, whetstones, flint stones to make arrow-heads, and cinnabar; and the khun and lu bamboos, with the hu tree, (all good for making arrows)--of which the Three Regions were able to contribute the best specimens. The three-ribbed rush was sent in bundles, put into cases. The baskets were filled with silken fabrics, azure and deep purple, and with strings of pearls that were not quite round. From the (country of the) nine Kiang, the great tortoise was presented when. especially required (and found).

They floated down the Kiang, the Tho, the Khien, and the Han, and crossed (the country) to the Lo, whence they reached the most southern part of the Ho.

8. The King (mountain) and the Ho were (the Boundaries of) Yui Kau'.

The I, the Lo, the Khan, and the Kien were conducted to the Ho. The (marsh of) Yung-po was confined within its proper limits. The (waters of that of) Ko were led to (the marsh of) Mang-ku.

The soil of this province was mellow; in the lower parts it was (in some places) rich, and (in others) dark and thin. Its fields were the highest of the middle class; and its contribution of revenue was the average of the highest class, with a proportion of the very highest. Its articles of tribute were varnish, hemp, fine cloth of dolichos fibre, and the boehmerea. The baskets were full of chequered silks, and of fine floss silk. Stones for polishing sounding-stones were rendered when required.

They floated along the Lo, and so reached the Ho.

9. The south of (mount) Hwa and the Black-water were (the boundaries of Liang Kau.

The (hills) Min and Po were made capable of cultivation. The

Tho and Khien streams were conducted by their proper channels. Sacrifices were offered to (the hills) 3hai and Mang on the regulation (of the country about them). (The country of) the wild tribes about the Ho was successfully operated on.

The soil of this province was greenish and light. Its fields were the highest of the lowest class; and its contribution of revenue was the average of the lowest class, with proportions of the rates immediately above and below. Its articles of tribute were ---- the best gold, iron, silver, steel, flint stones to make arrowheads, and sounding-stones; with the skins of bears, foxes, and jackals, and (nets) woven of their hair.

From (the hill of) Hsi-khing they came by the course of the Hwan; floated along the Khien, and then crossed (the country) to the Mien; passed to the Wei, and (finally) ferried across the Ho.

10. The Black-water and western Ho were (the boundaries of) Yung Kau.

The Weak-water was conducted westwards. The King was led to mingle its waters with those of the Wei. The Khi and the Khu were next led in a similar way (to the Wei), and the waters of the Feng found the same receptacle.

(The mountains) King and Khi were sacrificed to. (Those of) Kung-nan and Khun-wu (were also regulated), and (all the way) on to Niao-shu. Successful measures could now be taken with the plains and swamps, even to (the marsh of) Ku-yeh (The country of) San-wei was made habitable, and the (affairs of the) people of San-miao were greatly arranged.

The soil of the province was yellow and mellow. Its fields were the highest of the highest class, and its contribution of revenue the lowest of the second. Its articles of tribute were the khiu jade and the lin, and (the stones called) lang-kan.

Past Ki-shih they floated on to Lung-man on the western Ho. They then met on the north of the Wei (with the tribute-bearers from other quarters).

Hair-cloth and skins (were brought from) Khwan-lun, Hsi-kih, and Khu-sau;--the wild tribes of the west (all) coming to (submit to Yu's) arrangements.

1. (Yu) surveyed and described (the hills), beginning with Khien and Khi and proceeding to mount King; then, crossing the Ho, Hu-khau, and Lei-shau, going on to Thai-yo. (After these came) Ti-ku and Hsi-khang, from which he went on to

Part III Book 1. The Tribute of YÜ Section 2. Establishment of Order in a Kingdom

Wang-wu; (then there were) Thai-hang and mount Hang, from which he proceeded to the rocks of Kieh, where he reached the sea.

(South of the Ho, he surveyed) Hsi-khing, Ku-yu, and Niao-shu going on to Thai-hwa; (then) Hsiung-r, Wai-fang, and Thung-pai, from which he proceeded to Pei-wei.

He surveyed and described Po-khung, going on to (the other) mount King; and Nei-fang, from which he went on to Ta-pieh. (He did the same with the south of mount Min, and went on to mount Hang. Then crossing the nine kiang, he proceeded to the plain of Fu-khien. ... *the omitted text is similar...*

3. (Thus), throughout the nine provinces a similar order was effected:--the grounds along the waters were everywhere made habitable; the hills were cleared of their superfluous wood and sacrificed to; the sources of the rivers were cleared; the marshes were well banked; and access to the capital was secured for all within the four seas.

The six magazines (of material wealth)[1] were fully attended to[2]; the different parts of the country were subjected to an exact comparison, so that contribution of revenue could be carefully adjusted according to their resources[3]. (The fields) were all classified with reference to the three characters of the soil; and the revenues for the Middle Region were established.

4. He conferred lands and surnames. (He said), ' Let me set the example of a reverent attention to my virtue, and none will act contrary to my conduct.'

Five hundred Li formed the Domain of the Sovereign. From the first hundred they brought as revenue the whole plant of the grain; from the second, the ears, with a portion of the stalk; from the third, the straw, but the people had to perform various services; from the fourth, the grain in the husk; and from the fifth, the grain cleaned.

Five hundred li (beyond) constituted the Domain of the Nobles. The first hundred li was occupied by the cities and lands of the (sovereign's) high ministers and great officers; the second, by the principalities of the barons; and the (other) three hundred, by the various other princes.

Five hundred li (still beyond) formed the Peace-securing Domain. In the first three hundred, they cultivated the lessons of learning and moral duties; in the other two, they showed the energies of war and defence.

Five hundred li (remoter still) formed the Domain of Restraint.

[1] the magazines or 'stores' were the commodities - gold, silver, iron, copper, tin, and grain. At that time gold and silver were not stores of value.

[2] See also Sukra 4, 2, 25-29 (page 177).

[3] See Sukra 2, 207 (page 170).

4. Surnames were given for the organisation of the succession of land holding (2276 B.C.). Gorn translates the second sentence 'respectfully submit these my virtuous works to the people'. For details of the remainder of this section see below[1]

The (first) three hundred were occupied by the tribes of the I; the (other) two hundred, by criminals undergoing the lesser banishment.

Five hundred li (the most remote) constituted the Wild Domain. The (first) three hundred were occupied by the tribes of the Man; the (other) two hundred, by criminals undergoing the greater banishment.

5. On the east, reaching to the sea; on the: west, extending to the moving sands; to the utmost limits of the north and south:-- his fame and influence filled up (all within) the four seas. Yu presented the dark-coloured symbol of his rank, and announced the completion of his work.

Supplementary Notes

1. The Gorn translation of this verse reads. 'Five hundred Li was the region of the tribute holding. For one hundred Li the revenue consisted of the entire grain bearing plant. The second hundred Li brought in grain with half straw. The third hundred Li contributed grain in the ear. The revenue of the fourth hundred Li was grain in the husk and the fifth hundred Li, grain already threshed and winnowed.' He adds a footnote 'respect being given to the increasing cost and difficulty of transport'.

The entire arrangement is shown in the diagram. The inner domain supported the sovereign. The next in order of distance the great officers of the court, ensuring their proximity to the court and them

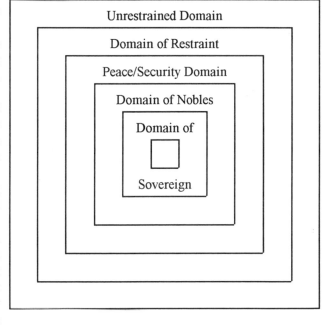

being under the observation of the higher authorities. The third domain was for the literati, artists and musicians under patronage and the military who secured all inside this circle. Outside this are foreigners upon whom restrain was required, and expelled felons. The final domain was not under control (hence unrestrained). Three and a half Li are equivalent to an English mile.

Šrimad Bhagavata

People perform actions for the sake of happiness;...

Book 3, Discourse 5
Object of actions

Wherever He will be in the course of His travels, the kings will acknowledge His supremacy with tributes and offerings... In obedience to Him as a supreme king, Earth will become a cow for Him (to milk the desirable items of wealth for the good of all). As a powerful patriarch He will provide for the livelihood of the people.

Book 4 Discourse 17 In praise of King Pṛitu the primordial monarch)

(20) The King Said...(21) As a ruler on this earth I have been assigned the role of punishing the evil-doers[1], protecting the people (against calamities)[2]; affording them the means of subsistence and keeping them severally within their bounds (the spheres allotted to them by the Sastras)[3]. ...(23) A sovereign who levies taxes but fails to teach the people their sacred duties (merely) reaps their sins and forfeits his fortune[4].

Book 4, Discourse 21 Role of a King [1] *See also L of M 7, 13 (page 67).* [2] *requiring accumulation of wealth, see Sukra 4, 2, 25 (page 177).* [3] *See also Confucius, Analects 16 (page 47), MhB, Adi 49 (page 75) & Santi 295 (page 103)* [4] *See also Mencius 3, A (page 111).*

(32) Constant pre-occupation with wealth and the objects of sense means the ruination of all the interests of man.

Book 4, Discourse 22 Preoccupation with wealth *See MhB, Santi 123 (page 97).*

Even as the sun drains (in summer) the moisture of the earth, and releases it (during the rains) and radiates heat, so he drew the wealth of the earth (by way of land revenue and other taxes), (freely) distributing it (among the people during famines etc[1]) and exercised his authority (over the people). (53-56)

Book 4, Discourse 22, 53

[1] *see Bible, Genesis 41, 28-57 for historical example.*

(15) Occupation of various kinds (such as agriculture, breeding of cattle. Trade and so on, accepting gifts without the impudence of asking, begging food grains daily and gathering ears of corn left by the owner while reaping the harvest or gleaning food grains lying scattered in a grain market after the heaps have been sold off or removed[1] - this is the four fold means of livelihood sanctioned for a *Brahman* (one belonging to the priestly class). (Of these four,) again, each succeeding one is

Book 7, Discourse 11 15-20 Occupations *See similar descriptions in L of M 1, 87-91 (page 65).*

[1] *See similar provisions in Bible, Leviticus 19, 9-10 (page 12) & note associated with*

preferable (to the preceding). (16) With the exception of a Kṣatriya, a man belonging to a lower grade should not adopt a higher vocation except in distress. (Of course, a Kṣatriya may adopt the means of livelihood of a *Brahman* other than accepting gifts made by another). In (times of) distress, however, all sorts of vocations are open to all without distinction. (17) One may live by (what is known as) Ṛta and Amṛta or (even) by Mṛta and Pramṛta. One may (also) live by Satyānṛta, but under no circumstance by Śwavṛti (a dog's living). (18) Gathering ears of corn left by the owner while reaping a harvest or gleaning food grains lying scattered in a grain-market after the heaps have been sold off or removed is called Ṛta (*lit.,* right or true); that which is got un-asked for is called Amṛta (nectar). Daily begging (of food grains) is Mṛta (death); while agriculture is called Pramṛta (*lit.,* greater death, so called because it involves the destruction of many living beings). (19) Trade is (what goes by the name of) Satyānṛta (a mixture of truth and falsehood); while service rendered to those belonging to a lower grade is (what is meant by) a dog's living. A *Brahman* as well as a *Kṣatriya* should always shun this detested calling. (For) a *Brahman* is an embodiment of all the (four) Vedas, while a Kṣatriya (*lit.,* a ruler of men) is the personification of all the gods. (20)

Mencius 3, A (page 111).

17. Relating again to the Brahman, refer also to L of M 4, 5-6.

18. Translators of an identical passage in L of M note that money lending is included with agriculture.

19. See foe example Plato, Laws 918 (page 141).

Yudhisthira said: O divine personage, I am anxious to hear (from you) about the eternal *Dharma* (course of right conduct) prescribed for men, along with the ethical code governing the (four) Varnas or grades of society, and Asramas (stages in life), by following which a human being (eventually) reaches the Supreme (either through devotion or spiritual enlightenment)... (4) Narada resumed Bowing (my head) to gain the favour of the birthless Lord (Narayana), the Promoter of righteousness among the people, I shall expound the eternal Law as learnt from the lips of (the divine sage) Narayana... (13) Study (of the scriptures and charity, which along with study of an obligatory nature; and three more; viz., teaching, officiating as a priest at sacrifices, and receiving gifts from those whose earnings are free from blemish, - which are recommended as a means of subsistence and are therefore not obligatory) are the six duties of a *Brahman.* Non-acceptance of gifts is a rule for the other one (viz., the *Kṣatriya,* or a member of the warrior class who comes next in order to the *Brahman*

Book 7, Discourse 11b Order of Society *See L of M 10, 115-131 (page 73) for similar description of the duties of the castes. But ultimately all men are the same, see MhB, Santi 319 (page 104).*
13. see Plato, Republic 2, 370 (page 129) for Division of Labour. See also L of M, 1, 87 (page 65).
Tf:- A king is entitled to receive voluntary gifts from his subjects & collect periodically tributes from feudal chiefs as acknowledgement of submission on their part or as the price of peace & protection.

and is allowed to earn his livelihood by the other two means, viz., teaching and officiating as a priest at sacrifices in distress. Of course, he is free to practise these otherwise than as a means of subsistence). Maintenance is to be sought by a Ksatriya, protecting the people, optionally by recovering taxes and fines from his subjects other than a *Brahman* (who is ordinarily exempted from such taxes and fines). A Vaisya (a member of the trading and agricultural classes) as a matter of fact should make his living by agriculture, breeding of cattle, trade and usury and should always follow the lead of the *Brahman* race. Service to the twice-born classes has been enjoined upon the *Sudra* (a member of the labouring and artisan classes) and service to his master has been ordained as his means of subsistence too.

He is justified in extending his dominion by conquering other territories as a preliminary for the performance of a Rājasūya sacrifice. If he is unable to meet his expenditure from these sources he is allowed the alternative of filling his coffers by recovering taxes from his subjects & fines by way of penalty from offenders.
NB. Priests are not to be taxed Bible, Genesis 47, 12 (page 9).

(in praise of Pṛthu) ...Even as the sun drains (in summer) the moisture of the earth, and relaxes it (during the rains) and radiates heat, so he drew the wealth of the earth (by way of land revenue and other taxes), (freely) distributed it (among the people during famines etc) and exercised his authority (over the people). 53-56

Book 7, Discourse 11b
Taxation a duty of kings
See Bible, Genesis 41 (page 8)

The glorious Lord began again:.. In the (very) first Satya Yuga (of the present Kalpa) the caste of men was (only one and) known by the name of Hamsa. People had their object (of life) accomplished by virtue of their (very) birth; hence they understood it by the name of Kṛitayuga (the aeon of blessedness) (10)... while I (alone as existing in their thoughts) constituted their piety appearing in the form of a bull (standing on all its four feet). Firm in ascesis (in the shape of one pointedness of mind and senses) and free from sin they contemplated on Me, the immaculate Lord (11). At the beginning of (the next Yuga known by the name of) Tretā (after the expiry of Kritayuga), O highly blessed Uddhava, was revealed from my heart through My respiration the threefold Veda (knowledge consisting of three limbs in the shape of Rik, Sāma and Yajus); (and) from the latter appeared I as (the institution of) sacrifice with the triple functions (of a Hotā, Adhwaryu and Udgātā). (12) (Again) from Brahmā (born of the Cosmic Person) appeared the four grades of society ....Control of the mind and the senses, meditation, (external as well as internal) purity, contentment, forgiveness, straight-

Book 11, Discourse 17 On the ages and orders of society
See Book 12, 3 below.
10. Satya Yuga & Kṛitayuga are the same, both names for the first period of human existence or the 'Golden Age'.

11. The 3 functions of sacrifice here are the names of 3 classes of priest involved, Hotā (the sacrificer, and invoker of the gods), Adhwaryu (non violent preparation), Udgātā (chanter of hymns).

forwardness, devotion to Me, compassion and truthfulness - these are the natural traits of a *brahman*. (16) Majesty, strength, fortitude, valour, forbearance, liberality, industry, firmness, devotion to the *Brahmans* and rulership - these are the (distinguishing) traits of a Kṣatriya. (17) Faith (in the scriptures as well as in the words of one's preceptor), firm adherence to liberality, sincerity (absence of hypocrisy) service to the *Brahmans* and remaining dissatisfied with hoards of money - these are the in born characteristics of a Vaiśya. (18) Sincere (guileless) service to the *brahman*, the cow and the gods too and contentment with whatever is obtained through such service - these are the inborn characteristics of a Sūdra. (19) Impurity, mendacity, thieving, want of faith, quarrelling without cause, concupiscence, anger and cupidity are inborn characteristics of a castless. (20) Non-violence, truthfulness, abstaining from theft, freedom from lust, anger and greed and doing what is pleasant and good to living beings - this constitutes the sacred duty of all the Varṇas (grades of society). (21)

(1) In the Kali age wealth alone will be the criterion of pedigree, morality and merit. Again, might will be the only factor determining righteousness and fairness. (2).....Justice will have every chance of being vitiated because of one's ability to gratify those administering it,..... (4) Want of riches will be the sole test of impiety... (6) Skill will consist of supporting one's family; virtuous deeds will be performed (only) with the object of gaining fame; and the terrestrial globe will be overrun by wicked people, the person who proved to be the most powerful amongst the *Brahmanas*, Kṣatriyas, Vaiśyas and *Sudras* will become the ruler. Robbed of their wealth by greedy and merciless Kṣatriyas, behaving like robbers, people will resort to mountains and forests and subsist on leaves, roots, meat, honey, fruits flowers and seeds. (7-9) Already oppressed by famine and (heavy) taxation, people will, perish through drought, (excessive) cold, storms, (scorching) sunshine, (heavy) rain, snowfall and mutual conflict.

Book 12, Discourse 2 Iron or Kali Age. *See also MhB, Udyoga 187 (page 85) & refer MhB, Vana 187.*

1. See Plato, Republic 550c (page 132).

4. See Plato, Republic 550d.

Sri Suka replied, In the Satayuga, O protector of men, *Dharma* (virtue) runs its course on (all) its four feet, and is held fast by the people of the age. Truth, compassion, asceticism and affording protection to all are the (four) feet (of virtue in its integral form). (18) People of that age are mostly contented,

Book 12, Discourse 3 The Ages

18-35 See also Book 11, 17 above, Plato, Republic 8 (page 131). See MhB, Adi 68 (page

compassionate, friendly (to all living beings), tranquil and forbearing. They practise self-control, take delight in the Self, look upon all with an equal eye and take pains for Self-Realization. (19) In the Tretā age a quarter of all the (four) feet of *Dharma* (virtue) gets gradually encroached upon by falsehood, violence, discontent and discord - the (four) feet of A*dharma* (unrighteousness). (20) In that age (of Tretā) people remain devoted to the performance of Vedic rites and austerities, they are not given to much violence nor lewd behaviour. They pursue the three objects of human endeavour *viz* religious merit, worldly possessions and sense enjoyment. People are advanced in Vedic rites and among (the four) grades of society the *Brahmans* form a majority, O protector of men! (21) Assailed by the four feet of A*dharma*, violence, discontent, falsehood and hatred, those of *Dharma*- compassion, austerity, truthfulness and a charitable disposition- diminish by one half each in the Dwāpara age. (22) The people of that age are fond of glory and given to the performance of great sacrifices, take delight in learning the Vedas, are affluent and happy and maintain big families. Among the (four) grades of society the *Brahmans* and Kṣatriyas are predominant. (23) In the Kali age, however, a quarter (alone) of the (four) feet of *Dharma* remains. (Nay) due to the feet of A*dharma* gaining ground that too steadily declines and ultimately disappears altogether. (24) People in that age turn out to be greedy, immoral and merciless, enter into hostility without cause and are unlucky and extremely covetous. The *Sudras*, fishermen and the like take the lead. (25)......

When duplicity, mendacity, drowsiness, excessive sleep, violence, dejection, grief, infatuation, fear and wretchedness prevail that is recognised as the age of Kali, characterised by the predominance of Tamas, as a result of which people become dull-witted (*viz* unable to judge things in their proper perspective) and are unlucky but voracious, voluptuous and destitute. And women (too) turn out to be profligate and unchaste. (30-31) Countries are infested with robbers; the Vedas stand condemned by heretics; rulers exploit the people; and the *Brahmans* remain devoted to gratification of sexual desires and intent on filling their belly. (32) Religious students will give up the course of conduct prescribed for them and fail to observe purity, and the householder will take up begging; hermits will take up their residence in villages and recluses will be seized

75) & refer to Plato, Statesman 272a for description of the Golden Age. See Rama 1, 5 (page 143) for description of the prosperity of the Dwāpara age.

18. Dharma is personifies as a cow.

20. See Plato, Laws (page 140), and see Purushârtha in Lexicon (page 194).

23. Kali Age

24. See Plato on Democracy, Republic 556 (page 133)

with an ardent longing for wealth. (33) Women will be short-statured but voracious, prolific and destitute of modesty. They will always speak harsh words and will be given to thieving and wiles and very daring. (34) Low minded traders will carry business transactions and practise fraud. Even when they are not in distress people will favour pursuits which are condemned. (35) Servants will leave their masters when reduced to penury, through superior in every (other) respect; and masters too will discharge their servants, when incapacitated for service (through ailment etc) even though he may be hereditary. (Even so) people will cease to maintain cows when they no longer yield milk. (36)

34. see also Plato, Laws 918 (page141).

35. For converse behaviour in former ages see MhB, Adi 49 (page 75).

See also Sukra 2, 819 (page 175) For duty of care to sick & elderly.

....The text continues with further description of life in the Kali Yuga.

Sukra-Niti

Dictionary definitions of Sanskrit terms used exclusively within this section are included in the Supplementary notes below[1]

Chapter 1 127-152
The qualities of a king

127-28 The king is the cause of the prosperity of this world, is respected by the experienced and old people and gives pleasure to the eyes (of the people) as the moon to the sea.

129-30 If the king is not a perfect guide, his subjects will get into trouble as a boat without a helmsman sinks in a sea.

131-32 Without the governor, the subjects do not keep to their own spheres. Nor does the sovereign flourish without subjects.

133-34 If the monarch proceeds according to the dictates of *Nyaya* or justice (Niti) he can supply himself as well as the subjects with Trivarga or virtue, wealth and enjoyments, otherwise he destroys both.

135-36 The king called *Vaisravana* could rule the earth through virtue, but through sin Nahusa got hell.

137-38 Vena was ruined through vice and Prithu was prosperous through virtue. So the ruler should cultivate his interests by placing virtue in his front.

139-40 The prince who is virtuous, is part of the gods. He who is otherwise is a part of the demons, an enemy of religion and oppressor of subjects.

141-43 The king is made out of the permanent elements of *Indra, Vayu, Yama*, Sun, Fire, *Varuna*, Moon, and *Kuvera*, and is the lord of both the immovable and movable worlds.

144. Like *Indra*, the sovereign is able to protect the wealth and possessions.

145. As *Vayu* or Air is the spreader (and diffuser) of scents, so the prince is the generator (and cause) of good and evil actions.

146. As the sun is the dispeller of darkness (and the creator of light) so the king is the founder of religion and destroyer of irreligion.

147. As *Yama* is the god who punishes (human beings after death) so also the monarch is the punisher of offences (in this world).

148. Like *Agni*, the prince is the purifier and enjoyer of all gifts.

149. As *Varuna*, the god of water, sustains everything by supplying moisture, so also the king maintains everybody by his

The qualities of a king

127. See also MhB, Santi 141 (page 101).

131. See Confucius, Analects 16, 1 (page 47). See also Brihad for requirements for flourishing (page 35).

133. Nyaya = That into which a thing goes back; a general or universal rule; a system or plan.

135. Vaisravana= another name for Kubera, the god of wealth. Nahusa= a king who took possession of Indra's throne & was afterwards turned into a snake.

137. See Confucius, Great Learning 10 (page 48)

141-152 see Brihad (page 35), L of M 7, 1-8 (page 67) & MhB, Santi 68 (page 90).

145-152. The king makes the age. Chap 4 Sect 1 adds 'The faults are to be ascribed neither to the age nor subjects but to the king. Men practise that by which the king is satisfied... Where the king is virtuous, the people are virtuous' see also MhB, Santi 69 (page 92).

147. Yama - the god of death

148. Agni - the god of fire

wealth.

150. As the Moon pleases human beings by its rays, so also the king satisfies everybody by his virtues and activities.

151. As the god of wealth protects the jewels of the universe, so the king protects the treasure and possessions of the state. *151. the god of wealth is Kubera*

152. As the moon does not shine well if deprived of one of its parts, so the king does not flourish unless he has all the parts described above....*the text continues with further attributes of the king.*

305-8. The science of discussion and Vedanta are founded on the science of Anwikshiki; virtue and vice, as well as the interests and injuries of man are based on the Trayi, wealth and its opposite on *Varta*, good and bad government on *Dandaniti*. Thus all the castes of men and the stages of human life are built into these sciences.......

Chapter 1 305-312 The science of government Anwikshiki =meditation, reflection; Trayi= triple science relating to Veda; Varta = subsistence, livelihood; Dandaniti = application of the rod (administration of justice), see L of M 7, 13-27 (page 67).

311-12. In *Varta* are treated interest, agriculture, commerce and preservation of cows. The man who is well up in *Varta* need not be anxious for earnings.

349-50. The man who is powerful, intelligent and valorous enjoys the earth full of its wealth, and such a king becomes lord of this world....

Chapter 1 349-362 Qualifications for acquisition and enjoyment of wealth.

351-53. Prowess, strength, intelligence & valour - these are great qualifications. The king who has other qualities but not these, though he is wealthy, cannot enjoy even a small region, but is soon thrown down from his kingdom.

354-55. Superior to the very wealthy king is the monarch, who though small in territory, has his commands unobstructed and is powerful. He can be such with the qualifications (mentioned above).

356. Men who are other than kings are not competent to (rule and) beautify the earth (land).

356. See Srimad 12, 2, 6 (page 164) For consequence of a king not ruling.

357-58. The earth (land) is the source of all wealth. For this earth (land) kings can lay down even their lives.

357. land is the source of all wealth, see also MhB, Bishma 4 & 9 (page 85) & Atharveda 12, 1, 6 (page 1).

359-60. Wealth and life are preserved by men for enjoyment. But what avails a man to have wealth and life who has not protected the land?

361-62. Accumulated wealth can never be sufficient for any amount of expenditure. Truly without perpetual incomes nobody's, not even *Kuvera*'s (is sufficient).

361. Kubera - the God of wealth.

375. The ruler has been made by Brahma a servant of the
people getting his share of the revenue as remuneration. His
sovereignty, however, is only for protection.

Chapter 1 375 The ruler is for
protection. *& cannot indulge
his wealth & power. See L of M
7, 2-3 (page 67), MhB, Bishma
109 (page 87) & Santi 58 (page
88).*

418-19. The ruler should always realise his share (revenue) of
produce from land according to Prajapati's system; but in times
of danger and difficulty, according to Manu's system, not
otherwise.
420. The ruler who extracts his share through cupidity (i.e.,
beyond his dues) is ruined with his subjects.
421-22. One should not give up even an angula of land in such
a way as to part with the rights to it; may, however, give away
(to persons) for their maintenance, but so long as the receiver
lives.
423-24. The wise man should always give away lands for the
gods, for parks and public grounds, and for dwelling houses to
the peasants.

Chapter 1 418-424 Rules of
Taxation *418. The taxable unit
of land is an Angula. By Prajapati's system of measurement
an angula is 8 yavas. By Man-
u's, 5 yavas. Yavas appear to
be an absolute unit. More tax
is paid for the same land &
rate under Manu's system.
421. Hence the right to the
revenue isn't surrendered as
happened later, see eg notes
with Ham 36 (page 53).
423. See MhB, Vana 199 (page
79) & Santi 191 (page 102) &
L of M 4, 227 (page 67).*

580. The outpost should be built by the police at the mouth or
end of a line of houses.
581. The king should hear reports of their work from them who
are to be maintained by wages raised from the householders.

Chapter 1 580-581
Local Taxation

599-600. Discord must never be created between husband and
wife, master and servant, brother and brother, preceptor and
pupil, as well as between father and son.
600-601. You must never obstruct the tanks, wells, parks,
boundaries or place hindrances to the use of religious houses,
temples and roads, nor must you check (the movements of) the
poor, the blind and the deformed.

Chapter 1 599-600 No discord to be created. *See Shantanand, the basis of economics
is the family- Conversation
1982 (page 153).*

631-635. The heads of the *grāmas* are to receive one twelfth of
the income from the *grāma*. The army is to be maintained by
three (such parts), charity (to be done to the extent of) half (of
such a part), (the people are to be entertained) with half (of
such a part), the officers (are to be paid) with half (of such a

Chapter 1 631-636 Distribution of Expenditure *Grama =
village. The division is 1/12 to
the head of the village; 3/12 to
the army; 1/24 to charity; 1/24*

part), personal expenditure (to be met) out of half (such a part). And the treasury is to be saved by the remainder. By dividing the income into six such divisions the king should yearly incur expenditure.

636. This rule is meant for and should be observed by rulers like Sāmanta and above, not by inferiors.

to the people; 1/24 to the officers; 1/24 to personal expenses. The remaining ½ to the treasury.

636 See also 2, 204 below. Sāmanta is, say at least, a prince.

741. The king should always take such steps as may advance the arts and sciences of the country.

Chapter 1 741 Government and the Arts *(A detail account of how painting should be done is included in the omitted parts of this text). See also Sukra 4, 5, 642 (page 183).*

1-2. Even if the work be a trifling one it can be done with difficulty by only one individual. What can be performed by an unfriended person for a kingdom that is considerable.

9-11. The wealth of intelligence is seen to be different with different men - according to (the various sources of knowledge) revealed wisdom, intuition, knowledge of *Sastra*, inferential reasoning, direct observation, analogies, adventurous instincts, craft and force.

12. There are diversities of human conduct as well as grades of excellence according to the degree in which they are high or low.

Chapter 2 1-2 The basis for co-operation in production. *See also Plato, Republic 2, 370 (page 129), Cicero, Offices 2, 4 (page 43) & Mencius 3, A, 4 (page 113).*

204-206. The Sumantra (Finance Minister) should communicate to the king the amount of commodities laid by, the amount of debts, &c., the amount spent, and the amount of surplus or balance in both moveables and immoveables during the course of the year.

207-208. How many cities, villages and forests are there, the amount of land cultivated, who receives of the rent, the amount of revenue realised.

209-210. Who receives the remainder after the paying of the rent, how much land remains uncultivated, the amount of revenue realised through taxes and fines.

211-212. The amount realised without cultivation (i.e. as Nature's gifts) how much accrues from forests, the amount realised through mines and jewels.

213-214. How much is collected as unowned or unclaimed by

Chapter 2 204-214 Collection of revenue. *Tf:- Financial affairs are split between the Sumantra in charge of the budget & Amantya a servant in charge of land settlement & records. Sources of revenue are:- rent from land; duties or taxes; fines; i.e. what is received without cultivation or care (nature's contribution); incomes from forests; mineral wealth; deposits (as in a bank); unowned (all unclaimed property belongs to the state); got*

anybody, got back from the thief, and the amount stored up, - *back from thieves.*
knowing these things, the Amantya should inform the king.

242-245. The Lord of Sahas, the headman of the village, the *Chapter 2 242-245 Adminis-*
collector of land revenues, the clerk, the collector of taxes (tolls *tration of villages. See MhB,*
and duties), as also the news bearer - these six are to be *Santi 87 (page 93)*
appointed in each village and town. *Sahas = powerful.*

345-346. The gardener collects flowers and fruits after having *Chapter 2 345-352 Taxes to*
duly nourished the trees with care. The collector of taxes is to *be Gentle. With regard duties*
be like him... *& taxes on goods, & revenue*
351-352. That man is a good collector of taxes and duties who *from land, the principle is the*
realises these from shop-keepers in such a way as not to destroy *same - not to destroy the sour-*
their capital. *ce. See MhB, Santi 87 (Page*
93), 72 (page 92, 93) & 120
(page 97), L of M 7, 129 (page
69).

523-526. 'I am sure to accomplish first what is absolutely *Chapter 2 523-531*
necessary for the king even though at the risk of life. Please *King and servant are both thie-*
command me' - Thus saying one should at once proceed with *ves.*
the work according to one's ability. And should sacrifice his *Tf This by their very functions.*
life even for great deeds and for kings. *So that this behaviour is legiti-*
527-528. The servant is for maintaining his kith and kin, never *mate in each case. Otherwise*
for other purposes. All servants exploit wealth, while the king *tyranny would result.*
takes life.
529-530. The king takes the life of servants in warfare and
other great deeds. And the servant takes away the wealth of the
king in the form of wages.
531. If they take otherwise they become destroyers of themselves.

547. One should not do anything that is good to the king but is *Chapter 2 547-548 New taxes*
harmful to the people. *are vexatious. See MhB, Santi*
548. Thus new taxes and duties are vexatious to the people. *87 (page 93).*

641-642...... Now is being described the other classes of writing *Chapter 2 641-672*
by which account of receipts and disbursements are kept. *Government Accounts-Income*
643-644. The documents for keeping accounts are of various *This is presented in a diagram*
kinds and are designated under different names according to *shown below[2].*
the differences in amount great or small, values and measure-
ments.

645-646. An income denotes the bringing under possession gold, cattle, grains, etc., annually, monthly or daily.

645. See L of M 10, 115 for forms of income (page 73).

647. An expenditure denotes the giving away of possession of wealth to others.

648. Income may be new as well as old.

649. Expenditure is of two kinds--for enjoyment or for exchange.

650-651. Accumulated wealth is of three kinds, that whose proprietary rights are known to belong to others, that whose owners are not known, and that which is surely one's own.

652. That wealth, the proprietary rights of which belong to others, i.e., the first class of accumulated wealth is again, of three kinds, that which has been kept as pawn or security by others, that which has been realised by begging, and that which has been collected though loan.

652 In contemporary terms the first and third of these would be items for which both assets and liabilities are shown on the balance sheet. Begging, presumably relates to 'favours', which may have to be repaid - say 'contingent liabilities'.

653-655. *Aupanidhika* wealth is that which has been placed with one by good people through confidence. *Yachita* wealth is that which has been collected without any consideration of interest, e.g, ornaments, &c., while *Auttamarnilia* wealth is that which is borrowed at some; interest.

656-657. That wealth whose owners are unknown (*i.e.,* -the second class of accumulated wealth) is illustrated by gems and jewels picked up in streets.

656. See also Plato, Laws 744 (page 140). Plato adds to this taxes on windfall profits, see Plato, Laws 744 (page 140). This is reflected in the English tradition. Refer Bracton, Laws of England.

658. That wealth which surely belongs to oneself (*i.e.,* the third class of accumulated wealth) is again, of two kinds, normal and artificial.

659-661. That income is said to be normal which grows regularly by days, months or years.

659. See 645-646 above.

662. Perhaps extra-ordinary items in today's terms. Adhika - additional subsequent, secondary, surplus.

662-664. Profits of sale, interest, wealth realised by services rendered, rewards, remuneration, wealth conquered, &c., all these constitute *adhika* (increase) class of one's own wealth. All else is normal.

665. Accumulated wealth is of two classes, last year's surplus or balance and the current year's receipts.

666-667. Each of *adhika* and *sadhajika* or normal, *I e.,* each of both the classes of one's own wealth is again of two kinds, *parthiva* (territorial) and *non-parthiva.*

668-670. *Parthiva* income is that which comes of land of the earth. That again is various owing to various sources,. *e.g.,* natural waters, artificial waters, villages and cities.

Income from the land is again divided into various classes owing to the divisions of land and great, small or medium amounts.

671-672. The duties, fines, royalties on mines, presents and contributions, &c., are known to constitute non territorial income according to writers and specialists.

673. Expenditure is named after the purpose for which wealth has been realised.

674. Expenditure falls into two heads -- that which will come back, and that which destroys the right for ever.

675. Expenditure also can be both great and small.

676-677. That disbursement is said to be *abritta*, *i.e.*, to have the attribute of being able to come back which is hoarded, deposited with others, exchanged, or lent to debtors with or without interest.

678-681. *Nidhi* is that which is hidden underground, *upanidhi* is that which is placed with others as deposit. That which is said to be *adhamarnika* which is given to others with or without an increase. Of these that with interest is called a loan or *Rina*, that without interest is called *yachita* or got by begging.

682. That which does away with proprietary rights is of two kinds, worldly and other worldly.

683-684. Aihika or worldly disbursement is divided into four classes -price or return of value, reward, salary and food (and other necessaries). Paralaukika or other worldly disbursements (is innumerable and) admits of infinite divisions.

686-688. *Paridana* is known to be that which is paid by way of price. *Paritosika* is that which is paid as reward for service, valour, etc. *Vetana* is that which is paid as salary or wages.

689-691. *Upabhogya* is said to be that which is paid for grains, clothing, houses, parks, cattle. Elephants, chariots, etc., acquisition of learning, kingdoms, wealth as well as for protection.

692-696. Houses are meant for gold, jewels, silver, coins, etc., musical instruments, arm and weapons, clothes, grains and other necessaries, ministers, arts, play, physician, cattle, cooking and birds. Expenditure on these items is called *bhogya*.

697. *Paralaukika* expenditure is of four classes -- that for penances, sacrifices, worship and charity.

699-701. Both income and expenditure are of two classes, avartaka and nivarti.

Chapter 2 673-684

Government Accounts - Expenditure

this is explained diagrammatically below[3]

674 - see verse 649 above.

678 - this is the inverse of 653-655 above. Rina - see notes on diagram below.

683. Aihika= literally, worldly.

Chapter 2 686-774

Accounts, Prices and Values

686. Paridana= restitution of debt, to give, or deposit depending on the context.

689. Upabhogya = serving for food, or causing enjoyment.

692. Bhogya = literally 'to be enjoyed, to be used (in the sense 'to be eaten').

699 avartaka = not abiding, existing, nivarti = causing to

702-703. The accountant or scribe who keeps accounts of income and expenditure should part with goods after writing and receive goods after writing in such a way as not to cause diminution or increase in amount.

704-706. Incomes and expenditures are of various kinds owing to the varieties of source, amount, relation, as well as measurement, number and weight.

707-708. For business purposes experts desire sometimes the number, sometimes the weight as methods of measurement.

709-710. A Mana is known to be the standard of the angula, Unmana is known to be the standard of the balance, Parimana is the standard of vessels. Samkhya is the standard of numerical notation one, two &c.

711. One should use these standards according to the needs of each case.

712-713. Dravya or goods is silver, gold, copper, coined for commercial purposes, cowries and gems for use.

714. *Dhana* or wealth is cattle, grains clothes and grass.

715-716. Gold which belongs to ownself acquires a value in commercial transactions and an object comes into existence on this earth through the concurrence of several causes.

717. The *Mulya* of a commodity is the price paid for acquiring it.

718-719. Prices of commodities are high or low according as they are attainable with or without ease and according as they do or do not possess attributes.

720-721. One should not fix a low price for gems and minerals. Their depreciation is due to wickedness of kings.......

741-746. Incomes should be written first, then the disbursements; or incomes towards the left and disbursements towards the right of the page.

747-773. *The lines omitted here were not included in the translation.*

774. Writing has been described in brief which is an aid to men's memory.

788-789. Time is divided according to three systems-solar movement, Lunar movement and according to Savana.

789-790. In making payments of wages one should always take the solar time, in augmenting interests one should take lunar time. And the Sāvana system should be followed in [giving] daily wages.

709. I.e. area, weight & volume respectively. Samkhya= to count.

713.Dravya= substance, thing, object; object of possession, wealth, goods or money.

714. Dhana = wealth ie excluding that which has had no work applied.

715. That is to say that until trade takes place the gold has no value.

717. Mulya = value.

718. Tf:- In determining the value or price of a commodity 2 points are to be noted:- ease or difficulty of attainment (cost of production determining supply); & its utility or power of satisfying wants etc, because of its properties - referring to the demand for it being determined by its uses. See Mencius 3, A, 4 (page 113).

720. Coinage is not to be debased.

Chapter 2 788-858
Wages

Savana - the three periods of the day (morning, noon and evening)

791-792. Remuneration can be paid according to time, work or according to both. It is to be paid therefore as arranged, *i.e.*, according to contract.

791. can be based on either time or effort, but in either case are a contract.

793-794. 'This weight is to be carried by you hither, and I shall give you so much for your work.' Remuneration calculated on this idea is according to work.

795-796. "Every year, month or day I shall pay you so much." Remuneration calculated on this idea is according to time.

797-798. 'So much work has been done by you in so much time I shall pay you therefore so much.' Remuneration thus calculated is according to both time and work.

Rates of Pay

799-802. One should neither stop nor postpone payment of salary. Moderate remuneration is said to be that which supplies the indispensable food and clothing. Good wages is that by which food and clothing are adequately supplied. Low wages is that by which only one can be maintained.

799. Note the harm that results if payments is delayed in the context of verse 809 below. See also Rama 1, 52 (page 147). NB moderate & good rates presumeably support a family.

802-804. According to the qualifications of the workers there should be rates of wages fixed by the king carefully for his own welfare.

805-806. Wages is to be so fixed that the worker may maintain those who are his compulsory charges.

805. Tf:- The equitable rate of wages is that which considers not simply the absolute necessaries of life but recognises the 'standard of life and comfort' as implied in implied in the care for family and dependants.

807-808. Those servants who get low wages are enemies by nature. They are auxiliaries to others and seekers of opportunities and plunderers of treasure and people.

809. Wages of *Sudras* is to be just enough for food and raiment.....

807. See also 2, 836 below & Mencius 3, A (page 111). The qualities of a good servant are detailed in 2, 118 onwards.

813-814. Servants are of three kinds - inactive, ordinary and quick. Their wages therefore have to be low ordinary, and high respectively.

809. Note, this implies that wages are not established by the market, & that the law of rent is not operational, at least for Sudras.

815-816. For discharge of their domestic duties servants should be granted leave for one yaama during the day and three yaamas by night. And the servant who has been appointed for a day should be allowed for half a yaama.

817-818. The king should make them work except on occasions of festivities, but in festivities also if the work be indispensable excepting in any case the days of Sraddha.

819-821. He should pay a quarter less than the usual remuneration to the diseased servant, pay three months' wages to the servant who has served for five years; six months' wages to the servant who has been long ill; but not more to anybody.

822-824. Even a slight portion should be deducted from the full

Chapter 2 819-835 Care of the Sick & Elderly

819. He being the king, this cost would be met from government revenues.

remuneration of a servant who has been ill for half a fortnight. And a substitute should be taken of one who has lived for even one year. And if the diseased be highly qualified he should have half the wages.

825. The king should give the servant fifteen days a year respite from work.

826-827. The king should grant half the wages without work to the man who has passed forty years in his service.

828-829 For life, and to the son if minor and incapable, half the wages or to the wife and well behaved daughters.

830-831. He should give the servant one eighth of the salary by way of reward every year, and if the work has been done with exceptional ability one eighth of the services rendered.

832-833. He should give the same salary to the son of the man who died for his work, so long as he is a minor, otherwise should pay the remuneration according to the offspring's qualifications.

834-835. He should keep with him (as deposit) one-sixth or one-fourth of the servant's wages, should pay half of that amount or the whole in two or three years.

836-837. The master by harsh words, low wages, severe punishments and insults brings out in the servant the attributes of the enemy.

Chapter 2 836-858 Management of Staff *See also MhB, Udyoga 133 (page 85), and 807 above.*

838-839. Those who are satisfied with wages and honoured by distinctions and pacified by soft words never desert their master.

840-841. The worst servants desire wealth, the medium want both wealth and fame, the best want fame. Reputation is the wealth of the great.

842-843. The king should satisfy both his servants and subjects according to their qualifications, some by spreading out branches, other by giving fruits.

844-845. He should satisfy the others by gentle looks and smiles, soft words, good feast and clothes, and betels and wealth;

846-848. Somebody by inquiries about health, etc., and the grant of privileges, bearers, ornaments and uniforms, umbrellas, chamar, &c.

849-852. By mercy, obeisance, respect, attendance, services, knowledge, love affection, association, offer of half one's seat or the full seat, praise or recital of the deeds done for the good of others.

853-855. He should mark those who have been his employees by the proper insignia of office placed on steel, copper, bronze, silver, gold and jewels.

856-857. For distinguishing from distance he should separate the officers by clothing, crowns, and musical instruments, &c.

858. The king should not give to anybody the uniform that is peculiarly his own.

1-2. Now this miscellaneous chapter I shall speak of the second section, *viz.*, that on Treasure. A collection of wealth by one person is called treasure.

3-4. The king should collect funds by hook or by crook and maintain thereby the commonwealth, the army as well as sacrifices.

5-6. The collection of treasure is for the maintenance of the army and the subjects and the performance of sacrifices. This leads to the king's happiness in this life and hereafter, otherwise to misery.

7-8 The collection that is made for wife and children as well as for self-enjoyments leads to hell and does not give happiness hereafter.

9. That which is earned wrongfully is the cause of sin.

10. That wealth increases which is taken from, or given to, good persons.

11. The good or deserving person is he who earns well and spends well. And the undeserving person is he who is the opposite.

12. The king who takes away all the wealth of the undeserving person is not a sinner.

13-14. One should take away by craft or force or by robbery, wealth of the king who is addicted to immoral ways of life -- and also from other kingdoms.

15-16. His kingdom is destroyed by enemies who has amassed wealth by forsaking morality and by oppressing his own people.

17-18. In normal times the king should not increase his treasure by augmenting the punishments, land revenues and duties, and by taking dues from holy places and properties consecrated to divine purposes.

19-20. When the king is preparing to maintain an army to destroy the enemy, he should receive from the people special grants of fines, duties &c.

Chapter 4 Section 2, 1 (Treasure)

3. See also MhB, Santi 130 (page 98).

5. See also MhB, Santi 133 (page 99), Mencius 1, B, 5 (page 110) & Plato, Republic 543a (page 131) for different aspects of this.

7. See 1, 375 above.

15. See also Plato, Republic 550d (page 132) & Confucius, Great Learning 10 (page 48).

17. Note that churches are not taxed.

19. See also MhB, Santi 130 (page 98).

21-22. The king should receive the wealth of the rich men in times of danger by supplying them wherewith to live. But when he is free from danger he should return the amount to them together with interest.

21. Swriddhikam = loans are prescribed from the rich person in difficult times. They should be repaid as soon as the danger is over together with interest.

23. Otherwise the subjects, state, treasure and the king -- all are ruined.

24. Kings like Suratha were reduced through severity of punishment inflicted by them.

25-27. The treasure should be so governed that it may maintain the subjects, and that the army may be maintained for twenty years without fines, land revenues and duties.

25. See also Mencius 1, B, 5 (page 110).

28-29. The treasure is the root of the army, and the army is the root of the treasure. It is by maintaining the army that the treasure and the kingdom prosper and the enemy is destroyed.

28. See also MhB, Santi 133 (page 99).

30. And by protecting the subjects, all these three results accrue as well as the acquisitions of heaven.

31-32. Goods are produced for sacrifice, sacrifices lead to happiness, heaven and long life. Absences of enemies, army and treasure -- these three lead to prosperity of the state.

31. See MhB, Santi 20 (page 88).

33--34. The state also prospers through the mercifulness of the king and his virtue and intelligence. So one should strive.

35-38. The best king is he who, by following the practice of the weaver of garments, protects his subjects, makes the enemies tributaries and increases the treasure by their wealth. The middling king is he who does this by following the practice of the Vaisya. And the worst by service and the receipts from fines, holy places and lands consecrated to gods.

35. Vaisya ie engaging in trade & rearing cattle.

39-40. Subjects whose wealth is little should be maintained, and officers whose wealth is moderate. Also officers whose wealth is considerable.

41. But the rich men whose wealth is excessive, and those who are richer than the king but of low character are not to be maintained.

41. See also Mencius 1, B, 5 (page 110).

42-44. That wealth is said to be low which is sufficient for twelve years. That is said to be madhyama or middling which is enough for sixteen years. And good wealth is that which is sufficient for thirty years.

42. Madhyama= middle in place, position.

45. The king should deposit this wealth with the rich persons in order in times of danger.

46-48. Merchants trade with their capital, not with interest. They sell when prices are high and store by when prices are low.

46. Note that contributes toward the stability of prices.

178

49. Otherwise the discontent of his own subjects destroys the king with his whole family.

50-57. *This section deals with the storage of grains and food supplies*

58-59. And the king should carefully replace every year by new installments the exact amounts of those consumed.

60-63. The accumulation of all these things that are useful and instrumental for the purposes of man, *e.g.,* medicinal plants, minerals, grasses, woods, implements, arms, weapons, gunpowder, vessels and cloths, etc., should also be made -- This is likely to be efficacious.

64-65. The king should also carefully preserve the wealth that has been collected. There is great trouble in earning, four fold difficulty in maintenance (of wealth).

64. See also MhB, Santi 133 (page 99) & Vana 32 (page 78).

66. That which has been disregarded for a moment is soon destroyed.

67-68. It is the earner who gets pain when the accumulated wealth has been destroyed. Even wife and children do not feel that, how could others?

69-70. If one is negligent in his own duties, will not others be so? But if one is mindful of his own business other will become his assistants as well as equals.

71-72. There is no greater fool than the man who knows how to earn but not how to maintain what has been earned. Vain is his exertion in earning.

73-76. The following men are also fools:-

The man who has two living wives, who trusts people over much, who hopes for great wealth, the idler, the man overpowered by women, and one who calls upon thieves, paramours and enemies as witnesses.

77-78. One should keep his wealth like a miser and give away at times, as it were, unconcerned; otherwise he displays his foolishness even in the matter of spending his own wealth.

79-80. One should always try to understand the real nature of goods. And the king should keep the jewels after having them tested by experts as well as by himself.

79. The modern expression of this is perhaps 'let the buyer beware'.

81-162....*These verses relates to qualities. categories and measures of gems.*

163. Excepting diamonds the value of small gems has to be determined by number (not weight).

Chapter 4 Section 2 163-211 Price and Value

164. But that of very fine and rare ones is to be determined by

164. The Sanskrit term used is

179

fancy (demand).

165. So also the sale price of very fine things has not to be determined by weight.....

171-172. There are natural defects in gems, but metals have artificial defects. So the wise man should determine their value by carefully examining them.

173-179 *The omitted text discusses the merits of different metals and how to test their purity.*

180. Iron in the form of tools, implements and weapons is very valuable.

181-206.... *The omitted text deals with prices & values of domestic animals...*

207. Those which are rare in this world are priced as gems.

208. One should fix the price according to Time and Space.

209. There is no price for worthless things that cannot be used for any purposes.

210-211. There are high price, low price and middling price in the valuation of all things. This is to be always considered by wise people.

212. *Sulka* or duty is the king's share received from the buyer and the seller.

213. The regions of *Sulka* or Duty are the market places, street and mines.

214. Duties are to be levied on goods only once.

215. The duty should not be realised more than once by the king through craft.

216. The king should receive the thirty-second portion from the seller or buyer.

217. The twentieth or sixteenth part, as the duty, is not a draw back upon the price.

218. The king should not realise duty from the seller when he receives what is less than or just equal to the cost.

219. He should receive it from the buyer after seeing that he is a gainer.

220-221. Having ascertained the amount of produce from measured plots of land, whether great, middling or small, the king should desire revenue and then apportion it among them.

222-223. The king should receive rent from the peasant in such a way that he be not destroyed. It is to be realised in the fashion of the weaver of the garland not of the coal merchant.

224-226. That agriculture is successful which yields a profit

kāma which translates loosely as desire or passion.

171. Prices are not always the same, see also Mencius 3, A (cont) (page 115).

Chapter 4 Section 2 212-260[4]

Amounts and Source of Government Revenue

Sulka = toll, tax, duty, customs (especially levied at ferries, passes and roads).

217. i.e. this will not affect demand & presumes that margins are such that it will not effect the sale price.

218. NB. fair taxation

220. Taxation rates are set by the king.

222. Tf:- The coal merchant sets fire to the woods to make charcoal and thus destroys the whole property, but the weaver of garlands plucks from the

twice the expenditure (including Government demand) after duly considering the variations in actual produce, *e.g.*, great, middling or small. Any thing less than that is unsatisfactory.

227-229. The king should realise one-third, one-fourth, or one-half from places which are irrigated by tanks, canals and wells, by rains and rivers, respectively.

230. He should have one sixth from barren and rocky soils.

231-232. If the king gets one hundred silver *karshas* from the cultivator he should give back to him twenty *karshas*.

233-235. The king should realise from the peasants, &c., after noticing the amount of profits.

237-238. He should realise one-third, one-fifth, one-seventh, one-tenth, or one twentieth from the collectors of grasses and woods &c.

239-240. He should have one eighth of the increase of goats, sheep, cows buffaloes, and horses, and one sixteenth of the milk of she buffaloes, she goats and female sheep.

241. The king should make the artists and artisans work one day in the fortnight.

242-244. If the people undertake new industries or cultivate new lands and dig tanks, canals, wells, &c., for their good, the king should not demand any thing of them until they realise profit twice the expenditure.

245-246. The king should promptly realise the land revenues, wages, duties, interests, bribes, and rents without any delay.

247. The king should give to each cultivator the deed of rent having his own mark (seal).

248-250. Having determined the land revenue of the village the king should receive it from one rich man in advance, or guarantee [for the payment] of that either by monthly or periodic installments.

251-252. Or the king should appoint officers called *gramapas* by paying one-sixteenth, one-twelfth, one-eighth or one-sixth of his own receipts.

253-254. The king should receive milk of cows, &c., rice, for the kith and kin but should not receive paddy and clothes from buyers for his own enjoyment.

255. The king should realise one thirty-second portion of the interest of the usurer.

256. He should receive rents from houses and abodes as from cultivated lands.

257. He should also have land tax from shopkeepers.

trees only those flowers that are in full bloom and preserves the rest as well as the trees for future use.

227. The gods, or natural agencies, and rivers are called the mothers of the lands. Areas fed by rivers are called the daughters or gifts of rivers. The variety of rates relates to the relative certainty or uncertainty of moisture from these different sources. See also verse 242 below.

230. See Shu King 3, 1, 2 for historical example of soil classification to affect tax rate (page 155).

241. See also L of M 7, 137 (page 69) & MhB, Santi 87 (page 93).

242. This shows how development of marginal land and new enterprises are to be encouraged. See also L of M 8, 248 (page 71), MhB, Anusasana 48 (page 105) & Shu King 3, 1 (page 155).

247. The formalisation of the gift of land.

251. Gramapas, from grama =village.

255. The Sanskrit word translated as usurer is 'vadhuśika', literally, one who lives by increase.

257. Land for houses & building is to be taxed at the same rate as that for cultivation.

258. For the preservation and repair of streets he should have dues from those who use the streets.

259. The king should thus enjoy fruits everywhere but should protect all like a servant.

260. Thus has been described in brief the section on treasure.

Land for stalls should be taxed. The sellers have to pay duties not only for the commodities sold but also for the use of the land. See also Mencius 2, A (page 111).

581-582. A man is not the owner of the property because it is held by him. Is it not found in the case of thieves that somebody's property is being held by somebody else?

583. Hence ownership is being admitted only if the Sastra sanction, it is not brought about by mere enjoyment.

584. Otherwise one should not say that so and so's wealth has been stolen by so and so.

585-6. In the Sastra sources of income as well as the castes are known to be various and that *Dharma* of the Sastras always binds even *Mlechchas.*

587. For the preservation of the community these have been fixed by previous sages.

588. Sons and wives are to be made equal sharers.

589. The daughter is to have half of the son's share, the daughter's son half of that.

590. Even if the father be dead, the sons, &c., are to receive their share according to the above proportion.

591-592. The son should give one-fourth to the mother, one-half of that to the sister, one half of that to the sisters son, and himself the remainder.

593-594. The son, the grandson , the wife, the daughter, the daughter's son, the mother, the father, the brother and the brother's son - these are to receive the wealth (in the order stated) each in the case of failure of the predecessor (in the list).

595. Absolute right is given to women in the matter of wealth that is called women's wealth as regards sale, and gift, even in immoveables.

597-598. The Saudâyika wealth is known to be that which comes to a married woman through gifts and dowries from parents' or husband's families or through presents by parents and relatives.

599-600. The man who earns anything without the help of ancestral wealth can enjoy that at his own will. This is indivisible.

601-602. Anybody who can save somebody's wealth from

Chapter 4 Section 5, 581-621

Property

583. See also Cicero, Offices 1, 7 (page 41). Sastra -scriptures.

585. Sastra= sacred legal texts, Dharma = Law or Virtue, Mlechchas = barbarians, foreigners.

597. Saudayika= that which is given to a woman at her marriage by a father or brother and always remains her property.

absolute destruction owing to ravages of deluge, thieves, kings and fire has the right to one tenth.

603-604. The goldsmith should get remuneration according to the labour undergone by each in cases where they combine to perform a work of art.... *omitted verses here deal with specific remuneration for specific peoples. This does not appear to be useful.....*

614-615. Those who deal in gold, grains, and liquids (collectively) will have earnings according to the amount of their share, greater, equal or less.

616-617. Whatever portion is stipulated indeed (beforehand), equal less or more, that (shall be accepted) exactly so. Expenditure he shall pay and do work (proportionately) and take profit too (in the same manner).

618. The same principle (of joint stock enterprises) applies to merchants as well as peasants.

619-621.The common property, the wealth that has been realised by begging, security, mortgage, slaves, the property of slaves, *amwâhita* (deposits) and the wealth if there be children - these nine are not to be made over to others by the wise even in times of danger.

628-629. A merchant should fix 1/32nd or 1/16th part as the profit in a business with due regard to the expenditure and to the conditions of the place and not more.

Chapter 4 Section 5, 628-634
Profit and Interest

630. (One might advance money to one who intends to be a merchant) and not demanding the interest, he should make him carry on the trade with half the profits always.

631-632. When (the amount) drawn from the debtor (in the form of) interest has reached twice the principle then the king shall make (the debtor) pay only the principal to the creditor and nothing more than that.

631. Note the limits imposed in other legal codes (eg Hammurabi's Code) to limit the potential damage arising from this.

633-634. Credit takes away people's wealth by compound rate of interest. So the king should protect the people from them.

642. The king should give wages to artists after noticing their works and qualifications.

Chapter 4 Section 5, 642-644 Artists Supported and Mining taxed.

643- 644. The king should daily receive (as duty) from the sales of silver one fifth, one-fourth, one third or half - not more.

Supplementary Notes

1.Dictionary translations of other Sanskrit terms used here are as follows:-

Adhamarnika - अधमर्निक one reduced to inferiority by debt.

Bhoga - भोग enjoyment; including (depending on context), eating, use, fruitition or use of a deposit, experiencing, possession, property revenue or wealth, wages.

Itara - इतर different from, the other, another, or contrary. In the context here (taxation and the kings income) it is other than Pārthiva income (that is from or associated with land). See for example notes on Sukra Niti (page 184).

Nidhi - निधिनि to put or lay down, deposit, lay up, preserve; to intrust; committ, present to; put into ~ to keep in mind, bear in mind, remember.

Paraloka - परलोक other or future world.

Paridana - परिदान restitution of a debt (परिदा) to give, grant, bestow, surrender, intrust to or deposit with, cause to be delivered to or given up.

Paritosika - परितोशिक satisfied, gratified, delighted.

Pārthiva - पार्थिव being in, relating to or coming from the earth. (Terrestrial - coming from rights of sovereignty over lands rivers, seas, lakes, tanks, wells, &c). Used here relating to income, or taxation. See also 'itara' for other income.

Rina - ऋण going, flying, fugitive (as a thief) having gone against, transgressed, guilty, anything wanted or missed, anything due, obligation, duty debt, a debt of money owed.

Sahajika - सहजिक original, natural, born or produced together.

Swaswatwa - स्वस्वत्व from स्व ones own, and स्वत्व property.

Upanidhi - उपनिधा to put or place down near to, conceal; to deposit, intrust; to bring near, near to; to produce, cause.

Ventena - वैतनिक living on wages, serving for wages; a hireling, labourer.

Yachita - यद्धि asked, begged (borrowed); solicited or asked for, entreated, importuned; asked in marriage, required, requisite, necessary; alms obtained by begging.

2.The following diagram show the arrangement of income.

Two divisions are admitted. Avartaka and Nivarti, applying to both income and expenditure. These translate as 'not abiding' and 'causing to return' successively. This implies a distinction between a single payment and a continual payment (and or receipt).

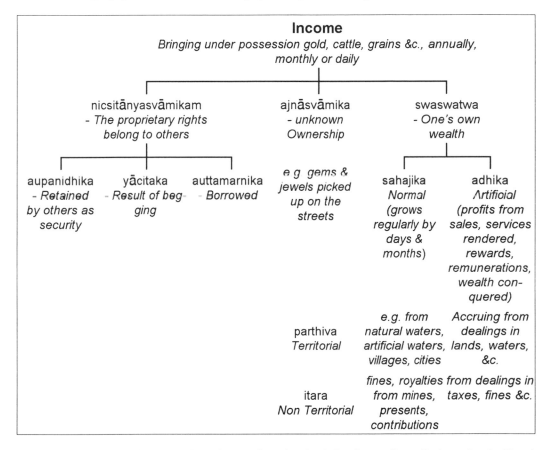

Other lists of sources of revenue include, rent from lands, duties/taxes, fines, that received without cultivation (natures contribution), Income from forests, mineral wealth, deposits, unowned & got back from thieves.

3. The following diagram show the arrangement of expenditure.

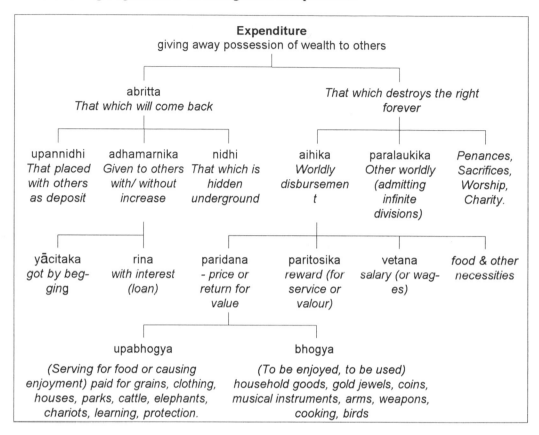

Expenditure
giving away possession of wealth to others

abritta
That which will come back

That which destroys the right forever

upannidhi	adhamarnika	nidhi	aihika	paralaukika	Penances,
That placed with others as deposit	*Given to others with/ without increase*	*That which is hidden underground*	*Worldly disbursement*	*Other worldly (admitting infinite divisions)*	*Sacrifices, Worship, Charity.*

yācitaka	rina	paridana	paritosika	vetana	food & other
got by begging	*with interest (loan)*	*- price or return for value*	*reward (for service or valour)*	*salary (or wages)*	*necessities*

upabhogya

bhogya

(Serving for food or causing enjoyment) paid for grains, clothing, houses, parks, cattle, elephants, chariots, learning, protection.

(To be enjoyed, to be used) household goods, gold jewels, coins, musical instruments, arms, weapons, cooking, birds

4.*Sukra Niti 4, 2 212-260 - The essence of the passage is as follows:- Sulka is the King's share of the increase in value as the result of trade (212/213). Land tax should be charged based on the amount of land held (220,221) and the productivity of the land (In this case based on the water source (227/230). The King should also have 'rents' from houses, and land tax from shop keepers (ie whether ever exclusive title is required). Some portion should be taken by the king from the profits arising from grazing and foraging (presumably on public land) (233/240). Artists & Artisans should work for the king, one day per fortnight (241). Some mitigating factors are also included; Sulka, should only be taken once, from the seller, but only if he profits. It may be taken from the buyer if it is not taken from the seller, if the buyer is seen to gain (214, 215, 218, 219, 256, 257). A tax rate of 5 or 6% is not perceived as an interference in the outcome of trade (217), not withstanding this, a tax of 3% is recommended (216). Usury also should be taxed at 3% (255). If people start new businesses, etc, revenue should not be demanded until the business has received twice the expenditure (242/244). The rate of tax should not harm the user of the land (222/223), The determining factor being that net of tax the surplus should be at least twice the cost (233/235).*

Yajnavalkya Smriti

6. When a gift is made, in due season, place and manner, in good faith and to a fit person - all this gives the idea of Law. *Alternate translation:- Whatever thing is fully given in (proper) country, at (proper) time, with (proper) means, accompanied by faith, to (proper) person, that is the cause of Dharma.*

Chapter 1, 6
Gift is the source of the Law

37. Where there is a pledge, the interest, month by month, shall be an eightieth part; otherwise, two, three, four or five parts, in a hundred, according to the order of cast.

38. They however who travel in forests give ten parts; they who go to sea, twenty parts, in a hundred. Or all must render to all, of whatever cast, the rate of interest settled amongst themselves.

39. But for cattle and women lent [the return] is, their off-spring;.....

Chapter 2, 37 - 39 Interest
Expanded in L of M 8, 140 (page 70)
37. The most reputable thus paying the least rate of interest.
38. In the first case where there is risk to property, and in the last case where nothing is expressly stipulated.
39. See L of M 9, 48 for expansion of this (page 72).

40. The monarch should not blame one who enforces a recognised debt. If he, against whom the debt is enforced, complain to the monarch, he may be punished, besides being compelled to pay the debt.

41. The debtor [as a general rule] shall be made to pay his creditors in the order in which he received them; but a *brahman* he is to pay [first], and, after him, the monarch.

42. The debtor shall be made to pay to the monarch ten parts in a hundred of the sum proved against him; and the creditor, when he has recovered his property, five parts.

43. One of inferior cast, who is without means, may be compelled to labour in discharge of his debt; but a *brahman*, wanting means [to discharge his debt at once], shall pay gradually in proportion to what may come to him......

Chapter 2, 40 - 6 Recovery of debts
40. Manu provides 5 means for recovering debts, persuasion, law-suits, artifice, harassment and by force (refer L of M 8, 49).

43. See Leviticus 25, 8 (page 14) for protection of those so encumbered.
The text goes on to list rights and duties in special cases.

90. Payment of a debt incurred upon a writing is obligatory only on the debtor, his son, and grandson; but a pledge shall remain in use so long as the debt is unpaid.

Chapter 2, 90 Does this imply a form of money arising from exchange of pledges?

150. When there is a dispute as to boundaries, the neighbours of the [disputed] land, old men and the like, cowherds, cultivators of the soil close to the [disputed] boundary, and all whose business is in forests -

151. These shall determine the boundaries, as they are indicated by elevated ground, by charcoal [-remnants], by husks, by trees, by causeway, by ant-hills, by depressions of the soil, by bones, by memorials, and such like.

152. Otherwise, four, eight or ten neighbours of the same village, wearing red wreath and red garments, and carrying earth, shall settle the boundary.

153. ...In the absence of any persons having knowledge of the matter, and of any indicatory signs, the monarch shall mark the boundary.

154. The same rule applies to fruit-gardens, to outhouses, to villages, to wells or tanks, to pleasure-gardens, to dwellings, as well as to watercourses caused by rain.

Chapter 2, 150 - 154
Boundaries
See also L of M 8, 254 (page 71).

166. Pasture-ground shall be allotted for cattle, such as the villagers agree upon, or in proportion to the whole area of land, or as the monarch wills.
*A twice-born man may, in every place, appropriate as his own, grass, fuel, and flowers.
167. There shall be a space of one hundred *dhanus* between a *grama* and the [surrounding] fields, of two hundred for a *karvata*, of four hundred for a *nagara*.

Chapter 2, 166 - 167 Common Land *See L of M 8, 237 (page 71).*
166. Common ground is provided around each village. Manu says this is for sacrifice & commentators associate this right with common land only Refer L of M 8, 339.
167. ie a distance of 100 bow lengths around a village, 200 for a larger centre & 400 for a town.

195. A master may treat as he thinks right one who disregards time or place, or [so acts that he] prevents profit being earned. The more that is done, the more shall be given.

Chapter 2, 195 - 158
Unworthy service

244. He who, in measurement, or [use of] the scales, defrauds [to the extent] of an eight, shall be made to pay a fine of two hundred *papas*, and thus proportionably for a more or less quantity.

245. He who adulterates medicine, or oily commodities, or salt, or perfumes, or corn, or sugar, or other saleable articles, shall

Chapter 2, 244
Measures to Mitigate dishonest trade.

be fined sixteen *paṇas*.

246. For making one sort of article to appear to be another sort, whether it be earthen goods, or skins, or precious stones, or threads, or corn, or wood, or bark of trees, or clothes, a fine [is ordained of] eightfold the purchase money.

247. For him who changes a covered basket, or gives in pledge or sells counterfeit drugs in a wrapper, the fines prescribed are,....

247. Tf e.g. substituting a basket of crystals for one of jewels.

249. The highest fine is imposed on those who, [although] aware of the rise or fall in prices, combine, to the prejudice of labourers and artists, to create a price [of their own].

250. The traders who combine, by [arbitrarily fixing] an improper price, to impede [the traffic in] any commodity, or to make [an injurious] sale of it, the highest fine is ordained.

250. Tf - i.e. combining to buy up at a low rate foreign goods, or to resell them at a dear rate.

251. The price in [transactions of] sale and purchase, daily, is regulated by the monarch; the difference is declared to be the traders' profit.

252. On goods of his own country let a trader clear a profit of five percent, and ten per cent on those of another country; provided he make prompt sale of his purchase.

253. [The monarch] is to determine the price in unison with the wishes of both purchaser and seller; first adding to the cost of the article the expense of bringing it to the market.

Zarathushtra

Zend Avesta, Fargard 3.

In Praise of the Earth

1. O Maker of the material world, thou Holy one! Which is the first place where the Earth feels most happy? Ahura Mazda answered: 'It is the place whereon one of the faithful steps forward, O Spitama Zarathushtra! with the log in his hand, the Baresma in his hand, the milk in his hand, the mortar in his hand, lifting up his voice in good accord with religion, and beseeching Mithra, the lord of the rolling country-side, and Rama Hvastra.'

2,3. O Maker of the material world, thou Holy one! Which is the second place where the Earth feels most happy? Ahura Mazda answered: 'It is the place whereon one of the faithful erects a house with a priest within, with cattle, with a wife, with children, and good herds within; and wherein afterwards the cattle continue to thrive, virtue to thrive, fodder to thrive, the dog to thrive, the wife to thrive, the child to thrive, the fire to thrive, and every blessing of life to thrive.'

4. O Maker of the material world, thou Holy one! Which is the third place where the Earth feels most happy? Ahura Mazda answered: 'It is the place where one of the faithful sows most corn, grass, and fruit, O Spitama Zarathushtra! where he waters ground that is dry, or drains ground that is too wet.'

5. O Maker of the material world, thou Holy one! Which is the fourth place where the Earth feels most happy? Ahura Mazda answered: 'It is the place where there is most increase of flocks and herds.'

6. O Maker of the material world, thou Holy one! Which is the fifth place where the Earth feels most happy? Ahura Mazda answered: 'It is the place where flocks and herds yield most dung.' ...

23. O Maker of the material world, thou Holy one! Who is the fourth that rejoices the Earth with greatest joy? Ahura Mazda answered: 'It is he who sows most corn, grass, and fruit, O Spitama Zarathushtra! who waters ground that is dry, or drains ground that is too wet.

24. 'Unhappy is the land that has long lain unsown with the seed of the sower and wants a good husbandman, like a well-shapen maiden who has long gone childless and wants a good husband.

The import of this text is twofold:-

first, that the deity is most pleased when the earth is being used fruitfully, and hence fulfils its function in the creation. The same conception is expressed in Genesis 1, 28 (see page 5); and second that men have a duty to work and care for the earth. By implication then, there is a duty to make sure the earth is available.

6. The omitted text describes the places that the earth is least happy, these are mostly where the earth has been defiled.

25. 'He who would till the earth, O Spitama Zarathushtra! with the left arm and the right, with the right arm and the left, unto him will she bring forth plenty of fruit: even as it were a lover sleeping with his bride on her bed; the bride will bring forth children, (the earth will bring forth) plenty of fruit.

26,27. 'He who would till the earth, O Spitama Zarathushtra! with the left arm and the right, with the right arm and the left, unto him thus says the Earth: "O thou man! who dost till me with the left arm and the right, with the right arm and the left, here shall I ever go on bearing, bringing forth all manner of food, bringing corn first to thee. When something good grows up, it will grow up for thee first'.

28,29. 'He who does not till the earth, O Spitama Zarathushtra! with the left arm and the right, with the right arm and the left, unto him thus says the Earth: "O thou man! who dost not till me with the left arm and the right, with the right arm and the left, ever shalt thou stand at the door of the stranger, among those who beg for bread; the refuse and the crumbs of the bread are brought unto thee, brought by those who have profusion of wealth."'

30. O Maker of the material world, thou Holy one! What is the food that fills the Religion of Mazda [lit: what is the stomach of the law?]? Ahura Mazda answered: 'It is sowing corn again and again, O Spitama Zarathushtra!

31. 'He who sows corn, sows righteousness: he makes the Religion of Mazda walk, he suckles the Religion of Mazda; as well as he could do with a hundred man's feet, with a thousand woman's breasts, with ten thousand sacrificial formulas...

34. O Maker of the material world, thou Holy one! Who is the fifth that rejoices the Earth with greatest joy? Ahura Mazda answered: 'It is he who kindly and piously gives to one of the faithful who tills the earth, O Spitama Zarathushtra! ...

Iva. 47. Verily I say it unto thee, O Spitama Zarathushtra! the man who has a wife is far above him who lives in continence; he who keeps a house is far above him who has none; he who has children is far above the childless man; he who has riches is far above him who has none.

Lexicon of Non English Terms

The following, non English terms from the texts are included where fuller explanation may be beneficial.

Aditi - Sanskrit - 'अदिति' Translated as infinity, unbounded, unbroken, but as a goddess, the source of creative power and space.

Agni - Sanskrit- 'अग्नि' fire, or the god of fire, depending on the context in which it is used.

Brahmaṇa - Sanskrit - 'ब्रह्मण' priest, holy man or sage. The highest of the four orders of Society 'varnas' described in the Vedic scriptures.

Canaan - Hebrew - The name of a region but originally - merchant, traffic, traffickers. Its use in the old testament is largely associated with improper trading. From a root word which implies 'to humble', or 'to be brought into subjection'.

Chaldees - Hebrew - Chaldea or Chaldeans = "clod-breakers". The people who occupied the lower Tigris & Euphrates valley. Often implying the 'wisest people'.

Dāna - Sanskrit - 'ठन' the act of giving; giving in marriage; giving up; communicating, imparting, teaching; paying back, restoring; donation, gift; oblation; liberality; bribery. From the root दा - to give, bestow, grant, yield, impart, present, offer to; to give (a daughter) in marriage; to give back; to give up or cede; to sell (with instruction on price); to sacrifice one's self; to offer an oblation; to communicate teach, utter (blessings), give (answer), speak (the truth), address a speach to; to permit, allow; to permit sexual intercourse; to place put or apply.

Daṇdanīti - Sanskrit - 'दण्डनीति' from 'दण्ड' a stick or staff, and 'नीति' science, hence the science of the application of the rod, or the science of chastisement. The principle science related to government, giving guiding principles to the people and establishing restraint of behaviour.

Dharma - Sanskrit - 'धर्म' that which is established or firm, steadfast decree, statute, ordinance, law; usage, practice, customary observance or prescribed conduct, duty, right, justice; virtue, morality, religion, religious merit. One of the three objects of human pursuit (the others being Artha and Kāma). Commonly translated as either, Law, Virtue or Religion

Dravya - Sanskrit - 'द्रव्य' a substance, thing or object; an object of possession, wealth goods, money etc.

Dwāparayuga - - Sanskrit- 'द्वापरयुग' the third age or yuga, also referred to as the bronze age. See Rāmayaṇa for description of the prosperity of the Dwāpara age (page 143). See Yuga below.

Egypt - Greek - the Hebrew original carries the meaning of 'limitation' associated in some derivations with 'fortress' and in others with 'misery'.

Hebron - Hebrew - "association" Sometimes translated as unity.

Hivites - Hebrew = "villagers"

Indra - Sanskrit - 'इन्द्र' (From the root 'इन्द्' - to be powerful; to see). The king of the gods (superseding Varuna). God of the atmosphere and sky; the akin to the roman Jupiter Pluvius or lord of rain (who rules over other deities of the intermediate region); he is the general

193

symbol of generous heroism; - not originally lord of the gods, but his deeds were most useful to mankind. In the Vedānta he is identified with the supreme being; a prince; Called also Sahasraksa 'thousand eyes' - who can see the whole universe at one glance.

Psychologically associated with the mind as ruler of the five senses (hearing, seeing, touching, tasting & smelling) and hence indirectly ruler of the five constituent elements of the manifest world (space, fire, air, water & earth).

Īsana - Sanskrit - 'ईशन' Within these texts, the sun as a form of Śiva, the word is also used in other contexts to mean 'owning, possessing, reigning, wealthy, a ruler, a master'.

Jnāna - Sanskrit - 'ज्ञान' Knowing, becoming acquainted with, knowledge, (esp) higher knowledge (derived from meditation on the one Universal Spirit); conscience.

Kaliyuga - Sanskrit- 'कलियुग' The Kali age or dark age (see Yugas). This age is said to have begun with the ascent of the Lord Sri Kṛṣṇa traditionally held to have been 17 February 3102 B.C. The age is said to run for 432,000 years. It is the last of the four Yugas, and the one in which virtue is least practised and the condition of man and the earth is least attractive. The extract from the Srimad (see page 164) is part of a much larger description. Refer also to Plato, Cratylus 398A.

Kāma - Sanskrit- 'काम' wish, desire, longing, love, affection, object of desire; pleasure, enjoyment; love especially sexual love. One of the three objects of human pursuit (see Purushārtha).

Karsha - Sanskrit - 'कर्ष' a measure of silver or gold, approximately 280 grains troy.

Kṛta yuga - Sanskrit - 'कृतयुग' the first age or yuga, sometime refered to as the 'Sat Yuga' and the equivalent of the Golden Age in the Western Tradition. See Yuga below.

Kshatriya - Sanskrit - 'क्षत्रिय' The second of the four orders of Vedic society (varnas) comprising kings and soldiers; literally, governing, endowed with sovereignty.

Kubera (sometimes Kuvera) - Sanskrit- 'कुबेर' the god of wealth, guardian of the north, commander of Yakshas (minor gods representing the force of nature like fauns satyrs and imps of the Greek pantheon) and Guhyakas (a race of cavemen noted as Kubera's treasure keepers). Kubera is half brother of Ravaṇa (the demon king of Lanka and principle opponent of Rama from the Ramayana story).

Mleccha - Sanskrit - 'म्लेच्छ' literally to speak indistinctly, but implying not speaking Sanskrit, and hence a foreigner and barbarian. One who does not conform to the sacred Vedantic tradition.

Mūlya - Sanskrit - 'मूल्य' being at the root; to be bought for a sum of money, purchasable, original value, value, price, worth, a sum of money given as payment; wages salary, payment for service rendered.

Prajāpati - Sanskrit - 'प्रजापति' literally the 'Lord of all creatures', the divinity presiding over procreation, but associated with other gods in this capacity, especially Brahma.

Purushārthā - Sanskrit - 'पुरुषार्था' any object of human pursuit; any of the four object or aims of existence (viz. *Kāma*, the gratification of desire; *artha*, acquirement of wealth; *dharma*; discharge of duty; *moksha*, final emancipation)....... intent on the 3 objects of man (*Kāma*, *artha*, and *dharma)*;

Rākṣasa - Sanskrit - 'राक्षस' A demon, or evil spirit. The king of these demons is Ravana whose brother is Kubera the god of wealth. The demons are also the servants of Kubera.

Rudra - Sanskrit - 'रुद्र' literally - crying howling roaring, dreadful etc. The god of storms and tempests, which can also include fevers and sickness affecting the body, and also the god who overcomes these. Rudra is sometimes associated with or another name for Siva.

Satyayuga - Sanskrit- 'सत्ययुग' First great age or yuga (see yuga). From Sat, (the verb to be) being.

Śāstra - Sanskrit - 'शास्त्र' Technically an invocation or praise sung from sacred hymns, but more generally in these works refering to accepted scriptures.

Śraddhas - Sanskrit - 'श्रद्धास्' Acts of faith, trust or devotion.

Śruti - Sanskrit - 'श्रुति' The most authoritive scriptures.

Śūdra - Sanskrit - 'शूद्र' the fourth order of Vedic society comprised of labourers and servants.

Śulka - Sanskrit - 'शुल्क' Variously, price, value; the prize in a contest; toll, taxes, duty customs (especially levied at ferries passes and roads). A variation of Sulk (to gain, to acquire; to leave or forsake), from the root 'Shubh' to beautify, adorn, embellish, to shine.

Tapas - Sanskrit - 'तपस्' warmth, heat; the 5 fires to which the devotee exposes himself during the hot season (viz 4 fires lighted in the 4 quarters and the sun; pain, suffering; religious austerity, bodily mortification, penance, severe meditation, special observance (ie 'sacred learning with Brahmanas, 'protection of subjects' with Kshatriyas, 'giving of alms to Brahmanas' with Vaiśyas, 'service' with Śūdras, and 'feeding upon herbs and roots' with Ṛishis). From the root 'Tap', to give out heat, to be hot, to shine; to make hot or warm; to consume by heat; to suffer pain, to torment one's self, undergo self-mortification, practise austerity; to cause pain; to be purified by aus-

terities...

Tretayuga - Sanskrit- 'त्रेतयुग' the second great age (see yuga). Implication being that this was the age when the three great forces came into operation in human affairs (the gunas) leading men to have 3 objects in life, the pursuit of Virtue (dharma), the pursuit of Wealth (artha) and, or the pursuit of Pleasure (kama).

Unmana - Sanskrit - 'उन्मन' A gem lying on the surface of the earth.

Vaiśravaṇa - Sanskrit - 'वैश्रवण' another name for the god of wealth, Kubera derived from his brother Ravana (the king of the demons - rakshasas).

Vaisya - Sanskrit - 'वैस्य' the 3rd order of society composing merchants and farmers.

Varṇa - Sanskrit - 'वर्ण' The four Orders of Vedic Society composing Brahmaṇa (sages), Kśatriyas (warriors and kings), Vaiśya (merchants and traders) and śūdras (labourers and servants). Literally a covering cloak or mantle. See Śrimad 7, 11 (page 162). The spiritual origin, function and authority are dealt with in the Bṛihadaraṇyaka Upaniṣad, 1, 4, 11-16, especially in Śankara's Commentary.

Varta - Sanskrit - 'वर्त' The science of wealth, 'in which are treated, interest, agriculture, commerce & and the preservation of cows' (Sukra Niti 1, 311). The term is also translated as 'subsistence' or 'livelihood' and occasionally as 'economics', but this is clearly a limited aspect of the contemporary term. No treatise on this subject has been found.

Varuṇa - Sanskrit - 'वरुण' All enveloping sky; name of a son of Aditi (infinity) and presiding over the night as Mitra over the day; often styled as the supreme deity, being then styled 'king of the gods' or 'king of both gods and men' or 'king of the universe' (equated with the Greek Ouranus, Uranus). From the root वृ

meaning to cover screed vield conceal, hide surround and obstruct. No other deity has such grand attributes and functions assigned to him; he is described as fashioning and upholding heaven and earth, as possessing extraordinary power and wisdom called *māyā*, as sending his spies or messengers throughout both worlds, as numbering the very winkings of mens eyes, as hating falsehoods. Often connected with water especially waters of the firmament and atmosphere. Called lord of the sea.

Vāyu - Sanskrit - 'वायु' wind, air or the God of Wind and air depending on the context. Associated with the breathing. One of the five primal elements.

Veda - Sanskrit - 'वेद'. In the context of the texts above this appears to be limited to the body of Vedantic literature said to contain all the law. There are three principle works which are refered to as the Veda, the Rig Veda, Sama Veda and the Yagur Veda. A four, the Atharva Veda, is often included when refering to these.

Yajña - Sanskrit - 'यज्ञ' worship, devotion, prayer, praise; act of worship devotion, offering, sacrifice; fire.

Yama - Sanskrit - 'यम' rein, curb, bridle, a driver, charioteer, the act of checking or curbing, suppression, restrain, self control, forbearance; but in the context of these extracts, exclusively the name of the god of death, who presides over the spirits of the dead, (he is regarded as the first of men and born from Vivasvat, 'the Sun' and his wife Saraṇyú. His twin sister is Yamī , with whom he resists sexual alliance, but by whom he is mourned after his death so that the gods can make her forget her sorrow and create night; in the Veda he is called a king or *स गमनो ज्ञानानाम्* the gatherer of men, and rules over departed fathers in heaven ... in Post Vedic mythology he is the appointed Judge and 'Restrainer' or 'Punisher' of the dead...

Yuga - Sanskrit - 'युग' An age of mankind of which there are four, the Satyuga (sometimes called krityuga), Tretayuga, Dwaparayuga and Kaliyuga, each having a fixed duration. The Sattayuga is said to have a duration of 1,732,000 solar years, the Tretayuga 1,296,000 solar years, the Dwaparayuga 864,000 solar years, and the kaliyuga 432,000 solar years. The Kaliyuga is said to have begun on the 17th of February 3102 B.C. See Śrīmad 12, 3 for description of the qualities of these periods (page 164). The ages are referred to in other traditions as the golden, silver, bronze and iron ages. Plato's description of the different forms of government (page 131) may reflect these. Of the material in this collection, it is traditionally held that the Ramayana is a description of the close of the Dwāparayuga, The Śrīmad Bhāgavata and the Mahābhārata are held to describe the close of the Tretayuga and the remaining material is of the Kaliyuga. The Mahābhārata contains two further extensive descriptions, Vana 148 and especially Vana 187.

Notes on Texts

General Observations

The majority of these texts are from civilisations which pre-date our own and have ideas and values with which we are not familiar. The essential ideas and teachings however are the same, and it is instructive to see these ideas presented in such a variety of ways.

All the texts have been transcribed as precisely as possible from the work of the translator. This leads to some inconsistencies, especially in the transliteration of foreign names into English, where the spelling of the same name may vary from one text to another. Where multiple translations are available, the traditionally accepted authority has been used.[1] Where no clearly authorative text was apparent, the translation which most clearly dealt with the subject has been selected. Reference to other translations are appended as notes where applicable.

The texts have been selected on the basis of scriptural or philosophic authority, and in some cases simply antiquity (where the historical context was educational). The remarkable feature amongst all of these works is the consistency of both the primary teaching, and the remarks applicable to economics. The texts are from either a Master Teacher, or a major figure in the same tradition. The texts collected here are from a number of traditions: -

Vedantic	Chinese	Hellenic	Hebrew/ Christian	Middle Eastern
~ Artha Veda ~ Brihaspati Smriti ~ Narada Smriti ~ Brihadaranyaka Upanishad ~ Sukra Niti ~ Ramayana ~ Laws of Manu ~ Mahabharata ~ Srimad Bhagavata ~ Shantanand Saraswati ~ Yajnavalkya Smriti	~ Shu King ~ Lau Tzsu ~ Confucius ~ Mencius	~ Hesiod ~ Plato ~ Cicero Philo[2] Ficino	~ Bible ~ Gospel of St Thomas	~ Hummarabi's Code of Laws ~ Zarathushtra

Some examination was made of source material available from Egyptian traditions. Despite the knowledge derived or inferred on the manner of life, trade, taxation and administration in ancient Egypt, no useful source material was found dated prior to the legal texts of the 18th Dynasty. By this time many corruptions had entered Egyptian society. Amongst the earliest legal writings are some pillars detailing laws enacted by the king to protect the people from the excesses of corrupt tax collectors and military officials.

Two religious traditions are obviously missing. The first being the Buddhist writings, which in the earliest times do not include any material relevant to the subject. The second being the Islamic sources which have been rejected only because of their relative lack of antiquity (see below).

In the Hellenic tradition, there is a body of material sometimes called pastoral texts which describe agriculture or management of households[3]. Similarly, in the Vedantic tradition there are number of books called 'Varta' which deal with similar subjects. These deal with practical matters rather than the distribution of wealth and have not been included.

Time Frame of Texts

The intent of this project was to find the oldest sources of economic material available. Generally speaking the material included predates the Christian era. The exceptions being 'Conversations with Shantanand Saraswati' (a Twentieth century master teacher of the Vedantic tradition), and Marsilio Ficino (a 15th century Platonist).

These texts all refer to a concept of time, and history of mankind which is larger than currently accepted in Western Europe (see below). This tradition, holds that some of these works were compiled in earlier ages and transmitted orally until it became necessary to write them down.

In some of these earlier texts there are occasional references to writing (such as for contracts), and goods which are not normally associated with such antiquity, which suggests that some alteration of the text occurred as time progressed.

The assumptions of time have been adopted from the philosophical traditions themselves, rather than the academic research. The time frame shown in the following diagram begins with the dawning of the current age (the Iron Age). Texts from before this time were transmitted orally and are held according to the religious and philosophical traditions of India to have been put into writing approximately 1700 BC.

The Texts

The Vendantic Tradition

The range of Sanskrit religious and philosophic material is vast. The original material is called the Veda (literally 'knowledge'), which are referred to as Sruti or 'Revealed Word' because they are held to be inspired directly by the Supreme Creator (like the divine frenzy of poets[4]) and merely recited by the Rsis. There are three principle Veda and a fourth, the Atharveda. The source through which these works became manifest remains unknown.

The main body of the Veda contain prayers and songs of praise, especially associated with religious ceremonies[5]. They are still used today as part of Hindu religious rites. The text quoted here is song in praise of the goddess earth from the Arthaveda.

Another body of texts is referred to as the 'Shastra'. These fall into a category called 'Smṛiti' - 'Remembered', and are all associated with the name of the sage who originally promulgated them. This does not make the origins less divine[6].

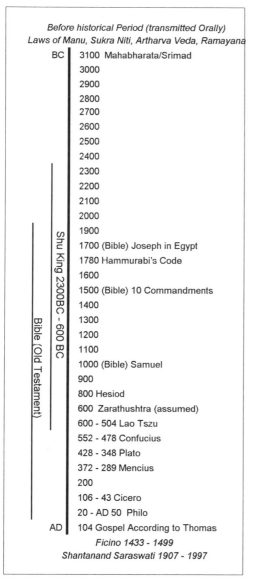

Before historical Period (transmitted Orally)
Laws of Manu, Sukra Niti, Artharva Veda, Ramayana

BC		
	3100	Mahabharata/Srimad
	3000	
	2900	
	2800	
	2700	
	2600	
	2500	
	2400	
	2300	
	2200	
	2100	
	2000	
	1900	
	1700	(Bible) Joseph in Egypt
	1780	Hammurabi's Code
	1600	
	1500	(Bible) 10 Commandments
	1400	
	1300	
	1200	
	1100	
	1000	(Bible) Samuel
	900	
	800	Hesiod
	600	Zarathushtra (assumed)
	600 - 504	Lao Tszu
	552 - 478	Confucius
	428 - 348	Plato
	372 - 289	Mencius
	200	
	106 - 43	Cicero
	20 - AD 50	Philo
AD	104	Gospel According to Thomas

Shu King 2300BC - 600 BC

Bible (Old Testament)

Ficino 1433 - 1499
Shantanand Saraswati 1907 - 1997

Timeline of the texts

These Law Books usually contain three sections (Kaṇdas), vis Achara (regulations relating to the performance of religious rites and ceremonies and the general duties of men), Vyavahara (civil laws) and Prayschitta (atonement for various sins committed). Not every text contains all three sections.

The most widely quoted (and translated) is the 'Laws of Manu', which is held to be next in sanctity to the Veda and the oldest of the Sacred Law Books. It is attributed to 'Manu' the son of the Creator (Brahma) and the first man. No dating of the text is possible. It is held by tradition to have originated at the end of the Golden Age or the beginning of the Silver Age. His Holiness Shantanand Saraswati recommended two others as having similar degrees of credence: the 'Yajnavalkya Smṛiti' and the 'Parashara'. The latter of these does not include a section on civil laws. These texts often repeat verses from Manu (or other authorities). In these extracts material is not duplicated unless there is sufficient variation to add further understanding.

Some commentators make further division of these texts into 'Dharma Shastra' (or law Shastra) and 'Artha Shastra' (or Wealth Shastra). The 'Sukra Niti' and the works of 'Brihaspati' are considered to be part of the latter group.

The other texts used within this collection are the Epics, of which the two principle works are the 'Mahabharata' and the 'Ramayana'. These Epics are the source of the majority of the subject matter of Indian art, poetry, and drama until this day. They comprise the moral lessons and great spiritual truths that have permeated a society for millennia.

The Mahabharata is the largest book ever written (consisting of more than one hundred thousand couplets). The text is attributed to the sage Vyāsa. The work is a saga describing the rivalry and subsequent war between two branches of a family (the Kurus and the Pandavas) which lead to the destruction of the entire governing class shortly before the death of Krishna (3102 BC). The story is interspersed with discussions by the participants on an enormous range of subjects. The most famous being the profound conversation between Krishna and Arjuna on the eve of the great battle known as the Bhagavad Geeta (The Lord's Song) containing the essence of the Vedantic teaching.

The majority of the extracts contained herein are from the book called the 'Santi Parva' which is a discussion between the Pandava family and their ancestor Bhishma after the battle. When the entire governing class of the world has been destroyed in the battle, the Pandavas, on the advice of Krishna, approach the dying Bhishma and ask him about the nature of government.

The Ramayana (or the life of Rama) is an epic tale of events that took place at the end of the Silver Age. The work comprises some twenty four thousand couplets in seven books. The composition is attributed to the sage Valmiki, originally a thief, who was told the story by the sage Narada. It was held that he taught the poem to others and that the vast work was transmitted orally for vast periods of time. From this story the only parts extracted are the descriptions of the capital of Rama's kingdom (during the reign of his father), and the description of the court.

The Srimad Bagavata is an epic of the life of Krishna and contains collections of stories and conversations like the above.

The final source used from the body of Sanskrit literature are the Upanishads. These, like the Veda are regarded as Sruti (heard) and the authorship is unknown (although some purport to be conversations between great sages). They are a body of 108 texts, of which 16 are held to be authentic and authoritative. The Bṛhadāraṇyaka Upaniṣad is one of these sixteen. The Upaniṣads are a part of the vedantic tradition, and the subject matter is entirely to do with the realisation of the Self (Brahman). Within this scope, principles of a number of other subjects are covered.

Shantanand Saraswati (1907 to 1997) was the Shankaracharya of Jyotir Math. This position is one of four 'seats' of a philosophic and religious tradition established by the great Indian sage Shankara. The occupiers of these 'seats' are accepted as senior leaders within the Hindu religion. The tradition of Shankaracharya provides that holders of these seats must also be masters of Advaita Philosophy. Westerners were also welcome 'at the feet' of the Shankaracharya, to ask questions of the great teacher. The extracts within this collection arise from various conversations of this nature.

Whilst the material in this collection deals with Principle and Law, readers' attention is also drawn to the 'Artha Shastra', an early book on government (2nd century BC), covering, in practice much of what is covered within these texts.

The Chinese Tradition

The most ancient of the Chinese classical books[7] is the 'Shû King', literally, 'The Book of Historical Documents'. It is a collection of documents relating to the period from around B.C. 2357 to B.C. 627. The collection as it comes to us today is certainly incomplete. It is not a chronicle, but includes descriptions of some momentous events, descriptions of the qualities of some kings and his ministers, and some speeches given by the kings and ministers. The collection has many of the qualities of the Old Testament in that each of the documents included has educational value at many different levels. It was quoted from extensively by Confucius and Mencius, both of whom clearly regarded it as having scriptural authority.

Lao Tsze (604 BC to circa 517 BC), is the earliest philosopher of the Chinese tradition. The name translates as 'Old Philosopher'. He wrote, late in his life, the Tâo Tê King, probably the most translated book ever written in the Chinese language. Lao Tsze's birth has been associated with miracles of the same nature as Jesus and Krishna. Lao Tsze is the spiritual father of the religion 'Taoism', which has many of the attributes of Gnostic Christianity. Only two books are attributed to him, both of which are quite short. His works are enigmatic and profound spiritual teachings.

Confucius (552 to 478 BC) was a philosopher and teacher, and founder of the popular Chinese religion known as Confucianism. Confucius was a contemporary of Lao Tsze. His father having died when he was three years old, the family grew up in a state of poverty. He describes however that at the age of fifteen he 'had his mind bent on learning'. Unlike Lao Tsze, Confucius spoke (and/or wrote) extensively on government. Part of his teaching was that the development of character in the governors was a prerequisite for effective government. Confucius is attributed by some with the compilation of a range of classical works including the 'Book of Odes', books on protocol, on music and on other subjects which have a bearing on social structure and behaviour.

Mencius (372 to 289 BC), or more correctly Meng K'e, was a follower and exponent of the teachings of Confucius, and is widely regarded as the greatest of his followers. Like Confucius he also quotes extensively from the Classics as authorities, especially from the 'Book of History' and the 'Book of Odes'.

The Hellenic Tradition

Very little is known of Hesiod (end of 8th century BC). He was probably a contemporary of Homer, and is accepted as having lived in Boetia (on the Greek mainland). It is through these two and especially Hesiod that we have our primary literary sources of Greek mythology and religion.

Plato (428 to 348 BC) was an Athenian, and student of Socrates. Plato wrote on a vast variety of subjects, mostly in the form of dialogues, which involved his beloved teacher. Socrates, who claimed to 'know nothing', was reckoned by the Delphic Oracle to be the wisest man in Greece. The majority of the material here is taken from the 'Republic' (a dialogue on the nature of justice) and the 'Laws', and dialogue in which Plato postulates a Constitution to govern a virtuous society in his own time.

The Platonic teaching continued with a long line of teachers after the death of Plato. It was revived periodically whenever another philosopher was able to penetrate and propound his teaching. Cicero (106 to 43 BC), was part of one such revival. He was a member of a noble Roman family and an active participant in the Roman Senate. His family and other early influences were Stoics, and he discovered Plato later in his life. Some of his books (The Republic and The Laws) follow the style and general theme of Plato's works by the same name but clearly have different objectives.

Philo (20 B.C. to 50 A.D.) was a Jewish Platonist living about the time of Christ, in Alexandria. Many of his works are commentaries on the Old Testament, to which he adds, with his insight into the Hebrew language and Jewish traditions, a keen understanding of Plato.

With the collapse of the Roman Empire most of Plato was virtually lost to Latin speaking Western Europe for almost a thousand years. He remained available to Greek speaking Eastern Europe and the Arab world. He was re-introduced to the West by the Byzantines in the early part of the fifteenth century. Marsilio Ficino (1433 to 1499 AD) was the head of the Platonic school which was at the centre of Renaissance Florence. Ficino was selected, as a youth, by Cosimo Medici to be educated to translate Plato from Greek to Latin. In addition to Plato he translated a large number of Philosophic works from Greek into Latin, wrote a number of works expounding Plato's teaching, and original works on a large variety of subjects. He corresponded with statesmen, religious figures, artists, poets, lawyers and other philosophers on a range of subjects. The extracts here are taken from his correspondence. Ficino also wrote on Economics[8], but these writings are no longer extant.

Hebrew - Christian Tradition

The Christian Bible is the cornerstone of this tradition. It is made up of two major divisions referred to by Christians as the 'Old' and 'New' testaments. The 'Old Testament' is accepted as scriptural authority by the Jewish, Moslem and Christian Religions. The 'New Testament' is unique to the Christian Religion. The Bible comprises a mixture of myth, history, law, poetry and song, all of which is devotional, instructional and inspirational.

The oldest historical material in the Bible dates from approximately 1800 BC when the Jews migrated to Egypt at the time of the great famine. The first five books are attributed to Moses, who was believed by Renaissance philosophers to have been directly instructed by Hermes Trismegistis[9] during the time the Jews spent in Egypt. The Mosaic Laws laid down in Leviticus are dated by biblical scholars at around 1500 BC.

The Gospel According to St Thomas is a document that was found in upper Egypt in 1945. It contains 114 'Sayings of Jesus', and attributes the collection to Didymus Jude Thomas. As it currently stands it has been dated from around 104 AD. Modern scholarship suggests that it pre-dates the four Gospels in the Bible, and may have been the source of some of the material used by the Gospel writers. The bulk of the work includes material that is available in the traditional gospels. The material included here is unique to that text.

Middle Eastern Tradition

Hammurabi's Code of Laws (circa 1780BC) is one of the several law codes surviving from the ancient Middle East. It is both the most comprehensive and intact. Hammurabi was the sixth king of the Amorite Dynasty of Old Babylon. It is best known from a beautifully engraved diorite stela now in the Louvre Museum which also depicts the king receiving the law from Shamash, the god of justice. This copy was made long after Hammurabi's time (circa 1780 B.C. - a little before the Hebrew Decalogue and the system of law expressed in Leviticus). It is clear that his was a long-lasting contribution to Mesopotamian civilization. It encodes many laws which had probably evolved over a long period of time. The pre-amble is an interesting reflection of both the duties of the king laid out in the Vedantic tradition, and, the changes in attitude that may have occurred in the short time since the end of the Bronze Age.

Zarathushtra was a Persian and probably a contemporary of both Pythagoras and Confucius. The religion attributed to him is believed to be a revitalisation of the traditional religion of the area. The texts currently available are only a small remnant of a vast religious and philosophic tradition. Some of the texts are in the original language of the region (similar to Sanskrit) and are probably from a tradition existing thousands of years before Zarathushtra.

It has been said of Zarathushtra that his favourite book was the Bhagavad Geeta which links him to the Vedantic tradition. The wise men from the East who attended Christ as a child were 'Magi' - of the Zoroastrian religion, which may link the teachings of Christ to Eastern sources.

Supplementary Notes

1.Such as the King James translation of the Bible.

2.Philo and Ficino partook of both traditions..

3. Such as Xenophon's 'Oeconomics' and, later Virgil's 'The Georgics'.

4.Refer Ficino Volume 1 Letter 7.

5.Other parts of the Veda deal with direction for performance of ceremonies and philosophic issues.

6.Mahabharata (Santi Parva 337) describes the origin of the Sukra Niti as follows.
"The seven celebrated Rishis, viz., Marchi, Atri, Angiras, Pulastya, Pulaha, Kratus, and Vasistha of great energy, who came together to be known by the name Chitra-sikhandas, uniting on the breast of that foremost of mountains, viz., Meru, promulgated an excellent treatise on duties and observances that was consistent with the four Vedas. The contents of that treatise were uttered by seven mouths, and constituted the best compendium of human duties and observances... Those seven Rishis constitute the seven (Prakriti) elements (of Mahat, Ahankara, etc) and the Selfborn Manu, who is the eighth in the enumeration constituted the original Prakriti. These eight uphold the universe, and it was these eight that promulgated the treatise adverted to... Reflecting in their minds in this way, those Rishis created worlds, and the science of morality and duty to govern those worlds. In that treatise the authors discoursed on Religion and Wealth and Pleasure, and subsequently on Emancipation also. They also laid down in it the various restrictions and limitations intended for the Earth as also for heaven. They composed that treatise after having worshipped with penances the puissant and illustrious Narayana called also Hari, for a thousand years, in the company with many other Rishis. Gratified with their penances and worship, Narayana commanded the goddess of speech, viz., Saraswati, to enter into the person of those Rishis... In consequence of the entrance of the goddess of speech into their persons, those Rishis, well conversant with penances, succeeded in composing that foremost of treatises in respect of vocables, import, and reason. Having composed that treatise sanctified with the syllable Om, the Rishis first of all read it to Narayana who became highly pleased with what he heard. That foremost of all Beings then addressed those Rishis in an incorporeal voice and said, -- Excellent is this treatise that ye have composed consisting of a hundred thousand verses. The duties and observances of all the worlds will flow from this your work! In complete accordance with the four Vedas viz., the Yajushes, the Samans, and the Atharvans of Angiras, the treatise of yours will be an authority in all the worlds in respect of both Pravritti and Nivritti... Even this treatise that ye have composed shall be regarded by all persons in the same light, viz., as a work of the highest authority. This is my command. Guided by this treatise, the Self born Manu himself will declare to the world its course of duties and observances. When Usanas and Vrihaspati will arise, they will also promulgate their respective treatises on morality and religion, guided by and quoting from this your treatise." Usanas became known in later times as Sukra. Other texts in this tradition have similar descriptions of their origin within the opening verses.

7.James Legge, in Sacred Books of the East.

8.Refer Ficino Letters Volume 1, letter 21.

A Scriptural History of Time

The following is a synthesis of the descriptions of human history within these texts.

All the scriptures introduce man to the creation in a 'Garden of Eden' or 'a state of bliss'[1], where man (collectively) was close to God and lived virtuously. The exercise of virtue arose from simply attending on what was required in any given moment and an outcome of this was happiness. This 'Garden of Eden' is referred to in other European traditions as the 'Golden Age' and in the Vedic tradition as the 'Sat Yuga'. It is also referred to in Chinese traditions but identified only in terms of sequence in the translations in this collection.

In this Golden Age, the desires of men were simple and did not cause harm to other men or other creatures. All were able to live in harmony. Nature (the earth) provided for all men's needs with no discomfort and men lived very long lives.

After a period of time, the harmony was disturbed by desires for personal gain and men were forced from the 'Garden of Eden' to labour to produce their bread and satisfy their desires. And, with the introduction of personal desire came the requirement for government and regulation of men in society.

The scriptural history of mankind is then a description of man's descent from this elevated state. The Silver Age, (although not the state of almost universal bliss), was a state of both abundance and general happiness and relative virtue. The Bronze Age was a further diminution of virtue and happiness, and in turn, in the Iron Age (this age), misery is predominant.

Each successive age is shorter, the life span of man is shorter and the power of men is diminished. Each age appears to have ended with some momentous event rather than a gradual slide from one age to another. The ages, are however vast periods of time, and for the most part all recorded (and archeological) history covers only the period since the dawn of the Iron Age.

In the Vedantic tradition, the end of the Iron Age, after a period of rest, is followed by another Golden Age, and this proceeds along larger cycles until the whole creation is withdrawn, to be reissued again, and again.

An understanding of these ages of men puts into perspective some of the material presented in the scriptures, especially as it relates to government and to economics.

The Golden Age

According to the Vedantic tradition, the Golden Age is 1,760,000 years long, and the normal life span of a man in this period is 400 earth years. Virtue (represented symbolically as a cow) is said to be complete, manifesting all the qualities of truth, compassion and asceticism.

Men of this age are described as supremely happy, and spend their time contemplating the Supreme Being, fearless of thieves or famine, and completely free from sin. Illness is unknown. No work is required to produce food, because the earth gives up her fruits unasked, and no mining is required because the surface of the earth yields in abundance. The necessities of life are described as 'obtained by being thought of'. Tastes and needs are simple and natural.

In such an age there is no requirement for private property, no buying or selling. Nor is there any requirement for trade (no need to go on ships - Hesiod), for the requirements of life are manifest where they are needed.

The age has no government, no social structure and no concept of private property. Descriptions of this age, in all the traditions are brief. The full operation of compassion requires that individuals address the needs of others rather than addressing their own, and especially that the individual's desires are not satisfied at the expense of others.

The End of the Golden Age

The Golden age ends when someone, somewhere, wants some for himself, and the equanimity is destroyed. Man is expelled from the garden of Eden 'to work the ground'. But some sages, for the benefit of subsequent generations, codified the knowledge available in the form of Scriptures and treatises on the Laws governing creation in forms that could be transmitted orally.[2]

The first manifestation of this Law in human affairs was the differentiation of men and the creation of the structure of society. The structure of society described in the Vedic literature is the genesis of the contemporary Indian social structure which has become much corrupted. It warrants some consideration.

At the top of the hierarchy is a class of people named the 'Brahmana'. People of this class reflect the qualities of the people of the Golden age. They live simply, with no aspirations for the accumulation of property, and are primarily concerned with learning, teaching, and living from alms (a reflection of the bounty naturally provided in the Golden age). The Brahmana are represented as derived from the mouth of the god Brahman. Harmlessness to all creatures is one of the tenets practised by this group.

Next, having the quality of activity much more predominant than those of contemplation and reflection, are the Kshatriya. They are a ruling and military class, represented as being born from the arms of Brahma. Their principle duty is the protection of the people (from internal and external threats). They also study the scriptures, as well as the sciences, especially the science of government. They bestow gifts, offer sacrifices, abstain from attaching themselves to sensual pleasure, and collect taxes[3] to support the function of protection of the people. They are fearless in battle, and prepared to sacrifice their lives to defend the kingdom. The king, in all the ancient texts, would always have Brahmanas about him to advise him on personal and public affairs.

Third, is a class comprising merchants and farmers (perhaps in contemporary terms 'entrepreneurs') and called Vaisya. The natural qualities of this class include those manifest in the Kshatriya class, but tempered by acquisitiveness. Their primary duty is to tend flocks, cultivate land and trade (the practice of arts, crafts and manufacturing was also included within these descriptions). They are also expected to bestow gifts, sacrifice and study the scriptures. Amongst the characteristics of this group are 'remaining dissatisfied with hoards of wealth'. Since the concept of property has been introduced, the concept can arise of wealth being lent and borrowed, and a sum being charged for this service (interest). This also is the province of the Vaisya. From the purely economic point of view, since the Vaisya command the production and distribution of wealth, only they have the means to pay the taxation demanded by the Kshatriya.

The final group, sometimes said to be casteless, are referred to as Sudra. They are devoid of the energy and discipline of the other groups and have only the duty to serve the other three castes. Sudras require care and protection that they cannot afford themselves. The Sudras are not permitted to accumulate wealth.

This order, being Divine Law, is populated by the same Law. Souls of particular qualities are drawn towards families of those qualities, so that the system appears to be sustained on a hereditary basis. Changes of caste, and intermixture of the castes are not condoned. Knowing one's place and duty within society is a prerequisite for happiness and contentment[4].

The distribution of wealth in this system, is instructive. The Brahmana are said to 'own' everything. The context for this is that 'property' is an illusion, and only the Brahmana are equipped with the knowledge and discrimination to understand this and not to become slaves to the desires and attachments commonly associated with it. The Brahmanas however make no claim to any property.

In a different context, the King is said to 'own' everything. Individual owners are perceived as custodians of wealth and land for periods of time. The wealth belongs to the king as the leader of society. He has the power to extend and withdraw custody of this wealth. Further, the wealth that remains in the custody of the king is for the benefit of the entire society. The king in fact requires wealth for all of the functions of government, especially to support the army (which is required for the protection of the people)[5].

For practical purposes wealth is held by the Vaisyas.

The Sudras do not, and are not permitted to accumulate wealth.

The Silver Age

The Silver Age opens with a quarter of the four feet of Virtue gradually encroached upon by falsehood, violence, discontent and discord. Without the equity people need protection, which is provided in the form of the social system described above, specific duties being assigned to different groups within the society. The majority of the people are said to be Brahmanas. The people of this age live in abundance[6]. Throughout their three hundred years of life, people remain devoted to the performance of religious rites and austerities and are not given much to violence or lewd behaviour. They pursue the three objects of human endeavour (religious merit, wealth and sense enjoyment). The chief virtue of this age is said to be 'knowledge'. The period of the silver age is 1,296,000 years.

There are a few books available which describe events (at least at the end of) the Silver Age, the best known being the Ramayana.

Plato describes this age as the Age of wealth. Having still virtue at a high level, the requirements for protection are relatively few and prosperity remains at a very high state.

The Bronze Age

The social structure of the Silver Age continues in the Bronze Age. People are fond of glory and given to the performance of great sacrifices. The Cow of Virtue is said to stand on only two legs in this age as violence, dissent, falsehood and hatred increase, assailing compassion, austerity, truthfulness and a charitable disposition. Sacrifice is the principle virtue of this age. Sacrifice is designed to win some end in either this world or the next. Those described in the Mahabharata often involved great amounts of wealth and were undertaken to win the support of the subtle powers for the birth of a son, to bring on rain, success in battle or expansion of the kingdom.

A human life span in this era is said to be two hundred years. The people are affluent and happy, maintaining large families and taking delight in the scriptures. Among the classes of society the priestly and regal classes are predominant.

After 864,000 years, the Bronze Age ends when the kings, cognisant that control of the earth is prerequisite to securing (for themselves) the wealth that the earth yields, become covetous of the Earth. Their ambition becomes unbounded and they fight. Still endued with courage and honour they fight to the death, and the entire race is destroyed in the battle of Kurukshetra.[7]

The Iron Age

The Iron Age is said to have begun with the death of Krishna shortly after the battle of Kurukshetra. By tradition, this is held to have occurred on the 17th of February 3102 BC using our current calendar. The battle destroyed the entire class of men who had the capacity to govern, and left the world unprotected. The Iron Age runs for 432,000 years.

At the outset of the Iron Age, the cow of virtue is said to stand on only one leg, but the descriptions of it's conclusion paint a very bleak picture of human existence. The life span of men at the outset of this period is said to be one hundred years, but by its conclusion only sixteen years. Women bear children at the age of eight. The caste system, dominant in the previous two ages, collapses completely at the beginning of this age. Possession of wealth becomes the sole criterion of pedigree, morality and merit; absence of it, the sole test of impiety. The Priestly class become addicted to sexual desires and satisfaction of the cravings of the stomach.

The chief virtue of this age is charity.

The forms of government vary[8]. Government during this age is by 'Merchants and Fishermen' (Vaisya and Sudra), who become merciless and greedy. Traders practice using false scales, and servants will leave their masters (masters too will discharge their servants - when they are incapacitated).

Supplementary Notes

1.Indeed, St Jerome translates Genesis 2:8 (And the LORD God planted a garden eastward in Eden; and there he put the man whom he had formed) as *'Moreover the Lord God had planted, from the beginning, a paradise in Eden (pleasure or bliss)'*. The Hebrew word translated in the 'King James Version' of the Bible as 'garden' can be rendered, garden, country, universe or any organised sphere of existence.

2.See for example the description of the source of the Sukra Niti as described in the Mahabharata included in the section 'Notes on Texts'.

3.Extracting taxes 'like a bee gathering honey from plants', so as not to harm the kingdom. The methods of taxation applied are discussed at length later.

4.See for example Confucius Analects Book 16 Chapter 1.

5.But even this is acknowledged to be an illusion (see Mahabharata, Santi Parva 321).

6.See for example the descriptions of the city of Ayodhya in the Ramayana

7.As described in the Mahabharata.

8.See for example Plato's Republic Book 8 for the different types of government and how they arise.

Abbreviations

Anal	Analects
Brihad	Brihadaranyaka Upanishad
Conf	Confucius
Deut	Deuteronomy (Old Testament)
Geeta	Bhagavad Geeta
Ham	Hammurabi's Code of Laws
Josh	Joshua (Old Testament)
KJV	Bible, King James Version
L of M	Laws of Manu
Lev	Leviticus (Old Testament)
Men	Mencius
MhB	Mahabharata
NAS	Bible, New American Standard
NBD	Nelsons Bible Dictionary
NIV	Bible, New International Version
Num	Numbers (Old Testament)
Rama	Ramayana
Srimad	Šrīmad Bhāgavata
Sukra	Sukra Niti
Tf	Translators Footnote
Yaj	Yajnavalkya Smriti

Bibliography

Ancient Near Eastern Texts relating to the Old Testament, Ed James Pritchard, Princeton University Press.

Artha Sastra, Translated by R. P. Kangle, Motil Banarsidass Publishers 1963, and Translated by L. N. Rangarajan, Penguin Books 1992.

Atharva-Veda, Sacred Books of the East, Translated by Maurice Bloomfield, Motilal Banarsidass.

Brihadaranyaka Upanishad (with Commentary of Sankaracarya), Translated by Swami Madhavanda, Advaita Ashrama.

Brihaspati Smriti, trans Julius Jolly, Sacred Books of the East, Motilal Banarsidass.

Commentary on the Code of Hammurabi by Charles F. Horne, Ph.D. (1915), The 11th Edition of the Encyclopaedia Britannica, 1910.

Cicero, The Offices, Trans Thomas Cockman.

Confucius, Confucian Analects, The Great Learning & the Doctrine of the Mean; Translated by James Legge; Dover Publications, Inc.

Dharma Shastra, Trans Manmath Nath Dutt: Cosmo Publications 1978 (originally printed 1906).

Gospel According to Thomas, Translated by A Guillaumont, Collins London 1959.

Hammurabi's Code of Laws (circa 1780 B.C.) Translated by L. W. King (1910) as well as translation by Theophile J Meek.

Hesiod, Works and Days, Internet, Project Gutenberg (translator not given).

Hesiod, Works and Days, Translated by Dorothea Wender, Penguin Classics 1973

Holy Bible, King James Version, New American Standard version & New International Version.

Laws of Manu, Sacred Books of the East Collection Vol 25 Translated by G Bühler, Penguin Classics Edition, Translated by Wendy Doniger & Brian Smith, and Munshiram Manoharlal Publishers, Translated by Arthur Coke Burnell (1884).

Notes on the Manu Smrti compiled by Mahamahopadhyaya Ganganatha Jha, University of Calcutta 1929.

Mahabharata, translated by Kisari Mohan Ganguli, Munshiram Manoharlal Publishers

Mencius, translated by D. C. Lau, Penguin.

Narada Smriti, Translated by Julius Jolly, Sacred Books of the East, Motilal Banarsidass

Nelson's Bible Dictionary, PC Study Bible 1994

Philo, The Works of Philo, Translated by C. D. Yonge, Hendrickson Publishers, 1985 (original published in Bohn's Ecclesiastical Lib 1854-55).

Plato, Jowett Translation.

George Gemistos Plethon, The last of the Hellenes, C.M. Woodhouse, Clarindon Press 1986.

Ramayana, Shatnisadam Publication, translated by Hari Prasad Shastri

Shu King (also known as the Book of History) Sacred Books of the East Volume 3 Translated by J Legge, and translation by Walter Gorn Old, Theosophical Publishing Society 1904.

Srimad Bhagavata, Translated by C. L. Goswami and M. A. Sastri, Published by Motilal Jalan at Gita Press, Gorkhapur (India).

Sukra Niti, Translated by Prof Benoy Kumar Sarkar, Published by The Panini Office, Bhuvaneswari Asrama, Bahadurganj.

Tao Te Ching, Shrine of Wisdom Pub, & Trans by Arthur Waley, Grove Weidenfeld Pub.

The Complete Works of Han Fei Tzu, Trans by W. L. Liano, Published by Arther Probsthain 1939.

The Man Who Wanted to Meet God, Stories from His Holiness Shantanand Saraswati, Bell Tower 1996

Yajnavalakya Smriti, see Dharma Shastra above.

Yajnavalakya Smriti, Translated by Rai Bahadur Srisa Chandra Vidyarnava, Published by The Panini Office, Bhuvaneswari Asrama, Bahadurganj 1918.

Yajnavalkya Dharma Sastra, Translated by Edward Röer, Published by R.C. Lepage & Co 1859

Zend Avestra (internet Zoroastra site).

Index to References

Abundance
  Mahabharata, Bishma Parva 9 (86)
Accounting
  Sukra Niti, Chapter 2, 686 (173)
Accounts, Government
  Sukra Niti, Chapter 2, 641 (171)
  Sukra Niti, Chapter 2, 673 (173)
Ages
  Hesiod, Works and Days 106-201 (59)
  Lao Tsze, Tao Te Ching 17 (63)
  Mahabharata, Santi Parva 232 (102)
  Srimad Dhagavata, Book 11, 17 (163)
  Srimad Bhagavata, Book 12, 3 (164)
Ages, Bronze Age
  Laws of Manu 1, 81 (65)
  Srimad Bhagavata, Book 12, 3 (164)
Ages, Duties vary
  Laws of Manu 1, 81 (65)
  Mahabharata, Santi Parva 232 (102)
Ages, Golden Age
  Bible, Genesis 2, 8 (5)
  Hesiod, Works and Days 106-201 (59)
  Laws of Manu 1, 81 (65)
  Mahabharata, Adi Parva 68 (75)
  Mahabharata, Santi Parva 263 (103)
  Mahabharata, Santi Parva 349 (105)
  Mahabharata, Vana Parva 148 (78)
  Mahabharata, Vana Parva 162 (79)
  Srimad Bhagavata, Book 11, 17 (163)
  Srimad Bhagavata, Book 12, 3 (164)
Ages, Iron Age
  Hesiod, Works and Days 106-201 (59)
  Mahabharata, Udyoga Parva 187 (85)
  Srimad Bhagavata, Book 12, 3 (164)
Ages, King Makes the Age
  Mahabharata, Santi Parva 141 (101)
  Mahabharata, Santi Parva 69 (92)
  Sukra Niti, Chapter 1, 127 (167)
Ages, Silver Age
  Ramayana, Book 1, 5 (143)
  Srimad Bhagavata, Book 12, 3 (164)
Agriculture and Trade
  Mahabharata, Santi Parva 68 (91)

Agriculture, Criteria for Success
  Sukra Niti, Chapter 4, 2, 212 (180)
Agriculture, World Depends on
  Mahabharata, Santi Parva 68 (91)
Anarchy
  Mahabharata, Santi Parva 67 (90)
Aristocracy
  Plato, Republic 543a (131)
Army
  Bible, 1 Chronicles 27, 1 (21)
  Laws of Manu 9, 294 (73)
  Mahabharata, Santi Parva 130 (98)
  Mahabharata, Santi Parva 136 (99)
  Plato, Republic 543 a (131)
  Sukra Niti, Chapter 1, 631 (169)
Army, Taxation is to Maintain the ..
  Sukra Niti, Chapter 4, 2, 1 (177)
Art & Science, to be Supported
  Ramayana, Book 1, 7 (146)
  Sukra Niti, Chapter 1, 741 (170)
  Sukra Niti, Chapter 4, 5, 642 (183)
Beggars, Supplied by Robbers
  Mahabharata, Santi Parva 88 (95)
Capital
  Bible, Matthew 26, 11 (31)
  Cicero, The Offices 2, 4 (43)
  Laws of Manu 8, 140 (70)
  Mahabharata, Santi Parva 8 (87)
  Sukra Niti, Chapter 2, 662 (172)
  Sukra Niti, Chapter 2, 673 (173)
  Sukra Niti, Chapter 4, 2, 227 (181)
  Sukra Niti, Chapter 4, 2, 46 (178)
Care of Elderly
  Mencius, Book 1, B, 5 (110)
  Mencius, Book 7, A, 22 (118)
  Sukra Niti, Chapter 2, 819 (175)
Care of Weak
  Mahabharata, Adi Parva 49 (75)
Charity
  Mahabharata, Vana Parva 257 (84)
Charity, Upholds Society
  Cicero, The Offices 1, 7 (41)
Citizen, Duty of

Ficino, Letters 1, 78 (49)
Ficino, Letters 2, 53 (50)
Mahabharata, Udyoga Parva 133 (85)
Mahabharata, Vana Parva 206 (79)
Srimad Bhagavata, Book 7, 11b (162)
Citizens, Should be as Children of King
Mahabharata, Santi Parva 69 (92)
Co-operation, And Prosperity
Mahabharata, Udyoga Parva 79 (84)
Co-operation, Makes Work Easier
Sukra Niti, Chapter 2, 1 (170)
Cycles, Economic
Mahabharata, Santi Parva Section 97. (97)
Debt
Yajnavalkya 2, 90 (187)
Debt, Measures to Mitigate
Sukra Niti, Chapter 4, 5, 628 (183)
Debt, Measures to Regulate
Hammurabi's Code 100-119 (56)
Debt, Recovery of
Yajnavalkya 2, 40 (187)
Debt, To be Avoided
Cicero, The Offices 2, 24 (45)
Debts, Grow unless Extinguished
Mahabharata, Santi Parva 140 (100)
Democracy
Plato, Republic 556 (134)
Desire, Motivates all Action
Laws of Manu 2, 1 (66)
Mahabharata, Santi Parva 167 (101)
Srimad Bhagavata, Book 3, 5 (161)
Desire, Requires Action
Mahabharata, Santi Parva 167 (101)
Desires, Three basic
Shantanand Saraswati, 1965 (149)
Division of Labour
Brihadaranyaka, Book 1, 4, 11 (35)
Cicero, The Offices 2, 4 (43)
Laws of Manu 1, 81 (65)
Mahabharata, Santi Parva 295 (103)
Mahabharata, Santi Parva 60 (89)
Mahabharata, Udyoga Parva 133 (85)
Mahabharata, Vana Parva 150 (78)
Mencius, Book 3, A, 4 (113)
Mencius, Book 3, A, 4 cont (115)
Plato, Republic 370 (129)
Plato, Republic 423d (130)

Plato, Republic 551c (132)
Ramayana, Book 1, 6 (144)
Shantanand Saraswati, 1974 (149)
Shantanand Saraswati, 1980 (152)
Srimad Bhagavata, Book 7, 11 (161)
Sukra Niti, Chapter 2, 1 (170)
Duties, Different in Different Ages
Mahabharata, Santi Parva 232 (102)
Duties, Have Their Root in the King
Mahabharata, Santi Parva 68 (90)
Duties, Not Fixed
Cicero, The Offices 1, 10 (42)
Duties, Of Orders of Society
Mahabharata, Santi Parva 295 (103)
Duty
Bible, Matthew 22, 36 (30)
Duty, of Citizen
Cicero, The Offices, Book 3, 6 (45)
Ficino, Letters 1, 78 (49)
Ficino, Letters 2, 53 (50)
Laws of Manu 10, 115 (73)
Mahabharata, Udyoga Parva 133 (85)
Mahabharata, Vana Parva 206 (79)
Srimad Bhagavata, Book 7, 11b (162)
Duty, of Government
Cicero, The Offices, 1, 25 (43)
Cicero, The Offices, 2, 21 (44)
Ficino, Letters 2, 53 (50)
Hammurabi's Code, Prologue (53)
Laws of Manu 10, 115 (73)
Laws of Manu 7, 1 (67)
Laws of Manu 7, 54 (68)
Mahabharata, Bishma Parva 109 (87)
Mahabharata, Santi Parva 130 (98)
Mahabharata, Santi Parva 56 (88)
Mahabharata, Santi Parva 58 (88)
Mahabharata, Santi Parva 68 (90)
Mahabharata, Santi Parva 69 (92)
Mahabharata, Udyoga Parva 133 (85)
Mencius, Book 1, B, 5 (110)
Ramayana, Book 1, 18 (146)
Ramayana, Book 1, 7 (145)
Srimad Bhagavata, Book 4, 21 (161)
Duty, of Kingdom
Mahabharata, Santi Parva 67 (90)
Earth, As Goddess
Mahabharata, Santi Parva 262 (103)

Earth, Created for Service of Man
Cicero, The Offices 1, 7 (41)
Earth, Source of Abundance
Mahabharata, Bishma Parva 9 (86)
Earth, Source of all Creatures
Bible, Genesis 1, 24 (5)
Bible, Genesis 2, 8 (5)
Mahabharata, Santi Parva 190 (102)
Earth, Source of all Wealth
Atharveda, 12 (1)
Mahabharata, Bishma Parva 4 (85)
Philo, On Virtues, 17 (121)
Srimad Bhagavata, Book 4, 17 (161)
Earth, Source of Existence
Atharveda, 12 (1)
Ecology
Atharveda, 12 (1)
Gospel According to Thomas 81, 28 (34)
Mahabharata, Anusasana Parva 48 (105)
Mahabharata, Bishma Parva 9 (86)
Mahabharata, Santi Parva 89 (96)
Mahabharata, Vana Parva 256 (83)
Zarathushtra, Zend Avesta, Fargard 3. (191)
Economic Cycles
Bible, Ecclesiastes 3, 1 (23)
Bible, Leviticus 25, 8 (13)
Mahabharata Santi Parva 97 (97)
Mahabharata, Santi Parva 224 (102)
Srimad Bhagavata, Book 7, 11b (163)
Economic Policy
Bible, Genesis 41, 28 (8)
Bible, Genesis 47, 13 (9)
Plato, Laws 739 (139)
Education
Mencius, Book 7, B, 14 (117)
Elderly, Care of
Sukra Niti, Chapter 2, 819 (175)
Expenditure, Government
Mahabharata, Santi Parva 133 (99)
Sukra Niti, Chapter 1, 631 (169)
Sukra Niti, Chapter 1, 741 (170)
Sukra Niti, Chapter 2, 204 (170)
Family
Shantanand Saraswati, 1982 (153)
Sukra Niti, Chapter 1, 599 (169)
Family, To be Cared For
Mencius, Book 1, A, 5 (109)

Farmers
Ficino, Letters 2, 53 (50)
Farmers, To be Supported and Encouraged
Mahabharata, Santi Parva 87 (93)
Gambling
Mahabharata, Santi Parva 88 (95)
Gift
Brihaspati Smriti 15 (39)
Hesiod, Works & Days 353 (60)
Laws of Manu 1, 81 (65)
Laws of Manu 10, 115 (73)
Laws of Manu 4, 227 (67)
Mahabharata, Anusasana Parva 62 (106)
Mahabharata, Santi Parva 191 (102)
Mahabharata, Vana Parva 199 (79)
Narada Smriti, Book 4 (120)
Sukra Niti, Chapter 1, 418 (169)
Yajnavalkya 1, 6 (187)
Gift, Duty of Iron Age
Laws of Manu 1, 81 (65)
Mahabharata, Santi Parva 232 (102)
Goods, Primary & Secondary
Mahabharata, Santi Parva 139 (100)
Government, Accounts
Sukra Niti, Chapter 2, 641 (171)
Sukra Niti, Chapter 2, 673 (173)
Government, Aristocracy
Plato, Republic 543a (131)
Government, Arts to be Supported
Sukra Niti, Chapter 1, 418 (169)
Government, Behaviour of
Mahabharata, Santi Parva 56 (88)
Government, Democracy
Plato, Republic 556 (134)
Government, Description of Virtuous Kingdom
Mahabharata, Adi Parva 109 (76)
Mahabharata, Adi Parva 64 (75)
Mahabharata, Sabha Parva 13 (76)
Government, Divinity of Kings
Laws of Manu 7, 1 (67)
Mahabharata, Santi Parva 67 (90)
Mahabharata, Santi Parva 68 (91)
Sukra Niti, Chapter 1, 127 (167)
Government, Duty of
Ficino, Letters 2, 53 (50)
Hammurabi's Code, Prologue (53)
Laws of Manu 10, 115 (73)

Laws of Manu 7, 1 (67)
Laws of Manu 7, 54 (68)
Mahabharata, Bishma Parva 109 (87)
Mahabharata, Santi Parva 130 (98)
Mahabharata, Santi Parva 56 (88)
Mahabharata, Santi Parva 58 (88)
Mahabharata, Santi Parva 68 (90)
Mahabharata, Santi Parva 69 (92)
Mahabharata, Udyoga Parva 133 (85)
Mahabharata, Vana Parva 206 (79)
Mencius, Book 1, B, 5 (110)
Ramayana, Book 1, 18 (146)
Ramayana, Book 1, 7 (145)
Srimad Bhagavata, Book 4, 21 (161)
Sukra Niti, Chapter 1, 375 (169)
Government, Expenditure
  Mahabharata, Santi Parva 133 (99)
  Sukra Niti, Chapter 1, 631 (169)
  Sukra Niti, Chapter 1, 741 (170)
  Sukra Niti, Chapter 2, 204 (170)
Government, Good
  Confucius, Analects Book 13, 16 (47)
  Mahabharata, Adi Parva 109 (76)
  Mahabharata, Adi Parva 63 (75)
  Mahabharata, Santi Parva 139 (100)
  Mencius, Book 1, B, 5 (110)
  Sukra Niti, Chapter 1, 127 (167)
Government, In the Iron Age
  Shantanand Saraswati, January 1978 (b) (150)
Government, Income
  Sukra Niti, Chapter 1, 631 (169)
Government, King is a Thief
  Sukra Niti, Chapter 2, 523 (171)
Government, Local
  Mahabharata, Santi Parva 87 (93)
Government, Ministers
  Laws of Manu 7, 122 (69)
  Laws of Manu 7, 54 (68)
Government, Oligarchy
  Plato, Republic 550 (132)
Government, Organisation of
  Laws of Manu 7, 54 (68)
  Laws of Manu 9, 294 (73)
  Laws of Manu 9, 48 (72)
  Mahabharata, Santi Parva 87 (93)
  Ramayana, Book 1, 7 (145)
Government, Punishment Governs

Laws of Manu 7, 13 (67)
Sukra Niti, Chapter 1, 305-312 (168)
Government, State rests on Justice
  Mahabharata, Santi Parva 69 (92)
Government, Timocracy
  Plato, Republic 547 (131)
Government, To Provide Protection
  Mahabharata, Santi Parva 69 (92)
  Mahabharata, Santi Parva 87 (93)
Government, Treasury
  Sukra Niti, Chapter 2, 204 (170)
Government, Treasury Must be Filled
  Mahabharata, Santi Parva 130 (98)
  Mahabharata, Santi Parva 133 (99)
Government, Tyranny
  Plato, Republic 562c (136)
Government, War to be Avoided
  Mahabharata, Santi Parva 69 (92)
Happiness
  Bible, Matthew 25, 14 (30)
Happiness, Pursuit of
  Mahabharata, Santi Parva 190 (101)
Inflation
  Shantanand Saraswati, 1974 (149)
Justice
  Bible, Genesis 47, 13 (9)
  Bible, Leviticus 25, 8 (13)
  Cicero, The Offices 1, 7 (41)
  Ficino, Letters 1, 73 (49)
  Ficino, Letters 2, 53 (50)
Justice, Is not Fixed
  Cicero, The Offices 1, 10 (42)
Kingdom, Duty of
  Mahabharata, Santi Parva 67 (90)
Labour, Division of
  Brihadaranyaka, Book 1, 4, 11 (35)
  Cicero, The Offices 2, 4 (43)
  Mahabharata, Santi Parva 295 (103)
  Mahabharata, Santi Parva 60 (89)
  Mencius, Book 3, A, 4 (113)
  Mencius, Book 3, A, 4 cont (115)
  Plato, Republic 370 (129)
  Plato, Republic 423d (130)
  Plato, Republic 551c (132)
  Ramayana, Book 1, 6 (144)
  Shantanand Saraswati, 1980 (152)
  Sukra Niti, Chapter 2, 1 (170)

Labour, For Tax
  Laws of Manu 7, 127 (69)
Labour, Relations
  Sukra Niti, Chapter 1, 599 (169)
Labourers
  Laws of Manu 10, 115-131 (74)
  Yajnavalkya 2, 195 (188)
Land
  Hesiod, Works and Days 106-201 (59)
  Laws of Manu 8, 97 (70)
Land, Acquisition of
  Mahabharata, Santi Parva 69 (92)
Land, As gift of God
  Bible, Psalms 24, 1 (23)
  Joshua 24:13 (18)
Land, Boundaries
  Bible, Deuteronomy 19, 14 (17)
  Laws of Manu 8, 246 (71)
  Mencius, Book 3, A, 3 (111)
  Plato, Laws 843 (141)
  Shantanand Saraswati, The Man... (153)
  Yajnavalkya 2, 150 (188)
Land, Common Land
  Bible, Leviticus 25, 23 (14)
  Hammurabi's Code 53-65 (55)
  Laws of Manu 8, 237 (71)
  Mencius, Book 1, B, 2 (109)
  Yajnavalkya 2, 166 (188)
Land, Distribution of
  Bible, Leviticus 25, 23 (14)
  Bible, Leviticus 25, 8 (13)
  Confucius, Analects Book 12, 9 (47)
  Plato, Laws 740 (139)
  Plato, Republic 543a (131)
Land, Duty of Care
  Atharveda, 12 (1)
  Hammurabi's Code 53-65 (55)
  Mahabharata, Adi Parva 49 (75)
  Mahabharata, Bishma Parva 9 (86)
  Mahabharata, Santi Parva 72 (93)
  Mahabharata, Vana Parva 256 (83)
  Zarathushtra, Zend Avesta, Fargard 3. (191)
Land, Earth as Goddess
  Atharveda, 12 (1)
  Bible, Leviticus 18, 1 (12)
  Mahabharata, Adi Parva 49 (75)
  Mahabharata, Bishma Parva 4 (85)

Mahabharata, Santi Parva 262 (103)
  Plato, Laws 740 (139)
  Zarathushtra, Zend Avesta, Fargard 3. (191)
Land, Gift of God
  Bible, Joshua 24, 1 (17)
Land, Gift to all Generations
  Bible, Genesis 13, 14 (7)
Land, is not wealth
  Mahabharata, Aswamedha Parva 89 (107)
Land, King to Give Land
  Mahabharata, Anusasana Parva 62 (106)
  Mahabharata, Santi Parva 65 (90)
  Sukra Niti, Chapter 1, 418 (169)
Land, Men Fight for Possession of
  Mahabharata, Bishma Parva 4 (85)
  Mahabharata, Bishma Parva 9 (86)
Land, No Property Rights in Nature
  Cicero, The Offices 1, 7 (41)
Land, Original Division
  Plato, Republic 543a (131)
Land, Origins of
  Bible, Genesis 1 (5)
Land, Possession of
  Bible, 1 Kings 21, 1 (21)
  Bible, Genesis 13, 14 (7)
  Bible, Genesis 15, 7 (8)
  Bible, Joshua 24, 1 (17)
  Bible, Leviticus 25, 23 (14)
  Bible, Leviticus 25, 8 (13)
  Cicero, The Offices 1, 7 (41)
  Hammurabi's Code 36-41 (53)
  Laws of Manu 9, 44 (72)
  Mahabharata, Vana Parva 199 (79)
  Mencius, Book 1, B, 2 (109)
  Plato, Laws 740 (139)
Land, Possessor owns the product
  Laws of Manu 9, 48 (72)
Land, Re-distribution
  Plato, Laws 736 (138)
Land, Rent payable for
  Hammurabi's Code 42-44 (54)
  Hammurabi's Code 45-52 (54)
Land, Required for Sacrifice
  Atharveda, 12 (2)
Land, Restraint on Sale
  Bible, 1 Kings 21, 1 (21)
  Bible, Joshua 24, 1 (17)

Bible, Leviticus 25, 23 (14)
Bible, Numbers 27, 6 (15)
Hammurabi's Code 36-41 (53)
Plato, Laws 744 (140)
Plato, Laws 923 (142)
Sukra Niti, Chapter 1, 418 (169)
Land, Source of all Wealth
Atharveda, 12, 4 (1)
Mahabharata, Bishma Parva 4 (85)
Mahabharata, Bishma Parva 9 (86)
Sukra Niti, Chapter 1, 349 (168)
Sukra Niti, Chapter 1, 375 (169)
Land, Source of Sustenance
Bible, Genesis 1, 26 (5)
Bible, Genesis 2, 8 (5)
Sukra Niti, Chapter 1, 349 (168)
Land, to be used for production
Zarathushtra, Zend Avesta, Fargard 3. (191)
Land, Trees & Wells to be Provided
Mahabharata, Anusasana Parva 48 (105)
Land, Virtues of
Mahabharata, Anusasana Parva 62 (106)
Law
Cicero, On Laws 3, 1 (46)
Philo, Every Good Man (122)
Plato, Statesman 294b (127)
Law, Natural
Bible, Exodus 20, 1 (10)
Shantanand Saraswati, January 1978 (a) (150)
Shantanand Saraswati, January 1978 (b) (150)
Law, Objective of
Plato, Laws 743 (140)
Plato, Republic 462d (130)
Law, Punishment Governs
Laws of Manu 7, 1 (67)
Sukra Niti, Chapter 1, 305-312 (168)
Law, Required for Government
Lao Tsze, Tao Te Ching 57 (63)
Law, Unity is the Objective
Plato, Laws 739 (139)
Plato, Republic 462d (130)
Leadership
Mahabharata, Udyoga Parva 133 (85)
Sukra Niti, Chapter 2, 836 (176)
Lending
Bible, Deuteronomy 15, 1 (15)
Bible, Deuteronomy 24, 6 (17)

Livelihood
Bible, Deuteronomy 24, 6 (17)
Man, Craves Wealth
Atharveda, 12 (3)
Man, Dominion over Nature
Atharveda, 12 (1)
Bible, Genesis 1, 26 (5)
Man, Foremost of Creatures
Mahabharata, Bishma Parva 4 (85)
Man, Pursues Happiness
Mahabharata, Santi Parva 190 (101)
Shantanand Saraswati, 1965 (149)
Man, Rich if he Thinks So
Shantanand Saraswati, February 1978 (150)
Man, Source of Authority
Bible, Genesis 1, 26 (5)
Man, Variety of Talents
Shantanand Saraswati, 1980 (152)
Management
Bible, Romans 13, 1 (32)
Shantanand Saraswati, 1982 (152)
Sukra Niti, Chapter 2, 836 (176)
Manufacture
Mahabharata, Santi Parva 87 (93)
Merchants, Duty of
Ficino, Letters 2, 53 (50)
Merchants, To be Supported and Encouraged
Mahabharata, Santi Parva 87 (93)
Money
Bible, Deuteronomy 19, 23 (17)
Bible, Exodus 22, 25 (11)
Bible, Genesis 47, 13 (9)
Bible, Luke 20, 22 (32)
Bible, Matthew 20, 1 (29)
Cicero, On Laws 3, 5 (46)
Hammurabi's Code 49 (54)
Hammurabi's Code 100-119 (56)
Sukra Niti, Chapter 4, 5, 628 (183)
Yajnavalkya 2, 90 (187)
Money, as power
Shantanand Saraswati, 1974 (149)
Money, In Distribution of Wealth
Plato, Laws 918 (141)
Money, Purpose of
Plato, Laws 741 (139)
Plato, Laws 743 (140)
Money, Requirement for Trade

Plato, Laws 741 (139)
Monopoly, Leads to Destruction
  Bible, Isaiah 5, 8 (24)
Nation, Parts of
  Laws of Manu 9, 294 (73)
Natural Law
  Shantanand Saraswati, January 1978 (a) (150)
  Shantanand Saraswati, January 1978 (b) (150)
Nature, All Creatures live off Others
  Mahabharata, Bishma Parva 4 (85)
Nature, Creatures Created to be Useful
  Mahabharata, Santi Parva 142 (101)
Nature, Not Property of Anyone
  Mahabharata, Vana Parva 154 (79)
Nature, Organisation of
  Mahabharata, Bishma Parva 4 (85)
Neighbours, Not to be offended
  Plato, Laws 843c (141)
Oligarchy
  Plato, Republic 550 (132)
Pleasure, Arises from Sacrifice
  Mahabharata, Santi Parva 20 (88)
Poor, Always with us
  Bible, Deuteronomy 15, 1 (15)
  Matthew 26:11 (31)
Poor, Care for
  Bible, Deuteronomy 15, 1 (15)
  Bible, Leviticus 25, 1 (13)
  Philo, Special Laws 2, 17 (123)
Poverty
  Bible, Zechariah 27, 1 (26)
Poverty, Cause of
  Lao Tsze, Tao Te Ching 75 (63)
  Plato, Laws 736 (138)
  Plato, Republic 551c (132)
Poverty, None in Golden Age
  Hesiod, Works and Days 106-201 (59)
Price
  Mencius, Book 3, A, 4 cont (115)
  Shantanand Saraswati, 1974 (149)
  Sukra Niti, Chapter 2, 686 (173)
Price and Value
  Sukra Niti, Chapter 4, 2, 163 (179)
Price Determination
  Sukra Niti, Chapter 2, 686 (173)
Price Fixing
  Mencius, Book 3, A, 4 cont (115)

Prices, Naturally Different
  Mencius, Book 3, A, 4 cont (115)
Priests, income of
  Deuteronomy 18:1-5 (16)
Priests, To be Protected
  Mahabharata, Santi Parva 56 (88)
  Mahabharata, Santi Parva 75 (93)
  Mahabharata, Santi Parva 89 (96)
Production, Not for the Producer
  Plato, Republic 345c (127)
Production, Ownership of
  Laws of Manu 9, 48 (72)
Professions
  Mahabharata, Vana Parva 206 (79)
Profit
  Plato, Laws 744 (140)
  Shantanand Saraswati, 1974 (149)
Profit, Result of Action
  Mahabharata, Santi Parva 167 (101)
Property
  Bible, Deuteronomy 23, 24 (17)
  Bible, Leviticus 25, 23 (14)
  Bible, Matthew 22, 17 (30)
  Bible, Psalms 24, 1 (23)
Property, Acquisition of
  Laws of Manu 10, 115 (73)
Property, All Belongs to the Brahmana
  Laws of Manu 1, 100 (65)
Property, An Illusion
  Mahabharata, Santi Parva 321 (104)
  Shantanand Saraswati, The Man... (153)
Property, Care of
  Hammurabi's Code 120-125 (57)
Property, Distribution of
  Bible, Leviticus 25, 23 (14)
Property, Does not Exist by Right of Nature
  Cicero, The Offices 1, 7 (41)
  Ficino, Letters 1, 73 (49)
Property, Held in Common
  Plato, Republic 543a (131)
Property, Nature is Everyone's
  Mahabharata, Vana Parva 154 (79)
Property, Possession is not Ownership
  Laws of Manu 8, 180 (71)
  Sukra Niti, Chapter 4, 5, 581 (182)
Property, Requires Law
  Cicero, The Offices 1, 7 (41)

Mahabharata, Santi Parva 68 (90)
Prosperity
  Mahabharata, Anusasana Parva 62 (106)
Prosperity, Arises from Virtue
  Bible, Job 8, 3 (22)
Prosperity, By Supporting Farmers
  Mahabharata, Santi Parva 87 (93)
  Mencius, Book 7, A, 23 (118)
Prosperity, By supporting Merchants
  Mahabharata, Santi Parva 87 (93)
Prosperity, Examples of
  Ramayana, Book 1, 5 (143)
Prosperity, from Co-operation
  Cicero, The Offices 2, 4 (43)
  Mahabharata, Udyoga Parva 79 (84)
Prosperity, God of is a woman
  Mahabharata, Anusasana Parva 46 (105)
Proverty, A Sin
  Mahabharata, Santi Parva 8 (87)
Public Works
  Cicero, The Offices 2, 4 (43)
  Laws of Manu 7, 80 (69)
  Laws of Manu 8, 246 (71)
  Mahabharata, Anusasana Parva 48 (105)
  Mencius, Book 3, A, 4 cont (115)
  Shu King, The Tribute of Yu 3, 1 (155)
  Shu King, The Tribute of Yu 3, 1, 2 (158)
Punishment, Protects all Creatures
  Laws of Manu 7, 13 (67)
Punishment, Required by Government
  Mahabharata, Santi Parva 69 (92)
Recession
  Shantanand Saraswati, 1982 (152)
Rent
  Sukra Niti, Chapter 2, 204 (170)
  Sukra Niti, Chapter 4, 2, 212 (180)
Rent, Collection of
  Sukra Niti, Chapter 2, 204 (170)
Rent, Payable for Land
  Hammurabi's Code 42-44 (54)
  Hammurabi's Code 53 - 65 (55)
Rent, To be Received from Peasants
  Sukra Niti, Chapter 4, 2, 212 (180)
Retail Trade
  Ficino, Letters 2, 53 (50)
  Plato, Laws 918 (141)
  Shantanand Saraswati, 1974 (149)

Retail Trade, and Taxation
  Sukra Niti, Chapter 4, 2, 212 (180)
Sacrifice
  Mahabharata, Santi Parva 20 (88)
  Mahabharata, Santi Parva 232 (102)
  Mahabharata, Santi Parva 248 (103)
  Mahabharata, Santi Parva 263 (103)
  Mahabharata, Santi Parva 343 (105)
Savings
  Mahabharata, Santi Parva 123 (97)
  Sukra Niti, Chapter 4, 2, 1 (177)
Self Interest, Motivates all Action
  Mahabharata, Santi Parva 138 (100)
Servants, Amounts to be Paid
  Sukra Niti, Chapter 2, 788 (174)
Servants, Care for
  Sukra Niti, Chapter 2, 788 (174)
Service, Everything Created for
  Mahabharata, Santi Parva 142 (101)
Service, Only Duty of Sudra
  Mahabharata, Santi Parva 295 (103)
Society, Aristocracy
  Plato, Republic 543 a (131)
Society, Democracy
  Plato, Republic 556 (134)
Society, Division of Original
  Plato, Republic 543a (131)
Society, Ideal Size
  Plato, Republic 423c (130)
Society, Ideal Society
  Plato, Laws 739 (139)
Society, Measures for Unity
  Bible, Leviticus 19, 9 (12)
Society, Objective of
  Cicero, The Offices 2, 4 (43)
  Confucius, Analects Book 13, 16 (47)
  Plato, Republic 369c (129)
Society, Oligarchy
  Plato, Laws 744 (140)
  Plato, Laws 923 (142)
  Plato, Republic 550 (132)
Society, Order of
  Confucius, Analects Book 16, 1 (47)
  Laws of Manu 2, 127 (66)
  Mahabharata, Vana Parva 150 (78)
  Mahabharata, Vana Parva Section 206 (79)
  Mencius, Book 4, A, 5 (117)

Society, Parts of
  Laws of Manu, Chapter 9 (73)
Society, Requirement for Unity
  Mahabharata, Santi Parva 58 (88)
Society, Requirements for Unity
  Confucius, Analects Book 12, 9 (47)
  Confucius, Analects Book 16, 1 (47)
  Ficino, Letters 1, 73 (49)
  Laws of Manu 9, 294 (73)
Society, Timocracy
  Plato, Republic 547 (131)
Society, Tyranny
  Plato, Republic 562c (136)
Society, Whole & Individual are Same
  Cicero, The Offices 3, 6 (45)
Specialisation
  Hesiod, Works & Days 225 (60)
Specialisation, Example
  Bible, Ezekiel 27, 1 (24)
Taxation
  Bible, 1 Samuel 8, 10 (18)
  Bible, Deuteronomy 18, 1 (16)
  Bible, Exodus 30, 11 (11)
  Bible, Ezra 7, 21 (21)
  Bible, Genesis 41, 28 (8)
  Bible, Luke 20, 22 (32)
  Bible, Matthew 22, 17 (30)
  Confucius, Analects Book 12, 9 (47)
  Lao Tsze, Tao Te Ching 75 (63)
  Laws of Manu 10, 115 (73)
  Laws of Manu 7, 127 (69)
  Laws of Manu 7, 80 (69)
  Luke 3:10-14 (31)
  Shantanand Saraswati, unknown (154)
  Srimad Bhagavata, Book 12, 2 (164)
  Sukra Niti, Chapter 4, 5, 642 (183)
Taxation & Trade
  Sukra Niti, Chapter 4, 2, 212 (180)
Taxation, as Labour
  Laws of Manu 7, 127 (69)
  Mencius, Book 2, A (111)
Taxation, As Military Service
  Bible, 1 Chronicles 27, 1 (21)
Taxation, As Punishment
  Mahabharata, Santi Parva 136 (99)
Taxation, Different Methods
  Mencius, Book 3, A, 3 (111)

Taxation, Effects of Good Taxation
  Mahabharata, Sabha Parva 32 (77)
  Mahabharata, Santi Parva 38 (88)
Taxation, Gentle Tax is Best
  Confucius, Analects Book 12, 9 (47)
  Laws of Manu 7, 129 (69)
  Mahabharata, Santi Parva 69 (92)
  Mahabharata, Santi Parva 88 (95)
  Mencius, Book 1, A, 5 (109)
  Mencius, Book 7, A, 23 (118)
  Sukra Niti, Chapter 1, 418 (169)
  Sukra Niti, Chapter 2, 345 (171)
  Sukra Niti, Chapter 4, 2, 212 (180)
Taxation, In Times of Distress
  Cicero, The Offices, 2, 21 (44)
  Laws of Manu 10, 115 (73)
  Mahabharata, Santi Parva 130 (98)
  Sukra Niti, Chapter 4, 2, 1 (177)
Taxation, Is for Maintaining the Army
  Mahabharata, Santi Parva 136 (99)
  Sukra Niti, Chapter 4, 2, 1 (177)
Taxation, Land Tax
  Mahabharata, Santi Parva 69 (92)
  Ramayana, Book 1, 52 (147)
  Shu King, The Tribute of Yu 3, 1 (155)
  Srimad Bhagavata, Book 4, 22 (161)
  Sukra Niti, Chapter 4, 2, 212 (180)
Taxation, Land Tax is Best
  Mencius, Book 2, A (111)
Taxation, Local
  Sukra Niti, Chapter 1, 580 (169)
  Sukra-Niti, Chapter 1 580-581 (169)
Taxation, New Taxes are Vexatious
  Sukra Niti, Chapter 2, 547 (171)
Taxation, On Merchants & Farmers
  Bible, 1 Kings 10, 14 (19)
  Laws of Manu 7, 127 (69)
  Mahabharata, Santi Parva 87 (93)
  Mencius, Book 2, A (111)
  Shu King, The Tribute of Yu 3, 1 (155)
  Sukra Niti, Chapter 2, 242 (171)
  Sukra Niti, Chapter 2, 345 (171)
  Sukra Niti, Chapter 4, 2, 212 (180)
Taxation, Only those Profiting are Taxed
  Sukra Niti, Chapter 4, 2, 212 (180)
Taxation, Oppressive
  Bible, 1 Kings 10, 14 (19)

Bible, Nehemiah 5, 1 (22)
Lao Tsze, Tao Te Ching 75 (63)
Mahabharata, Santi Parva 87 (93)
Mahabharata, Udyoga Parva 187 (85)
Taxation, People not to be Taxed
Cicero, The Offices 2, 21 (44)
Taxation, Priests Exempt
Bible, Ezra 7, 21 (21)
Bible, Genesis 47, 13 (9)
Mahabharata, Santi Parva 75 (93)
Philo, The Special Laws 1 (122)
Ramayana, Book 1, 7 (146)
Srimad Bhagavata, Book 7, 11b (162)
Sukra Niti, Chapter 4, 2, 1 (177)
Taxation, Required for Government
Mencius, Book 6, B, 10 (117)
Taxation, Rules Governing
Mahabharata, Santi Parva 120 (97)
Mahabharata, Santi Parva 87 (93)
Taxation, Source of
Mahabharata, Santi Parva 87 (93)
Taxation, Timing
Confucius, Analects Book 1, 5 (47)
Mahabharata, Santi Parva 88 (96)
Mencius, Book 1, A, 5 (109)
Mencius, Book 3 Part A, 3 (111)
Taxation, To be Increased Gradually
Mahabharata, Santi Parva 120 (97)
Mahabharata, Santi Parva 88 (95)
Timocracy
Plato, Republic 547 (131)
Trade
Ficino, Letters 2, 53 (50)
Laws of Manu 8, 180 (71)
Mahabharata, Santi Parva 88 (95)
Sukra Niti, Chapter 4, 2, 46 (178)
Trade, Example
Bible, Ezekiel 27, 1 (24)
Trade, Function of
Ficino, Letters 2, 53 (50)
Plato, Laws 918 (141)
Trade, Honest Trade
Mahabharata, Adi Parva 64 (75)
Trade, Honesty Required
Cicero, The Offices 3, 16 (46)
Cicero, The Offices, Book 3, 16 (46)
Yajnavalkya 2, 244 (188)

Trade, in Iron Age
Mahabharata, Udyoga Parva 187 (85)
Srimad Bhagavata, Book 12, 3 (165)
Trade, International
Bible, Ezekiel 27, 1 (24)
Plato, Laws 741 (139)
Trade, Is required
Mencius, Book 3, B, 4 (116)
Trade, Mixture of True & False
Srimad Bhagavata, Book 7, 11 (161)
Trade, Non in the Golden Age
Hesiod, Works & Days 225 (60)
Mahabharata, Vana Parva 148 (78)
Trade, Retail
Plato, Laws 918 (141)
Shantanand Saraswati, 1974 (149)
Sukra Niti, Chapter 4, 2, 1 (177)
Trade, Tax on
Bible, 1 Kings 10, 14 (19)
Laws of Manu 7, 127 (69)
Sukra Niti, Chapter 4, 2, 212 (180)
Trade, To be Exempt from Tax
Mencius, Book 2, A (111)
Treasury, Amount Required
Sukra Niti, Chapter 4, 2, 1 (177)
Trees, To be Protected
Mahabharata, Santi Parva 89 (96)
Tribute Money
Bible, 1 Kings 10, 14 (19)
Bible, 2 Samuel 8, 6 (19)
Shu King, The Tribute of Yu 3, 1 (155)
Srimad Bhagavata, Book 7, 11b (162)
Tyranny
Plato, Republic 562c (136)
Unity, All beings are Brahman
Mahabharata, Santi Parva 319 (104)
Unity, The Objective of Laws
Plato, Republic 462d (130)
Usury
Bible, Deuteronomy 19, 23 (17)
Bible, Exodus 22, 25 (11)
Bible, Nehemiah 5, 1 (22)
Hammurabi's Code 100-119 (56)
Laws of Manu 10, 115 (73)
Laws of Manu 8, 140 (70)
Philo, Special Laws 2, 17 (123)
Plato, Laws 743 (140)

Sukra Niti, Chapter 4, 2, 212 (180)
Sukra Niti, Chapter 4, 5, 628 (183)
Yajnavalkya 2, 37 (187)
Value
Sukra Niti, Chapter 2, 686 (173)
Value and Price
Sukra Niti, Chapter 4, 2, 163 (179)
Values
Plato, Laws 743 (140)
Srimad Bhagavata, Book 12, 3 (164)
Virtue
Plato, Laws 743 (140)
Virtue, Dimishes in Successive Ages
Laws of Manu 1, 81 (65)
Virtue, Its practise in This Age
Shantanand Saraswati, January 1978 (b) (150)
Virtue, Requires Wealth
Mahabharata, Santi Parva 167 (101)
Virtue, Source of Wealth
Bible, Job 36, 8 (22)
Bible, Job 8, 3 (22)
Brihadaranyaka, Book 1, 4, 12 (36)
Confucius, The Great Learning 10 (48)
Hesiod, Works & Days 225 (60)
Mahabharata, Santi Parva 123 (97)
Mahabharata, Vana Parva 31 (77)
Plato, Apology - 30 b (127)
Virtue, To be Pursued for Happiness
Cicero, The Offices 1, 2 (41)
Mahabharata, Santi Parva 190 (101)
Virtue, Wealth & Pleasue
Laws of Manu 2, 224 (66)
Mahabharata, Santi Parva 123 (97)
Virtue, wealth & pleasure
Mahabharata, Santi Parva 123 (97)
Wages
Bible, Leviticus 19, 9 (12)
Brihaspati Smriti 15 (39)
Narada Smriti, Book 4 (120)
Sukra Niti, Chapter 2, 836 (176)
Wages, Amounts to be Paid
Laws of Manu 10, 115 (73)
Laws of Manu 8, 180 (71)
Mahabharata, Santi Parva 60 (89)
Sukra Niti, Chapter 2, 788 (174)
Wages, Are a Contract
Bible, Matthew 20, 1 (29)

Sukra Niti, Chapter 2, 788 (174)
Wages, Basis for Payment
Sukra Niti, Chapter 2, 788 (174)
Wages, Not Related to Skill
Plato, Republic 345c (127)
Wages, The Fruit of Man's Work
Bible, Ecclesiastes 3, 1 (23)
Wages, To be Paid Immediately
Ramayana, Book 1, 52 (147)
Wealth, Accumulation causes Division
Plato, Republic 550 (132)
Wealth, Acquistion Involves Injury
Mahabharata, Santi Parva 8 (87)
Wealth, Acquistion of
Laws of Manu 10, 115 (73)
Mahabharata, Santi Parva 8 (87)
Mahabharata, Vana Parva 257 (84)
Plato, Republic 547 (131)
Wealth, All is Property of King
Mahabharata, Santi Parva 136 (99)
Wealth, Arising from Labour
Philo, Sacrifice of Abel (121)
Wealth, Arising from Virtue
Bible, Job 36, 8 (22)
Bible, Job 8, 3 (22)
Confucius, The Great Learning 10 (48)
Hesiod Works and Days 225-237 (60)
Mahabharata, Santi Parva 123 (97)
Mahabharata, Swagarahanika Parva 5 (107)
Mahabharata, Vana Parva 31 (77)
Plato, Apology - 30 b (127)
Wealth, Atributes
Mahabharata, Santi Parva 8 (87)
Wealth, Consequence of Pre-occupation
Srimad Bhagavata, Book 4, 22 (161)
Wealth, Desired by Men
Mahabharata, Vana Parva 257 (84)
Wealth, Disribution of
Mahabharata, Vana Parva 199 (79)
Plato, Laws 729 (138)
Wealth, Distribution of
Bible, Isaiah 5, 8 (24)
Bible, Leviticus 25, 8 (13)
Gospel According to Thomas 94, 1 (34)
Plato, Laws 741 (139)
Plato, Laws 918 (141)
Wealth, From Work on Nature

Cicero, The Offices 2, 4 (43)
Wealth, Income Required
  Sukra Niti, Chapter 1, 349 (168)
Wealth, Laws Governing Increase
  Mahabharata, Santi Parva 120 (97)
Wealth, Not a Result of Wisdom
  Mahabharata, Santi Parva 174 (101)
Wealth, Purpose of
  Mahabharata, Santi Parva 123 (97)
  Mahabharata, Santi Parva 20 (88)
  Sukra Niti, Chapter 1, 349 (168)
  Sukra Niti, Chapter 4, 2, 1 (177)
Wealth, Pursued by the Wise
  Mahabharata, Santi Parva 237 (102)
Wealth, Pursued for Happiness
  Mahabharata, Santi Parva 190 (101)
Wealth, Re-distribution
  Cicero, The Offices 2, 21 (44)
  Plato, Laws 736 (138)
Wealth, Required for Government
  Mahabharata, Santi Parva 130 (98)
  Mahabharata, Santi Parva 8 (87)
  Sukra Niti, Chapter 4, 2, 1 (177)
Wealth, Required for Virtue & Pleasure
  Mahabharata, Santi Parva 167 (101)
Wealth, Sources of
  Brihadaranyaka, Book 1, 4, 11 (35)
  Mahabharata, Santi Parva 167 (101)
  Mahabharata, Udyoga Parva 114 (84)
  Mahabharata, Vana Parva 32 (77, 78)
  Sukra Niti, Chapter 1, 349 (168)
Wealth, Supports & Sustians Life
  Mahabharata, Udyoga Parva 114 (84)
Wealth, To be Taken from the Wicked
  Sukra Niti, Chapter 4, 2, 1 (177)
Wealth, Virtue & Pleasure

Laws of Manu 2, 224 (66)
  Mahabharata, Santi Parva 140 (100)
  Mahabharata, Santi Parva 167 (101)
Wealthy, People are Devoted to
  Mahabharata, Santi Parva 322 (105)
Wealthy, To be Honoured
  Mahabharata, Santi Parva 88 (96)
  Mencius, Book 4, A, 6 (117)
Women
  Srimad Bhagavata, Book 12, 3 (164)
Women, Duty of
  Mahabharata, Anusasana Parva 46 (105)
  Mahabharata, Vana Parva 204 (79)
  Mahabharata, Vana Parva 231 (80)
Women, In Iron Age
  Srimad Bhagavata, Book 12, 3 (164, 165)
Women, to be protected
  Mahabharata, Anusasana Parva 46 (105)
Women, Wives Shared
  Plato, Republic 543a (131)
Work, And Results of
  Mahabharata, Bishma Parva 26 (87)
Work, Our Concern not with Product
  Mahabharata, Bishma Parva 26 (87)
Work, Our Concern with Profit
  Mencius, Book 3, B, 4 (116)
Work, Preferable to Idleness
  Bible, 2 Thessalonians 3, 8 (33)
  Bible, Matthew 20, 1 (29)
  Bible, Proverbs 6, 6 (23)
  Hesiod Works and Days 293-320 (60)
  Philo, Special Laws II, XV (122)
Work, Produces wealth
  Bible, Galatians 6, 7 (33)